More Comments from the Master Chefs

PEACE SOUP IS A MASTERFULLY CRAFTED BLEND of wisdom, humor, and heart. Chef Jerry Bartholow has taken many colorful elements of metaphysical truth and boiled them into a very tasty and practical gift. I know that anyone seeking to move their life to greater aliveness and love will receive a great deal from this wonderful book!

—*Alan Cohen*, *author of* THE DRAGON DOESN'T LIVE HERE ANYMORE

FOR ALL OF US WHO STRUGGLE each day with fear, anxiety and stress, at long last there is good news. **Peace Soup** is now being served by my favorite chef, Jerry Bartholow, just in time for the new Millennium. This is simply the best and most helpful book I have ever read. It's funny, it's wise, it works!

—*Fannie Flagg*, *author of* FRIED GREEN TOMATOES *and* WELCOME TO THE WORLD, BABY GIRL!

TAKING THE MEDITATION COURSE that Jerry teaches is easily one of the most significant things I have ever done. It was a life changing event. What I have learned in the course still impacts my life daily and I'm pleased to see that it's now in a book for everyone to experience.

—*Robert Hudson*, *author of* THE CENTER OF THE WHEEL

THIS BOOK IS A DELIGHT. We smiled with it and learned from it. "Chef" Jerry Bartholow has created a recipe guaranteed to satisfy the appetite of anyone hungering for total peace of mind, body and spirit. **Peace Soup** is fun to read, easy to digest, and overflowing with sound help. It will be a great blessing to all who are fortunate enough to read it.

—*Mary-Alice and Richard Jafolla*, *authors of* THE QUEST *and* NOURISHING THE LIFE FORCE

PEACE SOUP UPLIFTS with enlightening concepts and soothes with healing words.

—*Salle Merrill Redfield*, *author of* THE JOY OF MEDITATING *and* CREATING A LIFE OF JOY

THIS BOOK TRULY IS ONE for the new Millennium! It speaks to every level of our being—spiritual, mental, emotional, and physical. It has "lightness" and so much light! Many times I found myself chuckling out loud as I read, and other times I went, "umm-mm-m" as if I were tasting the **Peace Soup!**

—*Rev. Marilyn Reiger*, *Vero Beach, FL*

PEACE SOUP IS A CHARMING and transformational book, a veritable feast for anyone searching for meaningful answers, practical help and spiritual guidance. To call this a self-help book would be a gross understatement. It gives the "how to" yet so much more beside that is of a profoundly spiritual nature, rarely found in such books and seldom as clearly and simply expressed. I heartily recommend it.

—*Colin Tipping, M.Ed.*, *author of* RADICAL FORGIVENESS: MAKING ROOM FOR A MIRACLE

WONDERFUL! RIGHT ON THE MARK! The soul of everyone who reads **Peace Soup** will be nourished.

—*Neale Donald Walsch*, *author of* CONVERSATIONS WITH GOD

Comments from Preview Readers

AS I READ TOWARD the end of the book, I didn't want to put it down. Maybe that's a good sign. I think most classics are slow reading at first and just get better and better and, like a good classic, I look forward to reading **Peace Soup** again. I hope the whole world will read it (especially the people I come in contact with). I know that meditation and following your "recipe" changed my life. Thank you, Jerry.

—*R. W., Birmingham, AL*

IF YOU'VE EVER HAD A QUESTION about psychology or spirituality, you will find it answered in these pages. I know this is a bold claim, and there is no way for me to back it up, except to say, "Read this book and you'll see what I mean." Of course, you may not like Jerry's answers, but part of what this work is about is finding your own answers through meditation and reflection.

—*J. T., Birmingham, AL*

PEACE SOUP HAS ALL THE INGREDIENTS necessary to cook up a peaceful and happy life. After reading this book, my outlook on everything is different. I never knew the impact that my everyday habits have on my life. This book should be a regular part of everyone's menu. It tastes great and leaves you satisfied all day.

—*J. C., Chicago, IL*

MILLIONS WILL BE HUNGRY for a book like this to emerge serene and confident during the many unexpected surprises in the new millennium. God sent you as a special messenger to assist many to encounter Y2K and beyond. You are right on target and so valuable in this world.

—*C. C., New York, NY*

PEACE SOUP IS AN ABSOLUTE "MASTER-PEACE." I have loved reading it and will work from it always!

—*A. T., Birmingham, AL*

YOUR BOOK IS WONDERFUL! What a great place to live, here on this planet, if everyone followed your recipe.

—*B. W., Mountain Brook, AL*

MY SENSE IS—your book has the wisdom to heal the planet.

—*J. J., Birmingham, AL*

Peace Soup

Peace Soup

The Recipe
for a Peaceful Life
in the New Millennium

Chef Jerry Bartholow

PSI
Publishing
Birmingham, AL

Peace Soup—The Recipe for a Peaceful Life in the New Millennium

Library of Congress Cataloging-in-Publication Data
Bartholow, Jerry.
   Peace soup : the recipe for a peaceful life in
      the new millennium / Jerry Bartholow. – 1st ed.
   p. cm.
   Includes bibliographical references and index.
   LCCN: 00–131633
   ISBN: 0–9679005–0–6
   1. Peace of mind. 2. Self-actualization (psychology)
   3. Spiritual formation. I. Title.
   BF637.P3B37 2000   158.1
              QBI00-323

Book design by Kelly Leavitt
Cover artwork and design by Jack Cottle — jpc@magicnet.net
Production coordinated by Jackie Cottle

For additional copies: Contact your local bookstore or use the convenient order form on the last page of this book.

Attention Organizations, Healing Centers, Churches, Schools and/or Teachers of physical, mental or spiritual development: Quantity discounts are available. For information, please contact PSI Publishing, P. O. Box 55378, Birmingham, AL 35255 or call (205) 252-8000; fax (205) 328-8027.

1st edition: 10, 9, 8, 7, 6, 5, 4, 3, 2

To Imogene

My mother, my guide, my inspiration for peace.
She lives forever in the hearts of everyone she's touched.

Peace Soup

"The Table"
(of contents)

Peace Soup
(The Recipe)

Foreword

In the fall of 1990, the Unity church in Birmingham, Alabama was a well-known oasis for the soul—a weekly elixir for the members and a key destination for out-of-town travellers who had heard about the energy level of this special place.

Upon moving back to Birmingham—after being away for a long time—I heard about this church, too, and decided to attend a Sunday service. I had begun the writing of THE CELESTINE PROPHECY only months before, and what I needed was a spiritual shot in the arm. When I visited, I found just that—a remarkable church, ministered by a remarkable man, and the atmosphere exuded an aura of love, healing, and something else I couldn't quite put my finger on at first.

All I knew was that I couldn't stay away, and I spent the next three years hardly missing a service, wanting to just hang out in the back pew, regardless of whether it was a Sunday sermon that was occurring, a book study group, or one of the many workshops given by notable authors—heroes such as Barbara Marx Hubbard, Neale Donald Walsch and Catherine Ponder.

Not that I wanted to participate all that much. I didn't. I just needed to hang around in the energy, make notes about my own work, and get into a space where I could stay inspired.

It didn't take me long to understand the key feeling that characterized this church. It was a prevailing gestalt of *peace,* a sense of being safe and nurtured, the feeling of being at home. In retrospect, I would say that the whole place was blessed beyond belief by a true channel to the spirit, and still is. But I would also say that this channel has been established in large part by the consciousness and vision of its minister.

Jerry and his wife, Jane, set what I would now call a constant prayer-field—a huge, surrounding, glow of energy that establishes this mood of peace, and uplifts everyone and everything who gets close. Strangers drop in without knowing why. Animals congregate in the garden next door. You feel this energy when you drive by, or when you fly into the airport, for that matter, ten miles away.

From the beginning, Jerry has known that reaching higher spiritual experience is more than a matter of intellect, or belief—more, even, than willingness and determination. He knew that this experience often came from the subtleties of preparation, breaking old patterns, even diet. That's why life at Jerry's Unity has always been filled with exciting and progressive ideas, biofeedback machines, sensory deprivation tanks, therapy, psychodrama in the guise of May Day theatrical plays, and, above all, *meditation*—the discipline of moving past our distractions and opening up to the actual experience of the divine within. From this opening comes everything else: higher creativity and intuition, rich synchronicity, and an evergrowing sense of mission.

In a quiet way, Jerry has always taught how we can establish this connection for ourselves. For him there is only one God, one positive force in the universe. Everything else is merely the gyrations of human lostness and separation. All the joys of life come when we return home to that place of nurturing and peace.

Waiting for you is a cuisine of real spiritual experience that Jerry has been cooking for thirty years, and is now ready to share in this book. Sit down at the table and take the first sip. You won't be able to resist finishing the whole bowl.

— JAMES REDFIELD

Preface

Some call it a "New Age," the information age—the space age—the computer age. Some call it a revolution—the "super-industrial revolution," Alvin Toffler called it in FUTURE SHOCK. Some see it as a *spiritual revolution,* a leap in consciousness equivalent to the birth of a *messiah.* The "second coming" some are calling it...the *Rapture*...the *end times.* No matter what we choose to call it, we all agree we're in a time of great transformation on our beautiful planet Earth. Transformation involves tremendous change...and tremendous change means tremendous *stress!*

In my earlier life, I spent several years in the investment world as a stockbroker and financial planner and, in that environment, stress was rampant. I found few ways to cope with the stress...the *two-martini lunch* being the most common. I found this stress in every profession I encountered...it was *the world*...and it was diseased...sick with stress. I decided to find a way to solve the problem...and I did!

I have been teaching and counseling for the past thirty years, utilizing many stress-relieving ideas and techniques that have proven exceedingly effective in helping people from all walks of life to not only *relieve* the stress they've built up in their lives, but to learn how *not to let it build up again.* It hasn't seemed to matter what their religious or philosophical beliefs were (although some were closed to even *looking* at the techniques). Everyone who was open-minded enough to begin the first lesson and follow the recipe has seen dramatic results.

This process has been so effective that people have wanted to share it with their friends and family and many have urged me to put it in book form, or on cassette tapes or CDs, so it could be shared more widely than is possible in a classroom, workshop, or counseling setting.

This book, **Peace Soup**, and its peripheral tools represent *the recipe* that I have been using for so many years. It has been up-dated and, no doubt, will continue to be as new tools come to light. The way it stands now, however, it is more effective than most people dream possible.

I know how dramatic the results are through the transformation I've seen in the lives of those who have done the necessary work. Up until now, however, I didn't feel that very many people would be willing enough, and committed enough, to do the work on their own, without the support of the teacher and fellow classmates. With the upward movement in consciousness in just the past few years, I have changed my mind, and I'm now open to sharing these tools for transformation on a wider scale.

Just recently the idea came to me that, to *spice it up* a bit, I could present it in cooking terms. After all, the way to man's heart is through good food! I have enjoyed the process of converting the information to a *culinary delight* and it has taken on a somewhat different flavor. **Peace Soup** has a relaxing sound to it. Soup is warm and delicious... soothing to mind, body and soul. This is exactly what those of us who have followed the recipe over the years have experienced in our lives.

The new millennium can be the "thousand years of peace" promised in the *Book of Revelation*. Peace on Earth, the *True Peace* that is promised, will not come from the *outer world*. It must come from within the hearts of the people who inhabit this planet. When we reach critical mass, when enough of us have decided to create a peaceful life for *ourselves,* the entire race consciousness (social consciousness) will be lifted up and shifted toward peace.

There is a favorite song of mine that I've sung literally hundreds of times over the past thirty years, and it sums up the theme of this book and the theme of my life. *Let there be peace on Earth, and let it begin with me.* I invite you to sing this along with me as we cook up the recipe for Peace Soup.

> *Let there be Peace on Earth,*
> *And let it begin with me.*
> *Let there be Peace on Earth,*
> *The Peace that was meant to be.*
> *With God as our Father,*
> *Brothers all are we.*
> *Let me walk with my brother,*
> *In perfect harmony.*
> *Let Peace begin with me,*
> *Let this be the moment...now.*
> *With every step I take,*
> *Let this be my solemn vow.*
> *To take each moment,*
> *And live each moment*
> *In Peace eternally.*
> *Let there be Peace on Earth,*
> *And let it begin with me.*

> —PEACE SONG,
> by Jill Jackson and Sy Miller

Acknowledgments

The ideas presented in this recipe are not all originally mine. I have been studying, learning and integrating the ideas presented here all my life and, as we all have, I've gleaned much of what I believe and teach from *my* teachers and mentors. To acknowledge all of them would require a book in itself, but I would like to mention a few of the Master Chefs who have inspired me and shared with me the secrets of their favorite recipes.

I would like to begin where *I* began…*with* **God!** All the inspiration I have, originated with the true inspirer…God. In His infinite wisdom, God led me to my first contact here on Earth…my mother…**Imogene.** My mother fed me my first taste of Peace Soup and introduced me to my first great spiritual teacher, **Winnie the Pooh**, a "bear of little brain"…*but a big heart!* I acknowledge **Walt Disney** and his *imagination* which, even today, is one of my greatest inspirations. I acknowledge my **father** and **step-father** for "training me up" and my **sister** and **brothers** for sharing their insights.

Special thanks to **Dr. Victor Zarley**, the minister who introduced me to *Unity*, and to **James Gattuso, Jr.**, my teacher in *Alpha Theta Meditation,* the class that has given us many of the basic technical ingredients for this recipe. Thank you **Wally** and **Vrle Minto—Wally** for developing *Alpha Truth Awareness,* and brother **Vrle** for being my instructor in these valuable lessons. I acknowledge **Dr. Edwin P. Hall**, clinical psychologist, for providing a test of the recipe with his patients in a clinical setting, and **Dr. Michael Ryce** for the insights and tools of his healing work.

I acknowledge my teachers at **Unity School of Christianity**, especially **Reverend Dennis Neagle**, and his wife **Kit**, for their contribution to my awareness of the deep, mystical teachings of **Jesus**, who is my *greatest* teacher and my model for Peace. My thanks to **Bernhard Dohrmann** and my other instructors at **Income Builders International**. Thank you **Dr. Catherine Ponder** for your friendship and the inspiration of your teachings on the principles of life and prosperity.

You will find the spices and flavorings of *these* authors and teachers through the pages of this recipe:

James Allen, Wally "Famous" Amos, Richard Bach, Steve Bhaerman, Beverly Alberstadt Bartholow, Robert Becker, Hans Berger, Ben (Oh, Be One) Kanobi, Dale Carnegie, Al Carter, Emmanuel Cheraskin, Doc Lew Childre, Deepak Chopra, George Clason, Alan Cohen, Terry Cole-Whitaker, Roy Eugene Davis, J. Diamond, Berny Dohrmann, Henry Drummond, Wayne Dyer, Meister Eckhart, Thomas Edison, Ralph Waldo Emerson, Rocco Errico, Charles and **Myrtle Fillmore, Emmet Fox, Benjamin Franklin, James Dillet Freeman, Eric Fromm, Robert Frost, Mahatma Gandhi, Kahlil Gibran, Steven Halpern, David Hawkins, Louise Hay, Napoleon Hill, Ernest Holmes, Robert Hudson, Richard** and **Mary-Alice Jaffola, William James, Gerald Jamplosky, Ruth** and **Bonnie Jarrett, Carl Jung, Ken Keyes, Martin Luther King, Jr., Rudyard Kipling, Elisabeth Kübler-Ross, Maharishi Mahesh Yogi, Maxwell Maltz, David McArthur, Wally Minto, Raymond Moody, Earl Nightingale, Gary Null, Chad** and **Lytingale O'Shea, Mary Omwake, Patanjali, Catherine Ponder, Dean Portinga, Jan** and **John Randolph Price, Ramakrishna, Janeson Rayne, James Redfield, Richard** and **Marilyn Reiger, Tony Robbins, Jim Rosemergy, Michael Ryce, Richard Schultz, Jack Schwartz, Barry Sears, William Shakespeare, Norman Shealy, Ed Shear, José Silva, David**

Sohn, **Huston Smith**, **Richard Talbot**, **John Templeton**, **Mother Teresa**, **Thich Nhat Hanh**, **Alvin Toffler**, **Carlson Wade**, **Alan Watts**, **Andrew Weil**, **Jullian Whittaker**, **Yoda**, **Robert Young**, **Leroy Zemke**, **Zig Zigler**, and the masters **Krishna**, **Buddha**, **Lao-Tzu** and **Jesus**.

I acknowledge the members of the **Unity Church of Birmingham** (my home) and other churches and organizations where I've taught, for providing inspiration and feedback that has allowed this work to expand and evolve over the years. Each one of you has played a very important role in preparing this recipe and there will always be a special place in my heart for you. It was the classes, workshops and counseling sessions that provided the laboratory for putting the principles to the test. You all have helped this work to expand.

I give a special thanks to my close friend and golfing partner, **James Redfield**, and his wife, **Salle Merrill Redfield**, for setting the perfect example for success in writing and publishing THE CELESTINE PROPHECY and subsequent books, and for holding my hand through the process of getting this book published. I acknowledge also the **Counsel of Advisors** who helped me edit and proof the final manuscript. Their input inspired much of what you have in your hands as the finished recipe. Thank you, **Kelly Leavitt**, for typing the manuscript in its final form and for making all those valuable corrections. Thanks to **Robert "Bobby" Hudson** for sharing the valuable lessons learned in publishing THE CENTER OF THE WHEEL and for being my friend, and fellow teacher of this recipe. Thank you, **Patricia** and **Stanley Walsh-Haluska**, for sharing your consciousness and your expertise in publishing, and thanks to **Roger Phillips** for engineering the CD and the audiotapes and to **Jim Aycock**, **Ken Talley** and **Tena Wilson** for providing the musical inspiration for **Peace Soup**.

Most of all, I acknowledge my wife, **Jane**, whose unconditional love and dedication have provided me with inspiration daily. Her contribution to this book is incalculable. Thank you my wife, my partner in ministry, my friend, my pray-mate and my playmate…I love you!

I give a joyful hug and a loving thank you to our children: **Kathy**, **Laura** and **Scott**, **Lisa**, **Jon**, **Paul** and **Anne**, **Brandon** and **Christi**, and **Cami** for being living examples of peace for their generation, and to our grand-children, **Garrett** and **William**, as examples for theirs.

Finally, I acknowledge **YOU,** the reader of this work, for your courage in being willing to take a closer look at your life, and being open to exploring a process that will help you develop a more peace-ful, fun-filled, healthful, prosperous, love-filled, masterful life!

I love you…all ways…
Chef Jerry ♡

Introduction

Well, here we are. We, as adults, have been working for a number of years to get ourselves into the soup we're in—Stress Soup! We all started out pretty relaxed, peaceful and happy, as a little bundle of joy with not a care in the world. Boy, did that change. The bundle of joy has become a bundle of nerves! We're not at ease much anymore. Stress has become a way of life in our modern world.

Most of us began feeling the effects of stress at a very early age, probably even before we were born. Birth itself **is** a stressful experience and each day since, we've added more and more layers of stress as we've grown into adulthood. Most of us are now totally *adulterated!*

> **All stress is internally generated by our attitudes and we have control over these attitudes.**

According to medical research, and depending on which reports you read, anywhere from 50 to 90 percent of all disease is stress-related. I say it's closer to 100 percent! The word disease is really *disease,* meaning that some part of the body, mind or emotions is not at ease. Unless we learn to do something about it, the stress will keep weighing heavy upon us until it pushes us about six feet under!

Excess stress causes sickness and death, pain and suffering, but, as we'll discover, *all stress is internally generated by our attitudes* and *we have control over these attitudes.* Thank goodness there is a way beyond suffering, a way beyond stress, a recipe for a peaceful life. Thank goodness for **Peace Soup.**

The steps you are about to take in preparing this recipe will lead you along the road to peace. Notice I said *lead* you, not *carry* you! The path is laid out for you, but there are certain contributions you have to make in order to receive the full benefit of the soup. *You must follow the recipe!*

The process is carefully designed to take you from where you are to where you want to be, from a life of stress and turmoil to a life of perfect peace and serenity. In a cursory overview, this book may appear as a "smorgasbord," covering all areas of life, and you may feel that you can pick what you want and leave the rest. Of course you *can* do this, and it will be of some benefit, but the "ego" part of you would most likely want to leave out the parts that would be most helpful.

The recipe covers every aspect of life, *for a reason*. We tend to develop pockets of stress that keep us off balance and out of peace. We cannot achieve true peace, total peace, in any aspect if we are not perfectly balanced in *all*. This process takes you gently through all areas and cleans out the pockets of stress that you hold, both consciously and unconsciously.

Each step has been carefully researched, put to the test, and proven again and again by thousands of people over the past three decades. Many lives have been changed for the better in a relatively short period of time. Much of what you will learn is not new. Many of the techniques and lessons have been around for hundreds, even thousands of years.

These proven techniques for relieving stress and establishing a peaceful life have been taught by the masters of all ages, but until now they have been reserved for a few adepts who have had the time and discipline necessary to implement them in their lives—the monks in the monasteries...the priests in the temples...the swamis in the mountain caves. The excessive stress of modern life is now making it essential that we move these ancient techniques out of the cloister and into the mainstream. Meditation and relaxation are not just for the religious devotees anymore. New discoveries in psychology and physiology are proving that these ancient techniques will be extremely effective and invaluable in relieving the stresses of 21st century living. The effects of stress are not likely to ease in the new millennium. It's more likely that stress will continue to increase as each new discovery feeds on the previous ones, to bring about what Alvin Toffler has called "Future Shock!"

Fortunately, as we pile more and more stress upon ourselves, the universe, in its infinite wisdom, is providing us with the tools necessary to cope with the new stress. Not only do we have the ancient techniques of stress reduction in our recipe, but these and other new scientific discoveries in psychology and physiology are added to them: the mind/body connection; bio-feedback training; auto-suggestion; self-hypnosis; mind-control; neuro-linguistic programming; self-image psychology; quantum physics; the relaxation response; bio-chemistry; bio-electronics; life extension; hormone adjustment; and applied kinesiology. Discoveries such as these are all making our potential for self-development almost beyond belief. We're beginning to realize that we are not just human beings, we are *super-beings!*

We are not just human beings...we are super-beings!

The recipe for **Peace Soup** folds together the ancient techniques with the new scientific discoveries in a process that guarantees success—*if you follow the recipe!* I'm not saying that you'll become a guru in the relatively short period of time it will take you to complete the recipe, but you will have all the tools you will need to handle any stressful situation that may come up for you in a relaxed, calm, easy manner...peacefully. Then all you need do is sharpen your skills in the arena of life.

A Little Spice
"Peace Porridge Puns"
(You may want to take them with a grain of salt)

I will be spicing up the **Peace Soup** with more than a few sprinkles of humor...*my kind of humor!* If some of these spices don't "tickle your palate," just spoon them off and leave them out of your recipe. This porridge is intended to be light in every way, and the puns keep it from getting heavy and sticking to the bottom of the kettle.

The English language is complex and the multiple meanings and similar phonics make for some pretty humorous plays on words. The Kabbalist says, "Puns are the only acceptable humor...they hurt no one." (Some groan-ups do *groan,* however.)

Words are power! *Words are power,* as we'll discover in the first two chapters, and as we become more aware of our words, we'll begin to see how powerfully "punny" they can be. You can smile or you can groan...either way it's good for your digestion.

How to Listen to the CD (Compact Disc)

You'll find in the back of this book a CD with the techniques for relaxation and meditation that are such an integral part of this recipe. I added this tool with reluctance because the temptation is great to use my voice as a "crutch" and continue to listen to the outer expression instead of internalizing it and making it your own. The techniques will not be nearly as effective if you depend on the CD. It's helpful—for the first couple of times, to get a feel for the process—but then let it go, and do it yourself.

Pretend you're coming to class and listening to me, as your teacher, then going home to practice on your own. For decades, my students have been asking that I make a tape for them to listen to...and I've always said, *"No."* They could call me if they had a question.

With this book format, a phone call is not possible, thus the CD, but for your own good, it's best not to use it...except to firm up the techniques in your own mind.

"K.I.S.S."
—Simple and Easy—

I have been told that I have a way of making the complex seem simple. I like to say that this is an advantage of being simple-minded. In the interest of brevity, some of the ingredients in this recipe may seem overly simplistic or even technically inaccurate. It is meant to be "practically accurate," meaning not that it's *almost* accurate, but that it's accurate in a *practical* way. If I were to get too technical, each step in this recipe would be a book in itself and it would take forever to complete. The proof is in the tasting, and the soup made with this recipe has tasted wonderful to everyone so far. I trust it will taste good to you, too. So let's K.I.S.S. (Keep It Simple, Sweetie)!

You could probably read this book in a few days if you wanted to, but it will be much more effective if you will take a few weeks, even a few months, allowing each of the ingredients in each step of the recipe to work its magic before going on to the next step. You can't hurry a good soup. It must have time to boil and blend, stew and simmer, settle and be stirred again. Ideally, you would spend a week or more on each of the seven steps. Just remember, the longer a good soup sits in the pot, the richer it becomes...

You can't hurry a good soup.

Making **Peace Soup** is somewhat like making onion soup, in that you must peel the onion, one layer at a time, from the *outside in*. We have found over the years that stress must also be peeled away from the outer (physical) layer first. We have wound ourselves up into that tight bundle—the physical body—and we must un-wind or peel away the outer stress before we can get to the deeper *mental* layer and finally get into the core, the deep *emotional* layer.

It's taken some time for you to wind yourself up, so it follows that it will take some time for you to un-wind, but many have found it amazing how fast this recipe works. Most have noticed positive results in just the first few days of practicing STEP ONE. Always remember, it's a process—rush it and you'll get indigestion. Let the soup mellow, taking time to smooth out all the lumps and spoon off the foam. Relax and enjoy the refreshing aroma as the soup cooks. Feel the rich texture as you stir it gently—the joy, the love, the peace, the serenity. Take your time. You'll be ready to move on to the next step soon enough. Let go...un-wind...enjoy...in joy.

There is no required reading for making **Peace Soup** other than this recipe. I will be mentioning certain classic works of the great master chefs, past and present, and you may want to study their works (listed in the bibliography), but it's not essential. This recipe contains all the ingredients you will need, except the condiments you, personally, bring to the table. This is not a religious work, although I will be referring to several *spiritual* writings, especially from the great recipe book, THE BIBLE.

THE BIBLE is the basis of much of our Western culture and it contains much wisdom, even though it is largely misunderstood. I will take

It's the spirit of the law that makes a good soup.

the liberty to re-phrase (and even re-vise) some of the passages slightly to fit this recipe, but after all, as Chef Paul said in his second recipe for the Corinthians, "It's the spirit of the law that makes good soup....The letter of the law makes poison." (2 Cor 3:6, revised version)

My last 25-plus years of teaching and practicing the lessons outlined in this book have been so fulfilling for me because the recipe works. The soup tastes good and it's sooo…good for you. I have seen thousands of people all over the country change their lives for the better, overcoming stress and imbalance in every area of life. I have seen those who seemed lost, find themselves; those who were sick, heal themselves; those who seemed crazy, return to sanity; those who were fearful, angry, guilt-ridden or depressed, gain perfect emotional control; those who were financially destitute, become prosperous; and those whose relationships seemed hopeless, return to perfect love. *I* did not do any of this *for* any of them. They did it for themselves by following the recipe. You can do it, too. You *will* do it! Just by picking up this book, you have shown you are ready to enjoy the soup. All there is to do now is follow the recipe, step by step, for the most delicious soup…the most peaceful life possible.

I set before you the recipe for perfect peace. Peace of mind…peace of body…peace of emotions. It's up to you to prepare the soup. Once you have, it will last forever. The recipe is for eternal **Peace Soup**.

Enjoy…in joy…
Chef Jerry

1

Preparation:
Gathering the Basic Utensils

Utensil #1...A Clean Soup Pot or Kettle!

The kettle is your *consciousness*. Life is consciousness. Everything you've gathered so far in your life makes up your present consciousness. From the time you were conceived you have been influenced by input from the world around you—your parents, your teachers, your peers, your environment. You've learned everything by being told or observing certain information and believing it to be true. Whether it's true or not makes no difference; it's what you *believe* that makes up your consciousness. Your current belief system (b.s.) is a carry-over from the belief systems (b.s.) of those who have been your teachers. If I were to show you the computer I'm using to write this book and tell you it's an automobile, you would not believe me. You've seen an automobile and you've seen a computer and you know the difference. If, however, you had never seen a computer or an auto-

> **Whether it's true or not makes no difference; it's what you believe that makes up your consciousness.**

mobile and I, being your teacher and your friend, told you that this computer is an automobile (believing so myself), then the next time you saw a computer you would call it an automobile. You would believe this until someone you trusted more told you, "It's a computer, not an automobile," and you believed *them!*

You learn by receiving data and believing it to be true. Many of your teachers in life, including your parents, may have given you erroneous information based on their faulty belief system (b.s.), and you've bought their beliefs. If they did, then you are now living your life based in error and you're in bondage to these error beliefs. Acting on error beliefs is sometimes known as "sin." Sin has nothing to do with religion, although many religions use the term. The word *sin* comes from an Old English archery term meaning you "missed the mark." When your arrow missed the target, you sinned! Sin is simply error beliefs acted upon. Our lives are sinful because they are based in error. The old soup pot (old consciousness) is caked with the residue of our sins and it has resulted in Stress Soup!

We must, therefore, *wash the kettle clean,* which means to *have an open mind!* This doesn't mean that you are to believe everything I say. In fact, I'll be the first to tell you, as I've told every one of the classes I've taught, *"I cannot tell you the truth!"* I quote the Master Chef Lao-Tzu in the TAO TE CHING: "The Tao (truth) that can be spoken is not the eternal Tao...He who speaks does not know, he who knows does not speak." When one speaks, he or she must use the rational, thinking part of the brain. This left brain, as we'll explore in Step 4 of the recipe, contains all the old conditioned beliefs of the one who is speaking. So the spoken (or written) word is *tainted* by the belief system (b.s.) of the speaker (or writer) and, as we'll discover, "'t'ain't necessarily so!"

Get your own truth from your own heart, not from the heads of others.

What you will discover in this recipe is how to get your own truth from your own heart, not from the *heads* of others, *including me!* You will learn to open your mind to your heart, which is connected to the wisdom of the universe, and listen to the in-spiration...the truth that *breathes in you.* Jesus said, "You shall *know* the truth that sets you free," not that you will "read it in a book" or "hear it in a class or from a pulpit!" I will not tell the truth to you, nor will anyone else. Open your mind so you can cleanse your kettle of the "dregs" (error beliefs) of your old Stress Soup. Be ready to know the truth and be free.

Utensil #2...Four Mixing Bowls

Life is an eternal growth process. We're always learning, growing and remembering, and there are four steps (bowls) we need to make ready to draw from in mixing the ingredients of **Peace Soup**. So let's take a quick look at the contents of each of these mixing bowls. The first one is:

The Awareness Bowl

You already have a good beginning in filling your Awareness Bowl, or you wouldn't be reading this book. You are aware that there are things you can do to improve your quality of life, and you are willing to continue to expand your consciousness. The Zen master says, "You are only *alive* to the extent that you are *aware*." As you increase your awareness, you expand your *aliveness* and life becomes an ever-more exciting adventure! We will be adding to the Awareness Bowl throughout this recipe.

> **"You are only alive to the extent that you are aware."**

If your Awareness Bowl dries up, you fall asleep and the soup pot boils over, causing a mess that takes extra time and energy to clean up. Keep this bowl full and be ready for any contingency. As the Master Chef Jesus said, "Watch, therefore: for you know not when the master cometh...lest coming suddenly he find you sleeping...watch." (Mark 13:35-37) The first step in any growth process is *awareness*; so this is the first mixing bowl. The second is:

The Control Bowl

Many people say they don't like the idea of control (probably because they don't have any), but in this recipe we're talking about control as *discipline...self-discipline!* It doesn't matter how aware you are that you need to make changes in your life; if you don't develop the control, you will not make the changes. Just ask anyone who has tried to stop smoking or lose weight. It takes discipline! The word "discipline" has the same root as the word "disciple." A disciple is one who is disciplined (or becoming disciplined) in a certain teaching or way. In this recipe, we're becoming disciplined to the way of cooking up a peaceful life.

The exercises and techniques in each step of the recipe are designed to help you develop *self*-control. Just as learning to play a musical instrument or your favorite sport requires practice in developing discipline, so too does learning relaxation and physical-mental-emotional peace. If you want to become adept at anything, you must practice! Throughout the recipe, you will be adding to, and drawing from, *the* Control Bowl. To have control when you need it, you must practice the techniques. Without practice, the "dregs" of Stress Soup creep back in and destroy your peace.

Now that we have our first two mixing bowls in place—the Awareness Bowl and the Control Bowl—we're ready for the third:

The Balance Bowl

Life is a balancing act. Lose your balance and you'll fall off the path. The path of peace has often been called "the straight and narrow." When we are perfectly balanced, we are at peace and walking the narrow path without fear. We want to develop our balance to the point that we can walk the path blind-folded, much as Luke Skywalker (*sky-walker*) did in using The Force in STAR WARS. Balance is a large mixing bowl because it incorporates every area of life. We must establish and maintain balance in all areas if we are to complete the recipe and produce an ever-lasting supply of Peace Soup.

We have many hues... we "hue-mans."

We are many-faceted beings...have many hues, we "hue-mans." We are basically *spiritual* beings, created in the image and likeness of spirit, and we can get out of balance spiritually by embracing religions and cults (belief systems) that are error-based, some even requiring that we deny our spiritual nature altogether.

Beyond being spiritual, we know that we are also *physical* beings. Everyone knows what it feels like to be out-of-balance physically. This is the dis-ease I mentioned earlier and most everybody thinks it's just part of being human to get sick. It isn't! As you learn to draw from your Balance Bowl, you'll discover that you need never be sick. Perfect health is one of the great benefits of this recipe.

We are *mental* beings...*we think!* You have a mind of your own and a very complicated mind, at that. It's very easy to get out of balance mentally, and some even carry it to the extreme of mental illness. Depression, schizophrenia, multiple personalities and a myriad of other *dis*-orders come from having an empty Balance Bowl. Actually, all dis-ease is mental in its origin, as we'll discuss in the recipe. A full Balance Bowl will protect you from mental dis-ease.

We are *social* beings, meaning that we relate in a social setting with other complicated minds, and that really takes walking the straight and narrow! Relationships can throw you off-balance like nothing else you will experience. We will be dis-*cussing* relationships throughout the recipe, as you build your ability to understand yourself and others. Social balance is an attribute of the master chefs, but even they, as we'll discover, can fall off the path because of the next part of balance...*emotional balance!*

One of the most crucial steps in preparing **Peace Soup** is getting the emotions under control and keeping them in balance. This is not so easy. In the recipe, you will discover the difference between *feelings* and *emotions* and how to remain balanced even in the most disturbing and chaotic conditions by developing the feelings. This is a crucial step, but it, of necessity, comes late in the recipe. It won't work to skip there now, as you must have the foundation. It would be like trying to put the icing on a cake, *before* you bake the cake!

You will discover the difference between feelings and emotions.

In addition to being *spiritual, physical, mental, social* and *emotional,* we are also *financial* beings, meaning that we operate in a system of exchange that requires each of us to have something to exchange! It's very easy to get out of balance financially, experiencing lack and limitation in life. The Balance Bowl requires that you establish a connection with the unlimited supply of the universe and learn to be a good *stew*-ard.

Finally and foremost, we are *sexual* beings. Part of our responseability is to pro-create. It's the strongest drive most of us have, and it's *good,* when we keep it in balance! Sex can be creative or destructive, depending on how full your Balance Bowl is. Many people ruin the soup by going off the deep end—sexually!

You can see how important the third mixing bowl, the Balance Bowl, is in completing the recipe. The many "hues" can come together to make a beautiful rainbow, or they can be off-balance and create a destructive storm, a hurricane or tornado of strife and hardship.

This recipe is designed to help you maintain the Balance Bowl. Each step will lead you gently along to more *awareness, control* and *balance,* so that you fill the fourth mixing bowl automatically. I call this final bowl:

The Flow Bowl

Flow is the perfect expression of a peaceful life. When we're "in the flow," we don't have to *think* about peace—we *are* peace! I liken the flow to a river, flowing down a mountainside. When the river comes to a boulder, it doesn't bounce off or crash through the boulder, it simply flows around it and goes right on. The boulder is still a part of the experience of the river, and it may change its course, but it doesn't stop the flow.

You, like the river, will always have boulders in your life—this is the nature of life—but the boulders don't have to stop the flow, damming up the river. Life can be a continuous flow, no matter what's going on around you. As Rudyard Kipling said, in his poem *"You Are a Man,"* you can learn to "keep your head while those around you are losing theirs."

Some call the Flow Bowl "being in the zone." Great athletes don't have to *think* about what they're doing or how they're doing it—they *are* the activity! Basketball great Michael Jordan didn't have to *think* about how to "fly" to the basket, golfer Jack Nickolas didn't have to *think* about how to hit a 300-yard drive or sink a six-foot putt, the great football star Joe Montana didn't have to *think* about finding a receiver and throwing the perfect pass. Each of them had completed the steps of Awareness, Control and Balance in perfecting his particular sport. These athletes continually expressed in the Flow Bowl. In the **Peace Soup** recipe, our sport is life itself, and we'll have as much fun and be as *pro*-ficient in life as any accomplished athlete is in his or her sport.

As you prepare the soup recipe, you're becoming a *pro* at living a peaceful life. When you complete the *pro*-cess, you will no longer have to think about being peaceful—you will simply *be* peaceful, in the zone, in the flow of life!

You will be peaceful, in the zone, in the flow of life!

The second basic utensil is now in place—the four mixing bowls: Awareness, Control, Balance and Flow. In addition to the kettle and the mixing bowls, we need:

Utensil #3...The Measure

In His *Sermon on the Mount,* Chef Jesus said, "With what measure ye mete, it shall be measured to you again." (Matt 7:12) The Book of *Pro*-verbs says, "As a man thinketh in his heart, so is he." (Pr 23:7) This is the measure of your understanding of how life works, and having a full awareness of this *measure* is essential in preparing your recipe.

The measure has been known by many names. "The law of laws," Chef Ralph (Emerson) called it; others have referred to it as cause and effect, sowing and reaping, karma, the law of mind action. Earl Nightingale called it *"the strangest secret."* "Strange," he says, "that it remains a secret, since *all* the great teachers and philosophers through-out the ages have agreed on this one thing: 'You become what you think about.'"

You become what you think about, *when you believe it!* "A teenage boy might think about girls all day long, but he doesn't become a girl," Chef Earl says. The magic is in the believing. As you think, *in your heart,* so are you! "All things you shall ask, *believing,* you shall receive." (Matt 21:22, rev. ver.)

Another key in understanding the measure is that it can work in both a positive or a negative way, depending on your thoughts. When you concentrate your thoughts on positive things, you attract positive people and events into your life. When your thoughts are negative, the *cause* is negative and the *effect* will be negative, too. When you're hav-ing negative effects in your life, it's not bad luck, it's *bad thinking.* Stinkin' thinkin' makes sour soup. There is no luck and there are no accidents! As Ben (Oh, Be One) Kanobi said to Luke Skywalker as part of his training as a Jedi knight, "In my experience there is no such thing as luck." You'll have the same experience when you use *The Measure.*

Chef James Allen, in his classic book AS A MAN THINKETH, wrote what I consider to be one of the greatest treatises ever written on *The Measure.* In this great work, Chef James shows how our thoughts affect every part of our lives and then concludes with a short chapter entitled "*Serenity.*" Since our goal in making **Peace Soup** *is* Serenity, I share his enlightened and eloquent words with you:

> *Calmness of mind is one of the beautiful jewels of wis-dom. It is the result of long and patient effort in self-control. A man (or a woman) becomes calm in the mea-sure that they understand themselves as a thought-evolved being, for such knowledge necessitates the understanding of others as the result of thought, and as they develop a right understanding and see more and more clearly the internal relations of things by the action of cause and effect, they cease to fuss and fume*

and worry and grieve, and remain poised, steadfast, serene.

The strong, calm person is always loved and revered. They are like a shade-giving tree in a thirsty land, or a sheltering rock in a storm. Who does not love a tranquil heart, a sweet-tempered balanced life? It does not matter whether it rains or shines, or what changes come to those possessing these blessings, for they are always sweet, serene and calm. That exquisite poise of character which we call serenity is the last lesson of culture; it is the flowering of life, the fruitage of the soul...a life that dwells in the ocean of truth, beneath the waves, beyond the reach of tempests, in the eternal calm.

Chef James concludes his book with these inspiring words:

Tempest-tossed souls, wherever ye may be, under whatsoever conditions ye may live, know this—in the ocean of life, the isles of blessedness are smiling, and the sunny shore of your ideal awaits your coming. Keep your hand firmly upon the helm of thought. In the barque of your soul reclines the commanding master; he does but sleep; wake him. Self-control is strength; right thought is mastery; calmness is power. Say unto your heart, "Peace, be still!"

These inspirational words were written over a hundred years ago, but they are as valid today as they were then. Self-control *is* strength—the strength of discipline that we find in our second mixing bowl. Right thought *is* mastery—it's *The Measure* that makes certain all the ingredients in your soup are in perfect *pro*-portion. Calmness *is* power—the power that comes from *knowing* the source of all goodness, the power that comes when you complete the recipe and partake of the soup.

The most power-full beings ever to walk the planet—the master chefs who have influenced millions and millions with their spiritual strength—were *calm!* Jesus, Buddha, Krishna, Lao-Tzu, Mohammed and Gandhi were calm and powerful master chefs. Their recipes have influenced the lives of everyone and they, and others like them, have contributed *"measurably"* to this **Peace Soup** recipe.

We have the first three utensils in place: 1) the clean kettle *(an open mind);* 2) the mixing bowls *(Awareness, Control, Balance, Flow);* and 3) the measure *(the law of cause and effect).* Now we need an instrument for stirring the soup. This is:

Utensil #4...The Ladle

Nothing stirs up the creative process like *the spoken word.* The Law says, "We become what we think about," but until a thought is spoken out or acted upon, it is nothing (no-thing). We are creative beings, created "in the image and likeness" of The Creator, so we create as The Creator creates—by speaking the word. In the first

We create as the Creator creates—by speaking the word.

Creation Story of THE BIBLE, (the first book of the great collection of recipes), God *said*, "Let there be light, and there was light." (Gen 1:3) God *spoke the word* and it became a reality. In the creation story of the New Testament of THE BIBLE, we read, "In the beginning was the *word*, and the *word* was with God, and the *word* was God...All things were made by the *word*; and without the *word* was not anything made that was made." (John 1:1-3, rev. ver.) The *word* is the creative power—the *mind energy*—that brings thought into man-i-festation. You, and your life, and everything else that *is*, are a result of thought being spoken out—*becoming flesh!*

Every word you speak has the power to create—create good *or* evil, health *or* disease, peace *or* turmoil. The word can create or destroy, build up or tear down—and every word counts! Master Chef Jesus said, "Every idle word that men shall speak, they shall give account thereof in the Day of Judgment. For by thy words thou shalt be justified, and by thy words thou shalt be condemned." (Matt 13:36-37)

Your words create your world. Every day is judgment day and every word is power. The spoken word is the *ladle* that stirs the soup.

In using the ladle, it's important to understand that words are *not* words to the subconscious mind. When you hear the word "cow," it does not trigger a word c-o-w—it brings forth an *image;* in this case, it's a four-legged animal that gives milk and says, "Moo." *Words trigger images!* Words of fear and anger trigger images that are fearful and angry. Words of love and peace trigger images that are loving and peaceful. The recipe for a peaceful life requires a constant stirring with the ladle of positive, peaceful words, and the occasional spooning-off of the foam of negative, stressful words that make the soup bitter.

Realize also that *actions* have the same creative power as words. The home you live in, the automobile you drive, the building you work in, are all the results of actions. They could have been built without a word being spoken, but not without some action being taken. The creative tools we use in creating our lives are: *thoughts, words, actions* and *feelings*. We'll be exploring feelings in Step 5 of the recipe but, again, you're not there yet. Follow the recipe, one step at a time, and by the time you reach Step 5, your feelings will not be on your sleeve; they'll be in your heart.

The creative tools we use in creating our lives are: thoughts, words, actions and feelings.

The final basic tool we need before preparing the recipe is:

Utensil #5...Fire!
(Peace Porridge Hot!)

Without a burning desire for a peaceful life, you will not even begin to cook the soup. Without a commitment to yourself to devote the time and energy necessary, you will never savor the sweet taste, nor will you be blessed by the robust aroma and the rich, smooth texture of **Peace Soup**. You will remain in the same kettle of stress you've been in for much of your adult life.

Jesus put it this way in his "Be" Attitudes (attitudes of be-ing):

"Blessed are they which do hunger and thirst after righteousness, for they shall be filled." (Matt 5:6) You must have a *fire in the belly* that can only be quenched by the soothing effects of true peace. If you just give "lip service" to the recipe, the soup will not be cooked, and the healing properties will not get past the lips, through the digestive system and into your bloodstream to become a part of your life.

This process (the recipe) works, but only when you work it! You must make the investment in yourself by completing each step of the recipe, slowly and thoroughly. You must *believe* you can have peace—perfect peace—and then be willing to do what it takes to achieve it.

In the long run, you'll find it takes less energy to make **Peace Soup** than it does to make Stress Soup. The energy you waste in worrying, fearing, crying, or being angry, guilt-ridden, jealous or resentful can be re-channeled to help you accomplish positive, happy results. The rules that govern life work for good *or* evil, depending on how you use your creative tools and the recipe you follow.

Chemicalization

There is one other use of *Fire* that takes place in the cleansing of the kettle. This is the "burning out" of the old error beliefs or sins of ego. This use for the fire feels like *hell*, but it's a necessary part of the cleansing process for all kettles that are caked with the residue of old Stress Soup. This part is sometimes called *chemicalization*. You are actually changing the make-up of your mind, body and spirit, so it's like a chemical change taking place. During this *hot* phase, the temp-tation is to quit—to "get out of the kitchen." Don't do it! This is a natural part of growing up!

When it burns a little (or a lot), you're doing it right.

When you're "in *pro*-cess" and it burns a little (or a lot!), just know that you're doing it right, and it's all...come to pass! "This, too, shall pass" is a working phrase we use when the fire gets hot! Keep doing the work, keep practic-ing the exercises, and soon the burning will give way to the "healing water of truth." Soon, the heaviness will subside and the spirit of Peace that is your true nature will begin to shine through the darkness and reflect peace into every area of your life…from your shiny, *clean kettle!*

Are You Ready?

You have now completed the preliminary preparations for beginning the soup. You have looked at the contents, gathered your basic utensils and scrubbed them clean. You're now ready to move on into the most exciting adventure in the Universe—the journey *within*…within yourself! It takes courage and commitment to begin this journey and stay with it! *You* must provide the courage and commitment. The **Peace Soup** recipe will help make this journey as easy as possible by taking you gently by the hand and leading you around (and through) the major obstacles that block most people from experiencing true peace.

These obstacles, however, all come from you. You are the only one who can block yourself from peace. I'm going to suggest that you make a commitment to yourself to give this recipe a chance. Commit yourself *to yourself* for the next seven weeks and practice the techniques every day. You'll find that you will encounter resistance and perhaps make excuses, feel like a failure or decide it's not worth the effort—but this is all *you* resisting change in *yourself.* In Step 4 of the recipe, we'll explore exactly how this resistance occurs, but for now, just determine not to let your-*self* defeat you. I'm suggesting that you make up your mind to do something that will benefit you for the rest of your life and devote yourself to *you* for just seven weeks. You'll be amazed at the results!

> **You are the only one who can block yourself from peace.**

Step 1
Peeling the Onion
Developing Peace in the Physical Body

In the beginning, you were created in the image and likeness of Peace. But as we've seen, you've wound yourself up into a physical bundle of stress, and before you can re-establish peace in your mind and emotions, you must un-wind the physical body. The body is the man-i-festation (woman-i-festation) of all the thoughts–words–actions–feelings that have been accumulated by you in this lifetime, and by your ancestors before you (through your genes). The physical body is the garment you wear, the vehicle you move around in, but it's not *you*...not the *essence* of your being. We'll be exploring the essence later, but this first step requires that you understand the body and its function in a peaceful life.

The first step is to understand the body and its function in a peaceful life.

Just as your clothes and your automobile are designed for obsolescence, so, too, is your body. If the body didn't die, there would be no evolution, no improvements, no adaptation. Without this planned obsolescence, we might be walking around in pre-historic bodies, or floating in the ocean as one-cell amoebas. Each generation brings improvements to the physical body, even though they are usually imperceptible.

Bodies are designed to die, but not until having lived for a much longer period than the average life-span today. When you learn to take care of your body and obey the rules, as we'll discuss in Step 2, you can live for 120 years or longer (maybe much longer) and stay young and healthy the whole lifetime!

The Soup Stock

A relaxed, healthy body is the *soup stock* that is the foundation for the rest of the ingredients of the recipe. A healthy body is the result of healthy thoughts, words, actions and feelings, and you will prepare your soup stock by eliminating stress-causing elements. You prepare the stock by peeling away the layers of stress and dis-ease that you've allowed to build up over the years. The relaxation technique you'll learn later in this step will provide you with a *tool* for the peeling away of stress, but before we get there you will want to explore how you created the stress in the first place, and how to not create any more.

Prepare your soup stock by eliminating stress-causing elements.

You'll remember that the *ladle* we use for stirring our soup is the spoken word, and that the words we use trigger *images* in the subconscious mind. We're going to build on this awareness now by showing how you can lift up your consciousness for an even cleaner kettle and an even healthier, more robust soup stock.

You created Stress Soup and caked your kettle by speaking negatively and thus triggering negative images. "I *hate* it when you do that! I'm *sick* and *tired* of this! This just *kills* me!" What kind of images do these words trigger? *Hate, sickness, tiredness and death!* The subconscious mind doesn't have the power to reason or to think. It only *acts* on the data you feed into it. It's been likened to a computer, with the conscious mind as the programmer. The programmer types in the data and the computer spits out the results automatically!

Perhaps you've heard the computer term, "G.I.G.O"…Garbage In, Garbage Out. When you program your computer with negative images (garbage), what kind of soup do you think you'll cook up? *Garbage Soup!* That's what many people have cooked up for themselves—a life filled with stress, sickness, poverty, broken dreams, unfulfilling relationships…*Garbage!* If that's what you've created, it's time to clean up your act, and you begin by cleaning up your language.

It's time to clean up your act by cleaning up your language.

When you curse, using those famous "four-letter words," you trigger "four-letter images" in the subconscious mind, and produce four-letter stuff in your life. In addition to the common curse words, we often use more subtle negative words that curse our lives even more. "I can't. I'm afraid. I'm scared to death. I'm so stupid. I hate myself. I'll never get better. I quit. This is killing me. Damn it to hell!"

That's exactly what you're doing when you use negative words—damning your own life to hell, not a place you go when you die, but a place you create for yourself in your life *here and now.* Hell is not comfortable. It's hot...hot as hell! The heat is for your own good. When it gets hot enough, you'll decide to do something about it and create a more heavenly place, but you can decide to do that *before* you experience the real heat. The hot-as-hell experience burns out the negativity, the impurities, the curse—but instead of burning them out, you can gently *peel them away*...again, like peeling an onion, one layer at a time. You will probably still cry a little, but you need not go through hell! How do you keep from experiencing the fires of hell? The first step is to stop using negative words. Stop stirring the soup with a dirty spoon! Clean up your language. Stop saying words that trigger negative images in the subconscious mind. Put a new positive program into the computer and start bringing forth a *heavenly* print-out!

Let's take the word "hate" as an example. How many times do you say this word? "I just hate this, or that." Remember, the word "hate" is not a *word* to the subconscious mind—it's an *image.* When you say the word, it's not h-a-t-e (a word), it's the *image* of hate, and the computer pulls up everything you've ever known about hate and adds the new data to it. Every time you say the word "hate," you're becoming a little more hate-full. If you say, "I hate driving in the rain," you program that data, and every time it starts raining and you have to drive, you're hating it, and you're filled with stress. In this kettle of soup, you're much more likely to have an accident...or be miserable. I heard an otherwise positive person say recently, "It scares me to death to drive an automobile!" He still drives. What do you suppose he's creating for himself?

"Tricking the Guardian"
Opening the Trapdoor

We all want our lives to be filled with love and trust, not hate and fear, so how can the person who hates driving in the rain learn to be relaxed when it's raining and they're driving? They cannot say they "love" driving in the rain, or even that they "like" it, since they've been programming "hate" into the computer for years. There is a guardian that stands between the conscious mind and the subconscious mind,

The guardian is belief! and that guardian is *belief!* "As you *believe*, so shall it be done unto you." If you have programmed your belief system (b.s.) that you hate driving in the rain, you're not going to be able to say, "I *like* driving in the rain," and get it past the guardian. I liken this guardian to a trapdoor between the

conscious mind and the subconscious mind—and the key that opens the trapdoor is *belief* (See Figure 1.)

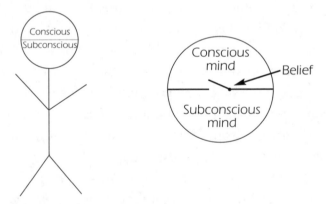

Figure 1

When you believe you hate something, then saying you "like" it won't open the door and get it into the subconscious mind to be acted upon. There is a way, however, to trick the guardian! You can open the trap door by saying something that's *believable* to the guardian, but still capable of pulling up a positive image and changing the belief system.

In this example, instead of saying, "I *hate* driving in the rain," which is believable, or "I *like* driving in the rain," which is *not* believable, you can say "I *don't like* driving in the rain." The "don't" makes the statement believable, opening the trap door and allowing the word (the image) "like" to be pulled up and reinforced. So you become more like-able—more able to like. Your life becomes lighter and, after a while, driving in the rain no longer creates excess stress.

Perhaps a better example of how this works is with the word "bad." When you say "bad," it's a downer. "This is *bad*" means there is no *good* in it. The word is designed to mean that—it's *designed* to be a negative word—but you don't want your life (your soup) to be *bad* (down)—you want it to be *good* (up), so you'll want to stop saying that any of the ingredients are bad. You *want* to stop saying the word, but you still *believe* that some things are just plain bad, so how do you get the "bad" out of your soup?

Instead of saying something is "bad," you can begin saying, "It's not so good!" What does this do to the trap door and the subconscious mind? It opens the door because "not so good" is believable, and the subconscious mind searches out and reinforces *good!* The "not so" is fluffed off because the subconscious mind doesn't weigh things. Good is good, even when it's not so good! It's a trick, and it works like magic to lighten up your life. Now, instead of the impetus being down (bad), it turns up (not so good). It's not so good, but it's getting better! This is the feeling you get. Again, you're lightening up the soup by stirring it with a good clean spoon.

Another example would be the word *hard.* "This is hard for me" creates an image of extreme difficulty that is another downer. You want life to be easy, but you make it hard by *saying* it's hard, and *believing* it's hard. Again, you can "lighten up" with our little trick. "It's not so easy" makes "easy" the image. "It's not so easy, but hey, I can do it!"

Can you see what's happening when you begin to trigger positive images instead of negative? You're giving yourself an "upper!" You're turning the world around, from the negative (down) to the positive (up), spooning off the dross of the old Stress Soup, making way for a

Trigger positive images instead of negative ones.

new peaceful life.

Many other negative words we use can be magically turned positive. "Worry" is one. We all know people who are professional worriers. I remember my grandmother used to worry a lot. She would say, "Well, somebody has to worry about it." She also would say, "I'm worried to death." She died at a young age. Worry is not a word—it's an image. I suppose you could learn to worry positively, but that's not the image you trigger when you say "worry." It's designed to bring up a negative image, a downer, and again you can begin lightening up with the word "concern" (a healthy concern). Better yet is *trust*. You can say, "I trust everything will be O.K."…and it will! Everything always works out for the best…so don't say "worry"…be happy!

Of course there are many negative words that you can turn around, and it's fun as well as helpful. Make it a game of awareness and elicit others to play along with you. You're changing the world to the positive, one word at a time!

You're changing the world to the positive, one word at a time!

Before leaving this section, there is one final word I'd like to emphasize that may be the most negative of all, simply because it masquerades as a positive word. This word is very plentiful in Stress Soup. It's *try!* "Just try," the world says. "You can do anything if you try." I bet you can't! Just try to close this book and then open it again. Did you do it? Then you didn't *try*—you *did* it! You're either going to *do* something or *not* do it. There is no such thing as *try*, but there is an image. It's the image of striving, of forever reaching. It's a "trying situation." Try and try again and you won't *do* anything. Trying creates stress—Stress Soup!

This was proven to me very vividly when counseling a young woman whose life was a genuine mess! She was so stressed that she couldn't eat or sleep. She cried most of the time. She was truly that "bundle of nerves" we talked about earlier. Every other word out of her mouth was "try." "I'm really trying. I've tried this. I've tried that. I'm trying to do what the doctors tell me. I'm really trying hard!" And she was, and it was destroying her! Her only assignment from me was to eliminate that one word from her vocabulary. It was amazing how fast her life turned around. In one week, she was noticeably better. She just stopped trying and began to *do* the things she needed to do. She cooked up a wonderful kettle of soup and lived happily ever after. It's so gratifying to see the recipe work its magic. It's great to see it work in other people's lives and it's even greater to see it work in yours, and you will—unless you try!

Most of us will probably not completely stop saying the word "try," since it's so entrenched in our vocabulary and in our lives. I've been working on it for over 30 years, and I still say "try" at times. The difference is that now, when I say it, I reach for the mixing bowl called Awareness. My internal response is, "Oh, I said 'try.' No, I'm going to *do* it (or not do it), but I'm not going to try!" When Luke Skywalker said, "I'll try," in THE EMPIRE STRIKES BACK, his teacher, the Jedi Master Yoda said, "No! Try not...do...or do not...there is no try!" Yoda makes a delicious **Peace Soup**.

Actions Do Speak Louder!

As powerful as words are in manifesting your life, *actions* are even more powerful. Actions are "the word made flesh." When you act a certain way, you are affirming (firming up) your consciousness. When you think you are a nervous person and *act* nervous, "the word becomes flesh and dwells among you." (John 1:14) You experience life as a nervous person. "By your fruits (actions), you are known," Jesus said (Matt 7:20, rev. ver.). In order to turn your world around to peace, you begin to *act* peacefully. *Speak* words of peace, and *think* peace. "Walk the talk and talk the walk," the great soup chefs say.

Actions are "the word made flesh."

Dale Carnegie has an affirmation that all his students remember forever, because they say it so many times during his classes. "*Act* enthusiastic and you'll *be* enthusiastic! *Act* enthusiastic and you'll *be* enthusiastic!" Over and over we affirmed this and even unto this day

(35 years later), I still affirm it, and I'm still enthusiastic about life! I *act* enthusiastic. I *believe* I'm enthusiastic. It's *firmed up* in my life and "made flesh." Actions speak louder than words!

Stress Replacement

Watch your actions! If you have any little nervous activities like twirling your hair, pulling your ear, clicking a pen, shaking a leg, tapping a foot—catch yourself *in the act!* Then use these nervous activities as *triggers* to relax! Turn the world around and use things that normally cause tension as triggers to relax. I call this *stress replacement.* You're taking what used to cause stress and replacing it with relaxation.

What do you normally do when the telephone rings? React! Bell rings, you act…sound familiar? Most of us learned in school about the experiment with "Pavlov's dogs." Pavlov, the Russian scientist, set up an experiment where he would ring a bell and feed his dogs until they became conditioned to eat when the bell rang. Then he would ring the bell and *not* feed the dogs, but they would react (salivate) the same as they did when they were eating.

How many bells (besides the telephone) do you have ringing in your life that you re-act to without thinking, without being aware of what you're doing? How many people can jerk your chain, or push just the right button to make you mad? We are all conditioned in many ways, just like the dogs!

See the conditioned reactions and replace them with relaxation.

Awareness helps you to *see* the conditioned reactions that cause tension and stress and replace them with relaxation. Let's use the telephone again as a general example, since we all have this bell ringing in our lives. You may want to become more aware when this bell rings and realize you don't have to answer it. You may want to, and probably will, but give yourself a chance to relax first! Bell rings…relax, then answer it, instead of bell rings…*react!* Catch yourself shaking your leg…relax; tapping your foot…relax; reaching for a cigarette…relax; turning on the TV when you enter a room… relax. It's a new habit—relaxation. (We'll discuss habits a little later.)

Body Language

What does body language tell you about yourself and others? A lot! Again, actions speak louder than words. The *Awareness Bowl* is essential in dealing with body language. When you catch yourself with your arms crossed, you are closed off to learning and growth. It's time to open up. Lighten up! When *you* open up, you'll find that others open up, too. When you shut down, *they* shut down. You'll find that you can help others who may be closed off by getting them to mimic you. Receive everyone with open arms and the whole world will be ready to receive you the same way. Open up and love. Open up and live!

Act the way you want to *be*. Act as the person who represents the values you prize most highly. When you catch yourself thinking about what you want to become…stop! Say to yourself, "I don't need to *become*, I will *be* this way now! *Act* enthusiastic and I'll be enthusiastic." The only thing that's preventing you from being all you can be is the idea of *becoming*. You are a human *being*, not a human *becoming*! Begin now to use every opportunity, every stressful encounter as a trigger to *relax*.

Act the way you want to be.

In just a few moments, you'll be learning how to relax, and how to practice *being* relaxed, but first let's look at a few more techniques in stirring the soup. You want to be stirring the soup gently, with good, positive images, spooning off the dregs of Stress Soup. You also want to…

Watch Out for Alligators!

Awareness is a big key in turning your world around, from negative to positive, from down to up. Another key is being gentle with yourself. You've been cooking up your Stress Soup for a long time, so it may take a little while to change it to Peace. Force won't help. Condemning yourself won't help. In fact, it just makes more stress. You cannot force yourself *not* to think about something negative. It's like my saying to you, "Don't think about an alligator!" What are you thinking about while you're "trying" not to think about the alligator? *The alligator!* He's a big one! You have to think about it in order to try *not* to think about it, and you just make it stronger. Let the alligator in, and then let him wander on out again, without giving him any power, and he won't bother you at all. Resist him and he will eat you up!

Instead of trying to block things out, let them gently flow through.

Instead of trying to block things out, let them gently flow through. For example, if you say the word "hard," simply be aware that you said it, and very gently change it to "not so easy." If you call something "bad," be aware and gently say, "Not so good." The difference between blocking it out or letting it flow through is very subtle, but knowing the difference determines whether you make **Peace Soup** or *Alligator Soup!* You must learn to let it flow through! We'll see more clearly how important this is as we move through the steps of the recipe and see how it's all about letting go!

The "Open Sesame" — Two Magical Words

You've begun now to use your first little cooking secret—being aware of your words and gently lightening up. One of the reasons we spend so much time and energy with words (besides the fact that your words create your world) is that the technique we're going to use in completing this first step of the recipe is built around words and images, especially the two most powerful words in your vocabulary. Can you imagine what they might be? There are a total of only three letters in these two words and we use them over and over in creating our lives. The two most powerful words you can utter are "I am!"

The two most powerful words you can utter are "I am!"

When you say, "I am," what do you think happens to the Guardian…the trap door between the conscious mind and the subconscious mind? It's like "Open Sesame!" (Open, says me!) When you say, "I am," you're saying, "I believe!" Belief opens the door and whatever you add to "I am" slides right through the door and into the subconscious mind to be acted upon.

In the Great Recipe Book, when Moses was in the wilderness listening to God speak through the "burning bush," what did God say His name (His nature) was? "I am!" "I am that I am…." (Ex 3:14) "I am" means "the essence of my being is," so the words "I am" give infinite power to whatever follows. When you take the name of God in vain by saying, "I am *sick,*" you are in error (sinning) and you feel the fire of hell (sickness). Who created the sickness? You did! You believed in sickness, you opened the trap door, and sickness (the word) became flesh and dwelt among you (in your body)! You are as you believe in your heart.

If you want to experience healing (wholeness), what must you believe? You must believe you are healed (whole). If you say, "I am well," will that make you well? If you truly believe it, it *will!* When Jesus performed a healing that was instantaneous, what did He always say caused the healing? Belief! "Your faith has made you whole! Go forth and sin (believe in sickness) no more." (John 5:14, rev. ver.) Those who experienced the healing had changed their belief from "sick" to "healed" and wholeness happened instantaneously, in the "twinkling of an eye!"

Go forth and sin (believe in sickness) no more!

Affirmations are positive statements of what you want to "firm up" in your life. However, negative statements can be just as powerful and are much more subtle because we don't realize what we're firming up. A student might affirm, "I'm terrible in math," not realizing that they've just reaffirmed the attitude that caused the problem in the first place. "I'm so angry!" never helped anyone overcome their anger. "I'm sick!" cannot help anyone feel better.

What about the use of "I am" with a negative image in the great healing organization of ALCOHOLICS ANONYMOUS? "I am an alcoholic" is an affirmation that's carried for a lifetime, but I believe it can be seen as a *step* in a much broader process. The next step is that of "recovering alcoholic." This, too, is but a step. "Re-covering" is covering the same stuff over and over. It's easy to get stuck in re-covery. The true goal is re-*covered!* "I am *covered again* in the peace of God and free of addiction to alcohol or any other substance or behavioral system. I see life with the vision of health and happiness." Beyond recovery is freedom. This is the final step in the process, and I see this

Beyond recovery is freedom. as the ultimate goal of *all* recovery programs.

Always follow "I am" with a positive image and you'll keep your life moving in a positive direction.

Watch your words and help your loved ones watch theirs. If you say, "This is hard," be aware of the image (hard) and gently, in your mind, change it to "not so easy." If a loved one says, "This is bad," gently say, "It's not so good." As we begin making these subtle shifts, life will become a little "gooder," until finally we will be able to say, "It's *all* easy and it's *all* good!"…a giant step made possible by many little baby steps. Watch…be aware. The soup is beginning to boil. Feel the smooth texture, see the ingredients blending together and smell the sweet, peaceful aroma. It's time now to add *relaxation.*

Learning to Wear "The Habit"

The physical body is designed to function best in a relaxed, calm, flowing condition. Witness professional athletes. When they are at their peak of performance, there is no sign of stress. All

Grace is the fulfilling of the law…the measure of greatness. activity is easy and grace-full. Grace is the fulfilling of the law; it is the measure of greatness. Grace comes from long and patient practice in developing the habit of perfection.

We are all creatures (creators) of habit. We have created ourselves with our thoughts, words, actions and feelings. Now those thoughts, words, actions and feelings re-create *us* automatically. They are habit! If stress is your soup, it's because (the cause be's) you have been adding the ingredients of stress to your kettle (your consciousness) for so long that you have developed *the stress habit*. If you want to form a new relaxation habit, you must begin thinking, speaking, acting in a relaxed manner. It's interesting that the garment worn by the calm, gentle loving nun in the Catholic discipline is called a "habit." To make a good **Peace Soup**, we, too, must begin to wear this mantle—the habit of peace and tranquility.

Habits Are Un-breakable!

Once you have programmed a habit into the computer, it will always play back the same. You will never be able to *break* a habit. The only way to erase it completely is electric shock treatment. This is definitely not recommended, as it erases good patterns along with the not-so-good ones! A habit that is to be changed must be "over-ridden" by a stronger habit. This stronger habit is developed in the same way that the old undesirable habit was, through long and patient practice…using the mixing bowls of Awareness, Control, Balance and Flow.

Where There's Smoke, There's Fire!

An example of this process that most of us are familiar with is the smoking habit. Smoking is learned. No one I know of ever came into this world with a cigarette in his or her mouth. He or she first had to become *aware* of smoking. The first cigarette usually doesn't taste very good, but it's the *cool* thing to do, so *control* is developed in overcoming the unpleasant taste through smoking more, and a chemical adjustment begins to take place in the body to *balance* the new substance (nicotine). After a while, the chemical change begins to "taste good like a cigarette should" and this allows the person to begin to *flow* with the activity of smoking. He or she can then say, "*I am* a smoker" and automatically go through the motions of lighting up with no conscious thought. I have known people to have three cigarettes lit at the same time as they were engrossed in some activity that was taking their conscious awareness.

The only way to change a habit, once it is established, is to develop a new, stronger habit…in this case, the non-smoking habit. The person reads the Surgeon General's report on smoking, attends the showing of a horror movie depicting the polluted lungs of smokers who have died from lung cancer, starts listening to his or her own "hacking" cough, and begins to become more aware that non-smoking is a healthier way to live. To develop *control* in this case is not so easy because smoking isn't a single habit. The activity of smoking involves reaching, touching, lighting, sucking, breathing, smelling, blowing, observing and remembering, plus the chemical reaction—the addiction to nicotine.

The only way to change a habit is to develop a new, stronger habit.

The fire of desire has to be turned up *high* in this case, and quitting often feels like hell! If one is persistent, finally a *balance* is established and the *flow* of a clean system makes it all worthwhile. Then they can thankfully say, *"I'm* a non-smoker…*I am* clean!" But the old habit is still there! It is not broken, just overridden, and it can take over again. We often see people who stopped smoking many years before all of a sudden take it up again. Why? They re-membered (put back together again) the Stress Soup that caused them to smoke so many years before and automatically started smoking again.

In order to maintain a new, positive habit, you must stay awake and continually increase the awareness of the way you want to be. You must maintain control by continuing to think, speak and act out the positive image. You must maintain your balance by continually pulling yourself back when you start getting out-of-balance, and then you can flow peacefully with the river.

> *"Row, row, row your boat, **gently down** the stream.*
> *Merrily, merrily, merrily, merrily, life is but a dream…."*

Let's dream…let's relax now. The soup is cooking, the sweet smell of peace is beginning to fill the air, so let's now add…

The Relaxation Technique

The technique you'll be working with in developing a relaxed physical body is called "Autogenic Training." This training was developed in Germany in the early 20th century by two psychologists, Dr. Johannes H. Schultz and Dr. Wolfgang Luthe. They discovered that if they gave their clients certain phrases to repeat *silently,* within their own minds, these phrases caused a shift in the clients' physical conditions. This proved to them that there definitely is a mind/body connection and they also found that the two magical words "I am" seemed to get the phrases more deeply entrenched in the mind and in the body. They discovered that well-designed phrases tended to pro-gress the client toward deeper relaxation.

Over their years of practice, Schultz and Luthe developed many different techniques, and autogenic training is still used in many hospitals in Europe to help patients relax before surgery. In the United States, we are drug-oriented, and the doctors simply *shoot the patients* (full of drugs)!

While these German doctors developed many exercises that affect different parts of the body, the technique we will use in this recipe is designed to relax the whole body in one session. I have been teaching people to use this exercise for years and we've seen phenomenal results in relieving physical stress. It works more effectively than any other system I've discovered, and I know it will do wonders for you. It's very simple and easy to learn.

Relax the whole body in one session.

Begin by finding a comfortable chair with a fairly straight back. You could do this exercise while lying down, but you would probably fall asleep before completing it. Of course, there's nothing wrong with sleep, but if you don't complete the exercise, you will leave pockets of stress that will make your soup stock lumpy and thick, instead of achieving the rich, smooth, flowing texture you want. Another reason for sitting up is that all of the techniques in the successive steps of the recipe call for a sitting position so, by sitting up, you are practicing for the next steps in making your **Peace Soup**.

Keep in mind that this autogenic exercise is relaxation, not medita-tion. As you'll discover in Step 3, one of the major differences between the two is that meditation is a *preparation for* activ-ity, while relaxation is a *release from* activity. Meditation is usually performed early in the day, while relaxation is done later, maybe after the work day and the rush hour drive, or just before bedtime, sitting up in your chair. Once you've completed your training exercise, relaxed the whole body, and it's time to go to sleep, you may want to begin the exercise again, while in bed. You will then fall asleep very quickly. I've never known anyone who has learned this technique to still have insomnia. They just don't go together. Another side benefit of this recipe is that you won't need as much sleep as you did with Stress Soup. You will get more quality sleep in a shorter time and you will have more awake time to be alive and enthusiastic about life. That tired, drained feeling you used to have is thrown out with the Stress Soup.

Meditation is preparation for activity; relaxation is a release from activity.

So, you're now sitting up in your comfortable chair, leaning against the chair, if you wish, with your back straight to allow energy to flow through your spinal column. This is a releasing exercise, so you want to keep your hands separated, resting in your lap, and your feet sepa-rated, resting on the floor. When you put your hands or feet together, you *close in* the body instead of allowing the releasing energy to flow through, and the stress to flow out.

Be sure to keep your head upright and balanced on your shoulders. If you allow your head to fall forward or to the side, you put stress on your neck. Balanced and upright, there is no stress, and you can sit for hours without moving (although 20 to 30 minutes is all that's needed in making **Peace Soup**).

Now, allow your eyes to *fall* shut. It's easier to relax and meditate with your eyes closed because approximately 80% of your sensory input comes through sight. Closing your eyes begins the relaxation process. Be aware of your breathing. Feel an easy, flowing breath. Keep in mind that this is the first step, and you will probably still find yourself full of stress and possibly feeling a little anxiety and apprehension. This is perfectly normal. Just accept yourself as you are, no matter how uptight or tense you may be, knowing that each step of the recipe is taking you closer and closer to perfect peace and serenity.

I remember a case where a woman came to me who was so nervous she couldn't sit down for more than a minute without jumping up and walking around. She was so stressed that I literally had to teach this autogenic exercise to her while she was walking around the room, and she had to practice at home, while walking, for the first few days. Within a week, she was able to sit through the whole exercise and within two weeks she was beginning to relax completely. Her family called it a miracle! It was just the **Peace Soup**. The recipe works…the soup is *so* delicious and *so* relaxing….

Hopefully, you are in better condition than this woman was, so I'll assume you're sitting in your chair now, eyes closed, head upright, breathing smoothly *(refer to Track 3 on CD)*….

Now, take a deep breath…inhale…hold it for three seconds… now let it out completely, feeling all the tension and stress flowing out of the body as you exhale. Do this once again…deep breath…hold it…1…2…3…exhale completely…all stress flowing out onto the floor. Now, just breathe normally as we begin this autogenic training.

Begin by being aware of your *right foot*. Become completely and totally aware of your *right foot* as a part of your body. Now, for just a moment, tense and contract the muscles of this foot…squeeze…1…2…3…now relax! Feel the sensation of "letting go" into a deep state of relaxation. Now, to place this foot into an even deeper state of relaxation, repeat this phrase "silently" (to yourself)…

"My foot is relaxed...
I am relaxed...
I am at peace with my body."

Now move your awareness to your *left foot*. Become completely and totally aware of your *left foot* as a part of your body.
Now, for just a moment, tense and contract the muscles of *this*
foot...squeeze...1...2...3...now relax! Notice how much better it feels to be relaxed rather than tense. Now, to place this
foot into an even deeper state of relaxation, repeat this
phrase...silently...to yourself...

"My foot is relaxed...
I am relaxed...
I am at peace with my body."

Now, feel this warm, comfortable feeling move to your
ankles...to your legs...to your hips. Feel your ankles, legs, hips
becoming *warm...heavy...comfortable.* Now, for just a moment,
tense and contract the muscles of the legs...squeeze...
1...2...3...now relax! Feel that sensation of letting go into a
deep state of relaxation. Now, to place this area of your body into
an even deeper state of relaxation, affirm silently to yourself...

"My legs are relaxed...
I am relaxed...
I am at peace with my body."

Now, allow this warm, relaxed feeling to move into your stomach...and into your chest, internally, and affirm to yourself...

"I feel quite, quiet...
I am at peace with my inner self."

Now, become aware of all your internal organs and glands, all
of the wonderful "working parts" of your body...and see them

all functioning in a calm, relaxed, efficient manner...and again affirm to yourself...

"I feel quite, quiet...
I am calm...serene...relaxed."

Now, very gently allow this warm, relaxed feeling to move into your shoulders...then slowly down into your back...feel the upper back relax...the lower back relax...and affirm to yourself...

"My back is relaxed...
I am relaxed.
I am at peace with my inner self."

Feel this warm, comfortable feeling move now into your arms and hands. For just a moment now, very gently tense and contract the muscles of your hands and arms...squeeze... 1...2...3...now relax! Feel that sensation of letting go into an even deeper state of relaxation...and now silently affirm...

"My arms and hands are relaxed...
I am relaxed...
I am at peace with my inner self."

Now, feel this warm and comfortable feeling move into your neck...and into your scalp...feel all the tiny muscles of your scalp gently letting go and relaxing...imagine soft, well-trained fingers gently massaging your scalp as you become more and more relaxed.

Feel this warm, relaxed feeling move down into your forehead...feel the forehead becoming smooth and relaxed...the eyebrows relax...the eyes relax...the nose relax...the cheeks relax...the ears relax...the chin relax...and finally release any tension that might be centered around the jaw…allow your jaw to relax…to let go…now affirm silently to yourself…

> *"My face is relaxed…*
> *I am relaxed…*
> *I am at peace with my inner self."*

Now become aware of your entire body…from the tip of your toes to the top of your head…and affirm silently…

> *"My whole body feels warm…heavy…*
> *comfortable…and relaxed….*
> *I withdraw my thoughts from the surroundings,*
> *and I am serene and still….*
> *I am alert in an easy…calm…*
> *inward-turned way….*
> *My mind is quiet…and at ease."*

And then once again…

> *"My whole body feels warm…heavy…*
> *comfortable…and relaxed….*
> *I withdraw my thoughts from the surroundings,*
> *and I am serene and still….*
> *I am alert in an easy…calm…*
> *inward-turned way….*
> *My mind is quiet…and at ease."*

Now just sit quietly with yourself for a couple of minutes and then begin to allow your eyes to drift open very slowly…just a slight glimmer of light and then *very slowly* open your eyes…then sit quietly for another few moments with your eyes open…. Now you can move and stretch….

The wonderful thing about this exercise is that you can do it yourself. In fact, you *must* do it yourself! It's called *auto*-genic. "Auto" means *self*. It's nice to have someone else say the words for you, but that won't generate the fire you need to cook the soup. Learn the phrases (memorize them), then use them. They're very simple. In fact, it's basically the same phrase for every part of the body. The only change is when you get to the stomach and chest internally, the third line changes to "I am at peace with my *inner self*." With the feet, ankles, legs, hips, it was, "I am at peace with *my body*." These are the most physical parts. Also, we begin with the feet for a reason. Besides bearing all the weight of the body, the feet also contain the nerve endings that run to every other part of the body. If you've ever had a foot massage or "shiatsu" massage, you know how working on the feet can relax every other part of your body.

I have used this autogenic exercise with people who had previously used hypnosis, self-hypnosis, massage, yoga, and many other effective techniques, and most of them agree that they feel this autogenic technique works better than any of the others, and sometimes even when the others have failed. It works, when you practice, and each time you practice, you will become a little more relaxed, a little more in control, and another layer of stress will be peeled away! Relaxation is becoming second nature to you. You're beginning to wear the habit of peace...the mantle of serenity. You're beginning to prepare the soup.

Each time you practice, another layer of stress is peeled away!

Practice this exercise at least once a day for the next 7 to 14 days (twice a day is twice as good) and you'll see wonderful things begin to happen. This is a powerful exercise and it's only the first step of our recipe. The next steps will build on this *soup stock*—your relaxed physical body. Be sure to take your time and build it up so that your foundation will be strong and secure. Don't rush to the next step. It will be of benefit only when the first step has been sufficiently mastered. When you *do* feel that you have this first step under your belt, you'll know you're ready to move on to...

Step 2

Completing the Soup Stock

The Mind/Body Connection

As we discussed in Step 1 of the recipe, the subconscious mind does not think, it only acts on what the guardian (belief) lets through the trapdoor. Another interesting and important fact about the subconscious mind is that it cannot distinguish between what is *real* and what is *imagined* to be real. It will respond in exactly the same way to both. This can cause great peace in your life, or great turmoil, depending upon your imaginings! If you worry a lot, or fill your mind with fear,

The subconscious mind cannot distinguish between what is real and what is imagined.

you will bring about chaos and turmoil. When you learn to create good, positive images, the subconscious mind will set about producing good, positive results in your life.

You may be familiar with the famous experiment involving three basketball teams, each seeking to improve their free-throw percentage. The researchers gathered the three teams, five men on each team, and tested the shooting percentage of each team. They then gave each of them their instructions for practice over the next 20 days.

The first team was to practice in the traditional manner, with each member actually shooting free-throws for 20 minutes each day. The second was instructed to practice by having the members sit in chairs around the free-throw line and just *imagine* they were shooting the basketball for 20 minutes each day. When they imagined they missed a shot, they would correct the next shot accordingly. The third team was instructed not to practice at all for the 20-day period. At the end of this time, the three teams were tested again, with very interesting results.

The team that didn't practice, of course, showed no improvement. The one that actually shot the free-throws improved *24%*, but the most surprising statistic was that the team that had *imagined* themselves practicing, improved *23%!* There was only a 1% advantage in physically shooting the basketball, versus simply using the imagination to make the shots.

In sports, and in any activity of life, the imagination can be a powerful tool for self-development when you use it *con*-structively. It can be an instrument of self-*de*struction, or at least detrimental to your well-being, if you fill it with images of fear, anger, jealousy, resentment, sickness or death.

The second step in the recipe requires that you learn the *con*-structive use of the imagination, and then put it to work in building a peaceful, productive life. The exercise you will learn in this step will help you develop the discipline you need to do this, but before you get to the Control Bowl, you must add some more ingredients to the Awareness Bowl.

There is a difference between truth and reality!

I like to say that there is a difference between *truth* and *reality!* Everyone has a different "reality," based on what they've learned about the world and believe to be real. What's real to you, may or may not be real to me. It depends on how similar our training has been. If you grew up (became "adulterated") in a country or a culture quite different from mine, our realities could be quite a bit different. For instance, if our religious training and beliefs have been different, then what I believe about religion can seem very unreal to you.

The truth, however, is absolute. It is the same for everyone, no matter what the realities may be. Most people live their lives based upon *their* reality, not on *the truth*. One of the attributes of **Peace Soup** is to be able to live as close to *the truth* as possible, and this takes *aware-ness*...remembering that *no one can tell you the truth!* No master teacher, no holy book, no religion, no *one* or no *thing* can express the absolute truth. Anyone who says they can is a "false prophet" and if you believe them, they will lead you down the road of false imaginings and ultimately to distress and destruction!

No one can tell you the truth!

The truth can only be known in your own heart! Master Chef Jesus said, "You shall *know* the truth and the truth shall set you free." (John 8:32, rev. ver.) When Master Chef Lao-Tzu said, "The truth that can be spoken is not the eternal truth," he was absolutely correct. The finite mind cannot comprehend the in-finite. Don't read many books, don't listen to many speakers, or ask the opinions of others, or get "add-vice." We have enough vice already, we don't need to *add more!* Listen to your *heart* and you will begin to know "the truth that sets you free." Listen to your *heart*, not your *head!* Your head is filled with false imaginings. This is where your ego resides, as we will explore more fully in Step 4 of the recipe. For now, what we want to emphasize is the power of the imagination and its effect on how you live your life.

Don't Feed the Bears!

If you were walking down a secluded path in a deep dark forest... all alone...and suddenly a giant grizzly bear jumped out in front of you, what would you do? Some people say they would run; others, who understand the nature of bears, say they would stand perfectly still; others say they would find a tree to climb, but the answer is really the same...we would all react to the bear, because we're all aware that grizzly bears aren't good for our health!

Now, let's say there's an actor who knows all about grizzly bears. He has a grizzly bear costume that looks real, and he knows how to act just like a bear and sound just like a bear. He gets some grizzly bear perfume to put on and hides on that same secluded path, waiting for you in the deep, dark forest. When he jumps out in front of you, looking, sounding, acting and smelling just like a giant grizzly bear, how are you going to react? The very same way! The truth is, this is an actor dressed up like a bear. The reality is, "That's a bear," and you respond according to your belief.

Most of us are living our lives with grizzly bears hiding in the bushes and we continue to feed them with our false beliefs...our false imaginings. Our lives are figments of our own imaginations. This is great if we imagine good things—peace, success, abundance, perfect health, perfect relationships. It's not so great if we imagine ourselves as "losers"—broke, ugly, depressed, unloved, unwanted, sick, tired, old, stress ridden. Many of us have an image of ourselves that is false and inadequate, yet we live our lives as if the image were true.

Our lives are figments of our own imaginations.

A good, positive self-image is an important ingredient in **Peace Soup**. We develop a large percentage of our self-image in the "formative years," the first six years of our lives, and especially the first year! Our parents have a dramatic impact on our belief systems. They are the authority figures, and we *believe* what they tell us. Much of their reality becomes our reality. Of course, our parents did the best they could, based upon what they believed, but some of that, maybe much of that, was error. Some of the error beliefs or false images they imparted to us have been controlling our lives in unfortunate ways.

If you were told you were "clumsy," you may have *believed* it and acted upon it. You were probably no more clumsy than anyone else, but you created a personality based on false information and have been living a clumsy, accident-prone, haphazard life. Maybe you were taught to believe that you are "messy" or "shy" or "stupid" or whatever, and you've been living your life based on this belief. The power of belief is awesome.

Although parents probably have the most profound effect on our self-image, they aren't the only ones in authority roles who label us. When a doctor calls you "diabetic" or "schizophrenic," it's like putting a stamp on your forehead and you, and everyone around you, begin to see that image, as *you!* It's not you, it's just a situation, a condition that you're here to heal.

Labeling or *general semantics* has a powerful impact on all of us, and we want to watch the labels we put on ourselves and others as much as the labels others put on us. The image they create can change the course of one's life, for the good as well as the not so good.

Labeling has a powerful effect on all of us.

When a teacher or school principal calls a student "backward" or a "slow learner," that student is stamped for life. There's a story of a little boy who was having trouble with his schoolwork, and the school notified his parents that he was going to be transferred to a slow learner class. The father immediately took his son out of that school and enrolled him in a private school, where he flourished. He ultimately went to a military academy and chose the military as his career. The child's name…John Glenn! If his parents had allowed the "slow learner" stamp, someone else likely would have been the first (and later the oldest) American to orbit the Earth and U.S. Senator from Ohio.

Learn to use positive, up-lifting labels that create a belief in a positive self-image. The imagination will then begin to blend it, stir it, fold it in with the other healthy ingredients to produce the perfect **Peace Soup**. Label yourself and others as "good…beautiful…loving…joyful…peaceful…happy…prosperous…healthy," and watch your life and theirs mellow and become more de-light-full.

As the great soup chef, Napoleon Hill says: "What the mind of man can *conceive* and *believe,* it can *achieve.*" I believe it not only *can* achieve it, but it *will* achieve it…when you truly believe. When you conceive and believe in negative ideas and images, your life will reflect negativity. When you conceive and believe in positive ideas and images, your mind and body will go to work to bring them about…bring them to fruition in your life.

What the mind of man can conceive and believe, it can achieve.

What this recipe is designed to do is to help you conceive of, and believe in, a peaceful life, and to give you the tools necessary to achieve it. To complete the recipe, you learn to let go of the false images of "sickness, suffering and death" that have been, and are continuing to be, fed into your computer by the world and its great image makers.

One of the chief image makers in our modern adult(erated) world is the media and its vehicles, especially television. The world is *tele-ing* us the vision, and we're buying it. Boy, are we buying it! We're being bombarded daily with images—images of murder and mayhem, broken lives, broken dreams, broken marriages, sickness, suffering and death.

We're being bombarded daily with images.

These images look real and the "authorities" say they're real, so we believe them and begin to act, think, speak and feel as if they are *true*, then we re-create the problems in our lives…over and over…"as the world turns!" This is the re-creation of the world, but we don't play that game anymore. "Days of Our Lives" is not our image any more. The talk show images of crazy, suffering, angry people are not a pattern for us. The negative, stressful, sensational, nightly news is a dirty ladle that stirs Stress Soup. It's time to wash the dishes, the *kettle*, the *ladle*, the *measure* and establish good images that will produce good soup. It's time to turn *off* the television set and turn *on* the power of your own imagination.

In the *Laboratory of the Mind* exercise at the end of this chapter, you will learn to turn on the television of your own mind. You will learn to "tele" your own mind to conceive, believe and achieve the vision of health, prosperity, love, joy and peace—the vision of **Peace Soup.**

Before you can catch the vision of peace, you must make sure this vision is founded in a good soup stock—a good, balanced, physical body. As we've seen, your body is the result of the thoughts, words, actions, feelings, beliefs and habits you've developed throughout your life, and in order to create and maintain a healthy body, you must be aware of, and abide by, the rules of the body!

You have created your body and are re-creating it every day, every moment, and you have the power to change your body into anything you can imagine—even a perfect body. Can you imagine that? If you can, and if you will obey the rules, you *will* create the perfect body, a body that looks good, feels good, acts good all the time. Even those who may find themselves in a de-

You have the power to change your body into anything you can imagine—even a perfect body.

formed body can re-form it to perfection. Roger Bannister, as a young boy, had his legs burned to the point that the doctors said he would never walk again. He re-formed his body and not only walked, but was the first man to *run* the four-minute mile!

You cannot have peace without health. You may have all the money you can ever use, a perfect family life, a wonderful profession or livelihood, but without your health you are only existing, you're not living. The exciting thing is, you can have it all, all ways, when you abide by the rules. So let's explore…

The Four Rules of the Body

Remembering the K.I.S.S. (simplicity) that makes the soup easy to digest, I will be brief in the discussion of these rules. As I've said, however, it is of utmost importance to build a solid base for your soup stock. The rules are basic, but they're also fluid. New discoveries are being made daily in health and well being, so each of us must keep our ingredients fresh by staying abreast of what's new, and adding to the basic recipe so we can extend our healthy, peaceful life even longer.

Choosing health requires an individual responsibility, the ability to respond to the needs of your body. All bodies are different and there is no magic formula for *every*-body. Learn to listen to *your* body and *don't* listen to every*body* else. Don't give your response-ability to doctors, drugs, surgery, germs, viruses, accidents—*any one* or *any thing*. "They" are not responsible for your health (or your sickness)—you are! Everything that is expressing (pressing out) in your life comes from the kettle you're cooking in—your consciousness. To develop a health consciousness, you must first clean the kettle of old ideas about, and beliefs in, sickness. The cleansing process began with the first step in this recipe. The first of the four rules of body is *Rest and Relaxation*. Relaxing and resting the body and the mind makes ready the kettle for the ingredients of **Peace Soup**.

The second of the four rules is *Nutrition*. The physical body is a chemical machine, a biochemical mechanism. Actually, it's *electro-chemical,* as we'll explore later, but the chemical part is what we're involved with here, and biochemistry can be very complicated and controversial. This recipe is about neither of these. It's not meant to be highly scientific, and certainly I'm no scientist or expert on nutrition. This recipe comes from a simple formula that has worked for me and has worked in thousands of lives over the past three decades. The ingredients of this formula have been gathered from some highly acclaimed scientists—biochemists—who all say the same thing:

"The body is designed to run on food, and only food!" "The body is designed to run on food, and only food!" Food is the fuel for the body and the main reason our society is in a health crisis is that we're not giving our bodies the fuel they need. We're not eating real food!

If you were to begin putting water into the gasoline tank of your automobile, a machine that's designed to run on gasoline, would that automobile run properly? No, it would "spitter and sputt" and finally conk out. If you put too much of anything other than food into your body, it, too, will begin to "spitter and sputt" and finally conk out. So nutrition becomes essentially very simple: *"Eat only food...Don't put 'non-foods' in your body!"* Sounds simple, but it's not so easy because of the technology of our modern society.

Where did you learn how to eat? From your parents, basically. Where did your parents learn to eat? From *their* parents, and they from their parents. If you go back to your great-grandparents or before, where did they get their food? They raised it, or bought or bartered it from neighboring farmers. It was all fresh—live and vital. They had their own gardens, slaughtered their own meats, got their eggs from the chickens scratching in the front yard, got their milk fresh from "Old Bessy." They canned their own foods to see them through the winter.

Where do we get our food today? From the supermarket (not so *super*), or the fast food restaurant (maybe fast, but seldom food). We're *trying* to eat a balanced diet, just like our great-grandparents, but the food's just not the same. The milk is pasteurized or homogenized, the eggs are not fresh or fertile, the vegetables and fruits come from hundreds or thousands of miles away and are days, weeks, even months old. The fats are hydrogenated, the meat "hormone-ized," the canned foods full of preservatives. It's all processed in some way and the vitality, the life, the nutrition is gone. What we think is food is not food, and beyond that, *it's full of toxins.* We're not feeding our bodies, we're *toxifying* them! Is it any wonder that the sickness care industry (*health care* is a mis-nomer) is the second largest in our country and growing like a cancer across what used to be "the fruited plain?" We're not feeding our bodies the fuel they need and they're spittering and sputtering and conking out at an ever-more rapid rate.

What we think is food is not food.

This doesn't have to happen. It *is* possible to feed your body properly and keep it running smoothly and efficiently and never get sick. This sounds impossible, according to the worldly standards. The world is sickness-oriented. Why? Most people *believe* in sickness. They *think* about sickness, they *talk* about sickness, they *act* sick. The worldly belief system (b.s.) says you *"catch* colds and flu, germs and viruses," but germs and viruses are always around. You don't catch *them,* they catch you! They catch you with your immune system down (impaired) because it hasn't been fed.

There are many people who don't get sick. They don't *catch* things because they think, speak and act healthily, and they eat good food. This is essential for all of us who are "cooking up a peaceful life" with this recipe. You must first wash your kettle clean of the old sickness beliefs and then go back to the four mixing bowls.

First, you become aware of what *is* food and what *isn't*. Then you gain control by learning to eat only food, and eliminating the non-foods from your diet. You then establish balance by getting the right amounts of each of the essentials and, finally, you're in the *flow* of perfect health.

What Is Food?...What Isn't!

The human body has been around on planet Earth for hundreds of thousands of years and, while it has evolved over this time, it takes a long time for it to adapt to a new substance and consider it a food. The scientific estimates as to how long this takes range from 2,000 to 10,000 years. So what the body considers food, fuel to keep it running smoothly, must have been being ingested for at least 2,000 years!

Much of what the average person on the Standard American Diet (S.A.D.) eats today has been "invented" in the 20th century, most in the second half of the century. It's not food, and our bodies are not designed to handle it. The human body is a very resilient machine and it can handle *some* of it (for a while), but much of this non-food actually poisons or toxifies the body and the spittering and sputtering begins at an increasingly younger age.

Before we get into these non-foods that are so common today, we want to explore what *is* food—the fuel that makes a healthy body. Keep in mind that nutrition is an in-exact science at best. It's probably closer to an art than a science because, as I've said, "Every *body* is different" and what I say, in general, may not be true for *you!* I'm happy to say that there *is* a way you can always determine what's right for you, and your body will tell you. We'll be exploring this later in this section, but for now, let's look at nutrition *in general.*

The Seven Essentials

There are basically seven nutrients that the body *has* to have in order to function properly. Without an adequate supply of any of these, there will be imbalance, stress and dis-ease.

Essential #1 — Protein

Protein is the only substance your body can use to rebuild tissue. The building blocks of protein are called *amino acids*. There are 22 amino acids; eight are known as *essential aminos,* meaning your body cannot make them, so they must be taken in through the food you eat. The eight essential aminos must also be in perfect ratio with each other.

> **Protein is the only substance your body can use to rebuild tissue.**

There are many good sources of protein that have the eight essential aminos in proper ratio, including eggs, dairy and meats. It's best, though, not to eat much of the heavier proteins such as chicken, duck, beef and pork, as they get progressively more difficult for the body to break down and assimilate. These heavy proteins can cause your soup stock to be thick, heavy and sluggish. What we want is a light, supple, rich-textured soup stock.

Use your Awareness Bowl when eating your essential protein and keep it light. Draw from your Balance Bowl: a few eggs, mostly the whites, although a little yolk can increase HDL (good) cholesterol; a little dairy (too much can be mucus-forming); some cold-water fish such as salmon and tuna; occasionally some turkey and chicken (skinless); perhaps a little red meat; *very* little pork; and *lots of fresh vegetables.*

It's important to note that no vegetable protein has all eight essential aminos in proper ratio, but a variety of vegetables will. If you want to become a strict vegetarian, you'd better learn which vegetables have which amino acids, or you may end up with a protein deficiency. Study diligently, or consider becoming "ovo-lacto," eating some eggs and dairy along with your vegetables. Whatever you decide, eat your protein—it's essential!

Essential #2 — Carbohydrates

Most people think of carbohydrates as pasta, grains, rice and bread—the starchy foods. These are, according to Chef Barry (Sears) in THE ZONE, the "unfavorable" carbohydrates. All fruits and vegeta-

All fruits and vegetables are carbohydrates. bles are carbohydrates, and this is ideally where we get most of this essential—the fresher, the better, and raised as close to you as possible. Fresh fruits and vegetables help connect you to your good Mother Earth. We need the energy that has been fueling our bodies through eons of time. It's a long-term connection, and it's essential!

Essential #3 — Fatty Acids

Again, simply put, the body needs a certain amount of fat to function properly—*good fat*. The "low-fat" or "no-fat" diets that are the "fad" are actually making people fatter (fadder). It **It takes fat** takes fat to burn fat! The good fats are commonly **to burn fat!** known as unsaturated fats. A quick way to determine if a fat is saturated or unsaturated is that a saturated fat is usually solid at room temperature, while an unsaturated fat is liquid.

The good fats are also divided into two categories, omega-6 fatty acids and omega-3 fatty acids. Omega-6 is plentiful in the high-fat American diet, too plentiful. According to Dr. Alexander Leaf of Harvard University, the human body ideally needs a ratio of omega-6 to omega-3 of 5 or 6 to 1. The current ratio in the S.A.D. is about 24 to 1. We need to decrease the omega-6 intake and increase the omega-3 intake. As we said, the best source of omega-3 is deep sea fish such as salmon, tuna and cod, and especially the oils of these fish. You can supplement your diet with fish oil capsules, or do as your great-grandmother did—take cod liver oil! If you prefer a vegetable source of omega-3, I believe that flax seed is the way to go. Not just the oil, but the whole seed. Flax seed contains 35% oil, 55% of which is the crucial omega-3 fatty acids. This seed is a high quality protein source and is loaded with soluble and insoluble fiber. One-fourth cup of flax seed has 11.7 grams of fiber and has been proven to lower cholesterol levels without the side effects of cholesterol-lowering drugs. However you decide to do it, get the good fat *into* your diet and the not-so-good, saturated fat out—it's essential.

Essential #4 — Vitamins

Whole books are written on vitamins and how vital they are, and new discoveries are being made constantly. Contrary to what many medical people may tell you, you cannot get all the vitamins you need in the food you eat. As I've said, "Food ain't food no more!" Not only are the soils depleted of essential nutrients, but the shipping and storage time, from harvest to table, greatly diminishes whatever vitamins might have been there at harvest time.

You cannot get all the vitamins you need in the food you eat.

Cooking also destroys vitamins. The National Food Review Board says that "cooking destroys up to 93% of the nutrients in many foods." If you must cook your vegetables, *steam them lightly.* Vitamins are alive...too much heat destroys life! In a study conducted by Dr. Paul Kouchakoff at Switzerland's Institute of Clinical Chemistry, it was found that the blood reacts to cooked foods the same way it reacts to toxic elements, infection or trauma. Uncooked foods caused no reaction, but food heated beyond a certain temperature (usually around 191°F), or processed in any way, always caused a rise in the number of white blood cells.

Interestingly, this study showed that if cooked food is eaten along with raw, uncooked or unprocessed food, there is no pathological reaction in the blood. The raw food seems to neutralize the detrimental effects of the altered food, so it may be wise to always eat raw food (a salad or raw vegetables) along with your cooked foods. This will keep your body from being traumatized, but it won't assure that you're getting your vitamins.

Even the raw vegetables at the supermarket aren't fresh. The produce just doesn't *produce* any more. It's lost its vitality, its vitamins, its life. So it's best to supplement your food with natural vitamins.

The produce just doesn't produce any more!

All vitamin supplements are not equal. There is definitely a difference between synthetic vitamins that are "created" in a laboratory and vitamins found in food. Actually, the synthetic vitamins should not be called vitamins at all; they are chemicals and are toxic to the body. Dr. Royal Lee, founder of the Standard Process Company, discovered that though synthetic vitamins have the same molecular structure, they are a mirror image or exact opposite of natural vitamins. Synthetic vitamins refract light the opposite of natural vitamin complexes. New Kirlian photography research is confirming these earlier studies. Research from Finland, published in the NEW ENGLAND JOURNAL OF MEDICINE, shows that taking synthetic vitamins may actually be worse than taking no vitamins!

It is essential to supplement all the vitamins, so find a good multivitamin that's all-natural. It is especially important to take extra vitamin C. This vitamin is necessary in helping to control stress, and without it, the immune system all but shuts down. Vitamin C is necessary for all bodies, but only humans, monkeys and guinea pigs do not make this vitamin. Other animal bodies make Vitamin C in large quantities, from 2,500 to 25,000 mg per day, but we three (humans, monkeys and little pigs) must get it in our diets and in supplements. How much do we need? Most researchers say 3,000 to 6,000 mg per day! You won't get anywhere near that in oranges or orange juice, so take supplements.

I will not attempt to tell you other vitamins you might need, but I recommend that you do some studying on your own and be sure to buy your vitamins from a reputable source, making sure they're natural. You will find health in a health store, not in a drug store. We want only the best ingredients in our soup.

Essential #5 — Minerals

While vitamins give us the lively, active vitality for a healthy body, minerals give us the stability. Minerals are the basis of the body, the blood, the flesh, the skin and bones. Being of Mother Earth, they are that ancient connection that is the essence of the physical body. Minerals give us "magical building blocks" for the hearty soup stock of our **Peace Soup.**

Unlike vitamins, minerals are not destroyed in cooking, provided they are there in the first place! Unfortunately (S.A.D.ly), they probably aren't. They're just not in the soil anymore. Our once "mineral-rich" soil in the United States has been depleted by so-called "modern technology," trying to produce as much food as possible, on as little land as possible. Excessive crops and pollution have stripped the minerals from the soil, from our food, and thus *from our bodies*.

> **Minerals are just not in the soil anymore.**

People who live in mineral-rich parts of the world—the Tibetans, the Hunzas, the Titicacas—live much longer and healthier lives than those in "developed" countries, and one reason is in the mineral-rich food they eat.

Proper nutrition requires putting the depleted minerals back into your body. There are at least 60 essential minerals; many of these are trace minerals, so make sure you're getting a good mineral supplement. Do some research yourself. Remember, you're response-able for your body. There are many good books on minerals. Study, learn the essentials and make sure they're in your diet.

Essential #6 — Enzymes

Enzymes are the body's nutritional delivery system. Without them, the human body cannot utilize vitamins, minerals, trace elements and other nutrients. Your body's self-healing and immune response capabilities all depend upon the quantity of enzymes in the blood, organs and tissues, and enzymes are essential to the body's ability to break down toxins, build protein into muscle, eliminate carbon dioxide from the lungs and ward off disease-causing organisms.

> **Enzymes are the body's nutritional delivery system.**

Enzymes are plentiful in fresh fruits and vegetables and in meat, eggs and dairy, but apply heat over 108°F and they're all gone! As with vitamins, cooking (and microwaving) eliminates these essential enzymes, so cook as little as possible and supplement with natural products—live and vital green formulas such as "green magma," "barley green," "blue-green algae," chlorella and spirulina. Good **Peace Soup** has the green tinge of live enzymes. They're essential!

Essential #7 — Water

Your soup stock (body) is mostly water, and this water must be replenished continually. Water is essential for life, but all water is not suitable for drinking; in fact, most water is not—especially tap water.

"Safe, approved" tap water may be one of our biggest health risks!

"Safe, approved" tap water may be one of our biggest health risks! The E.P.A. (Environmental Protection Agency) standards allow for many poisons, such as aluminum, lead, arsenic, mercury, radioactive particles, chlorine and fluoride, in addition to a long list of others, that have been shown to accumulate in body tissue over time and lead to serious illness and even death. The G.A.O. (U. S. General Accounting Office) has expressed deep concern that the E.P.A. has been unable to control the use of "over *450* toxic substances that may find their way into our water supply."

The chemicals used to "purify" drinking water and "make it better" are poisons themselves. Fluoride, which is supposed to strengthen teeth, has been shown to interfere with thyroid function and have detrimental effects on the brain! A fluoride dose of only 11 parts per million has been shown to affect the nervous system, and fluoride toothpastes and mouthwashes contain as much as *1,000* parts per million! Chlorine is put into the water to *kill* (bacteria), and it is *killing* (people)! Chlorine and its by-products have been linked to such diseases as cancer, heart disease, diabetes, kidney stones and gout. So how do we make sure our water is safe to drink?

Bottled water is a big industry, but be aware that all bottled water is not necessarily safe. Spring water may contain some of those 450 toxic substances deemed hazardous. Also, water stored in plastic bottles and exposed to the sun can pick up impurities from the plastic. Distilled water is less likely to react with plastic, since it has no minerals, but if you detect a plastic taste in any water, don't drink it.

Home water filters vary as to their effectiveness. Reverse osmosis is a good system, but costly and time consuming. Distilled water is probably the best alternative, but be sure to supplement the minerals, as we discussed earlier. Drinking distilled water can be especially helpful for those with persistent kidney problems, as the mineral-free water allows the body to rid itself of mineral deposits that may be causing kidney stones, as well as arthritis, joint problems and circulatory buildup (atheroschlerosis).

Distilled water is probably the best alternative.

When ordering drinking water from a restaurant, always ask for lemon and squeeze it into your water. The lemon will alkalize the water (yes, lemon *is* one of the best alkalizers) and help neutralize the toxins and wash them through the body. It's best not to drink much water with meals so as not to dilute the digestive enzymes. Undiluted, solid food will be more completely and rapidly digested. Drink your water between meals, at least 1/2 gallon every day, and your soup stock will stay clear and free.

Another Word on Balance

Another highly important (and I believe when the research is analyzed, the *most* important) aspect of nutrition is the maintenance of a proper acid-alkaline balance within the system…a ratio of approximately 80% alkaline-forming foods to 20% acid-forming foods. This alkaline balance helps strengthen resistance to disease, as it removes toxins and provides a healthy "terrain" where yeast, mold and fungus—the harbingers of death—cannot exist.

Dr. Robert O. Young, in his book, ONE SICKNESS, ONE DISEASE, ONE TREATMENT, says, "All sickness and disease that leads to death culminates with yeast and fungus. It begins with over-acidification of the blood and tissues from an inverted way of eating and living." I like to say that if you let the image makers (advertisers) of the world mold your eating habits, you end up *moldy!* The mold, yeast and fungus feed on the sugar (glucose) and protein of your body and produce waste products known as *mycotoxins.* "These mycotoxins," Dr. Young states,

If you're sick and tired, the answer is alkalize.

"make us sick and tired!" If you're sick and tired of being sick and tired, the answer is *alkalize.*

Dr. Theodore A. Baroody, in his book, ALKALIZE OR DIE says, "The countless names attached to illnesses do not really matter. What does matter is that they all come from the same root cause...*too much tissue acid waste in the body!*" Dr. Baroody says that even negative emotions can cause an overly acidic system and reduce energy, again making you sick and tired. You'll be "sifting out the emotions" in Step 5 of the recipe, but, for now, concentrate on getting your balance in the food you eat. Dr. Baroody says, "The body does have a great alkaline reserve, but it is only a back-up system with limited quantity to keep you from constantly poisoning yourself with too much acid-forming food. When the alkaline reserve is depleted, death follows."

Generally speaking, fresh fruits and vegetables alkalize the body. Grains, beans and meat are acid-forming. To keep the alkaline reserve replenished, eat the natural balance of 80% fresh fruits and vegetables (and their juices) and only 20% of the acid-forming foods. For a more complete list of the acid-alkaline content of different foods, refer to the above-mentioned books of Drs. Young and Baroody. (See Bibliography.)

"The Seven Poisons"

Along with the over-acidification of the body through improper balance in food, there are seven non-foods (poisons) that cause the "spittering and sputtering." These seven poisons make the soup indigestible and toxic. These are substances that are generally consumed in great quantity in our S.A.D. lifestyle. In the interest of "K.I.S.S.ing," I will keep this section brief, but don't let this detract from its importance.

Poison #1 — Sugar

Re-*fined* sugar is not fine. It's not only a non-food, it's an anti-food! To try to move the refined sugar through the body, we use up nutrients that are beneficial. The body is a very resilient machine which can handle *some* processed sugar, but the annual consumption of sugar has gone from an average of five pounds per person at the turn of the twentieth century to the current average of *150* pounds per person! That's the equivalent of eating more than a tablespoon of sugar every four hours, 24 hours a day! Sugar consumption in the United States is up 28 pounds per person just since 1970. Because of modern technology, sugar now includes not only refined white sugar, but other artificial sweeteners which are even more detrimental to our health.

These artificial sweeteners are mostly aspartame, which breaks down into methanol, formaldehyde and formic acid—all recognized poisons. Dr. H. J. Roberts, an authority on aspartame, says it causes, among other disorders, hyperactivity, confusion, dizziness, visual problems, tremors and insomnia, and our kids load up on it every day! Another interesting finding is that aspartame actually causes you to gain weight by increasing the appetite and throwing the insulin level out of balance, and most so-called "diet" foods contain aspartame. It's not food, but the image makers are pushing it, and it's poisoning the soup.

The body needs some sugar, but not re-fined, processed sweeteners. Get your "sweet" from fresh fruit and possibly a little honey or pure maple syrup. Pull out your sweet tooth (it's just a baby tooth anyway) and keep a "nose for the ose." Eliminate processed foods containing added sucr-ose, gluc-ose, dextr-ose, malt-ose, lact-ose and fruct-ose. They're all unnecessary and they're all contaminating the soup.

> **Pull out your sweet tooth...it's just a baby tooth.**

Poison #2 — White Flour

All re-fined bread and pasta turn to sugar in our bodies, throwing excess glucose into the system and, just like refined sugar, they cause the pancreas to pump extra insulin, throwing these crucial levels out of balance. These refined carbohydrates are also devoid of food value and act as an anti-food. They are empty calories and, since they cannot be properly digested, they clog and toxify the system.

I like to use the example of my first grade teacher who instructed our class in making paste for our art work. She asked us to bring white flour from home to mix with water to make paste. That's the way white flour products act in your body. They mix with the water, *and make paste*. It's "paste-a," not pasta! This can be a sticky subject for those who love pasta, but you can get healthy pasta made from whole foods. Buy your pasta from a health food store and, if you must eat bread, make sure it's 100% whole grain bread. Much of the brown bread (wheat bread) is just white bread with brown food coloring added. Don't eat white bread, white rice, white pasta, or any re-fined grains with any regularity, or you won't have any regularity! They thicken the soup and sicken the body.

White flour products mix with water... and make paste.

Poison #3 — Salt

As with sugar, the body needs natural salt, but not the refined, processed kind that "pours when it rains." In commercial salt there are 17 processes in refinement that deplete all the nutritional value and again produce an anti-food. The processing utilizes toxic chemicals and some brands even add sugar. That's adding "in-salt to injury!" Who needs it? No *body!* If it's recommended that you stop eating salt when you have high blood pressure, doesn't it make sense that eating salt has something to do with the *cause* of high blood pressure? **Peace Soup** doesn't need extra salt—there's plenty in the natural foods we eat. Watch especially for the extra salt in unnatural substances like potato chips, pretzels, salted nuts, popcorn, canned foods and cured meats. If you require a little more taste, "lightly" use iodized sea salt or, better

Peace Soup doesn't need extra salt.

yet, healthy salt made from vegetables or a little kelp (sea weed). Again, your body does need salt. So get your salt from nature…that's where your body comes from.

Poison #4 — Chemicals

The human body is biochemical and is not designed for man-made chemicals. Any chemical that's made in a laboratory is not food. Preservatives, additives, and other toxic substances clog up the cells and make the soup stock stale. There's a rule in nutrition that says, "First, eat fresh, raw fruits and vegetables. Second, if you can't get them fresh, buy them frozen, since they are flash frozen while still fresh. Third, *never eat canned foods."* What's in the can? Chemicals, toxins, preservatives, metal from the can— and no food!

Never eat canned foods.

Chef Gary (Null) conducted a research study on commercially canned food. He analyzed the nutritive value of a can of English peas (one of the top brands), and an equivalent volume of peas fresh from the garden. The canned peas had only 3% of the nutritional value of the fresh peas, plus all the chemicals. All you're eating from a can is toxic chemicals. Stop eating canned foods, but also realize that chemicals are not just in cans—they're everywhere in our environment…in the air, the water, our homes, our offices, our clothes. Do all you can to remove them from your environment and "for heaven's sake," don't put them into your body—they're poison.

Poison #5 — Drugs

"Say *no* to drugs!" That includes *all* drugs, legal or illegal, prescription or over-the-counter. Drugs are not food. The body is not designed to process them. What are known as "side effects" of drugs are not *side,* they're full-face effects. "Miracle drugs" means it's a miracle if they don't kill you! Even something as innocent as an aspirin is detrimental to your health. No *body* has ever been known to have an aspirin deficiency! All aspirin causes stomach bleeding, and research-

No body has ever been known to have an aspirin deficiency!

ers at the Boston School of Medicine have found that enteric-coated and buffered aspirin actually increase stomach bleeding over regular aspirin! Most aspirin is taken because of pain, but pain is nature's way of telling us that something is out-of-balance in your body. If you have a headache, don't treat the effect (the ache), treat the cause (the head)! Think about what you're eating…what you're putting into your body. Drugs cause much more pain than they cure. As Chef Michael (Ryce) says, "Every drug is a disease disguised as a cure." Our society has become a *drugged* society, but you don't have to participate. You *can't* participate and still be at peace. Drugs are not for bodies, nor bodies for drugs. The **Peace Soup** recipe requires that you don't do drugs!

That said, of course there are certain cases where drugs may be necessary to sustain life. In coming off drugs, it may take some time to "phase off," and in extreme cases the drugs may need to be continued over an extended period, maybe even for life. If you're already *on* drugs, don't quit cold turkey! That could kill you quicker than the drug. The body adjusts to foreign substances and the toxins are already built up in your body. To stop them suddenly could cause a reaction. Find a drug-free doctor to help you through the detox process—gently, easily and peacefully.

Poison #6 — Hydrogenated Fats And TFAs

The process of hydrogenation changes the molecular structure of whatever is being hydrogenated. An extra hydrogen molecule is forced into the substance, causing it to become different—and the physical body responds differently! Why is hydrogenation used in food processing? For the same reason preservatives and other toxic chemicals are put into cans—to increase shelf life.

If you've ever baked bread, whole wheat bread, at home, and left it sitting out on the counter for a few days, you know what happened. It spoiled…got moldy. It was alive. Processed foods last a long time because they're not alive. Hydrogenated fats are processed and are not food for the body. They clog up the system.

All margarine is hydrogenated. You may want to conduct this experiment. Take a little butter in one hand and some margarine in the other and feel the texture of each. The margarine feels like plastic. And that's exactly the way the body handles it, like plastic—it's not food! Commercial peanut butter (what all good mothers feed their children) is all hydrogenated...not food—poison. Fresh ground peanut butter is unprocessed (not hydrogenated) and it's fine, but the oil's on top and you have to stir it...too much trouble? The choice is between sickness and health, life and death. Choose life, not hydrogenation—it's poison!

Trans-fatty acids (TFAs), also made by food processors, are not food either, and they're everywhere. They're in fried foods in restaurants and in commercially baked cookies and crackers, as well as in peanut butter and margarine. The corn, safflower and other vegetable oils you buy in a grocery store are extracted and refined with chemical solvents, bleaches and deodorizing agents in a process involving very high temperatures. The food value is destroyed and then, to add insult to injury, many of these oils are even partially hydrogenated! Beware of TFAs...they'll spoil the soup.

Poison #7 — "The Social Poisons"

"How about a cup of coffee? Let's have a smoke! Meet me for a drink. Let's have a Coke!" These sound like sociable things to do, and most people are just *dying* to be liked. With the **Peace Soup** recipe, you learn you can be sociable without poisoning yourself or your friends.

— Caffeine —

Most of us are aware of what nicotine does to the body, and smoking is on its way out as a social pastime, but that "quick cup of coffee" can be just as detrimental to your health and that quick drink after work can be the most deadly of all! Everyone knows the dangers of drug addiction. Marijuana, cocaine and psychedelic drugs cause nightmares

Parents may be the biggest addicts of all!

for parents, but the parents, with their social poisons and pill popping may actually be the biggest addicts of all!

Dr. E. Cheraskin and Dr. W.M. Ringsdorf, Jr., say in their book, PSYCHODIETETICS, that "caffeine, nicotine, alcohol and other 'legal' drugs cause more damage to mind and body than all the psychoactive drugs combined." Most doctors will tell you that more than 200 mg of caffeine per day can be detrimental to your health, while they consume six or eight cups of coffee a day, each cup containing *90 mg!*

The drug caffeine is also found in cola drinks, cocoa and chocolate, and our kids are loading up on these daily. Is it any wonder kids get hooked on drugs? Caffeine is one of the xanthines, a class of chemicals that, by stimulating the central nervous system, causes brain and spinal cord disturbances. Your children need to know this.

Cola drinks may be the worst thing you can put into your body.

Next to concentrated sulfuric acid, cola drinks may be the worst thing you can put into your body, yet "soft" drink consumption actually surpassed water consumption in the early 1980s. The average annual consumption of soft drinks in the U.S. now exceeds 50 gallons per person. Cola drinks contain fluoride and phosphates that can destroy delicate nerve and brain tissue. Phosphates can rob the bones of calcium and cause muscle cramping. Fluoride accumulates in the brain and "can be indicative" of motor dysfunction, I.Q. deficits, learning disabilities and, after a lifetime of build-up, may even be a contributor to Alzheimer's disease. The brown coloring in cola drinks is an ammonia caramel compound patented for its ability to *suppress* the immune system (heaven forbid!). Don't put cola drinks in your shopping cart or your body—they're poison. If someone offers you a cup of coffee or a Mountain Dew™, just say, "No canned dew, I don't use it!"

— Nicotine —

Most people know that nicotine is detrimental to physical health, causing lung cancer and heart disease, but few people consider smoking a *cause* of emotional problems. Nicotine, which is absorbed into the bloodstream, adds to metabolic dysfunctioning and causes less blood flow to the brain. It thereby robs the brain of essential glucose and hampers mental functioning. Do people smoke because they're nervous or are they nervous because they smoke? Smoking and emotional imbalance go hand-in-hand. Some studies in England have shown that smoking creates a desire for caffeine and sugar. Smokers drink far more coffee, heavily sugared, than non-smokers. Twice as many smokers have been found among drinkers than among non-drinkers. Some AA meetings even take place in smoke-filled rooms, and what do they serve for snacks? Donuts and coffee! In any combination, caffeine, nicotine, alcohol and refined sugar put a tremendous strain on the body's ability to control blood-glucose levels, and physical and emotional disturbances escalate.

Do people smoke because they're nervous or are they nervous because they smoke?

— Alcohol —

Alcohol, as we all know, can destroy lives in more ways than just poor physical health. Mental, emotional, spiritual, social, financial and sexual health are all essential in "cooking up a peaceful life." Alcohol affects the central nervous system, destroys brain cells and, when we're under its influence, causes us to do things we wouldn't do in our "right mind!" Drinking alters consciousness in a negative manner, contaminating the kettle in which we're cooking our soup.

Recent research has shown that a glass or two of red wine, with meals, can increase HDL cholesterol (the good cholesterol) and help heart disease. This may be true; after all, mankind has been drinking wine for thousands of years. Red wine, especially, has many of the life-giving phytochemicals of plants that are very beneficial to the human body, but there are other, better ways of getting these phytochemicals into your diet. A glass of wine *with food* may be O.K., but can you stop there? A glass of wine, or any alcohol on an empty stomach (especially for women), is like shooting alcohol directly into the bloodstream. It's poison—best to stay away, completely.

Fires of Withdrawal

Withdrawal symptoms from these social poisons are the same as found in heavy drug users: nervousness; drowsiness; anxiety; headaches; energy loss; sweating; cramps; tremors; and palpitations. Ask any heavy coffee or cola drinker or smoker or alcoholic what it's like to come off their habit, cold turkey, and they'll tell you, "It's hell!" There's the fire again, burning the soup! You can bypass hell by not drinking coffee, colas or alcohol, and by not smoking or taking drugs. If you have been using these social poisons, it's time to detoxify. Give your body a chance to function as it's designed to function—perfectly! This is a requirement for the full enjoyment of **Peace Soup**.

A Nutshell

The **Peace Soup** recipe for *nutrition,* the second rule of the body, boils down to this simple formula: Eat only food (the seven essentials) and don't eat non-food (the seven poisons).

Of the seven essentials, protein, carbohydrates and fatty acids are known as "macro-nutrients." All balanced meals and snacks will include all three of these in proper ratio: 30% protein, 40% carbohydrates and 30% essential fatty acids. A good rule of thumb is to always eat more carbohydrates (natural, not processed) than protein, and eat no more protein than can fit in the palm of your hand. Fatty acids are essential in every meal, as they slow the entry rate of carbohydrates into the bloodstream. Good fats are monounsaturated—those found in olive oil, canola oil, olives, macadamia nuts, avocados, and natural nut butters (almond, peanut).

Along with the macro-nutrients, take your "micro-nutrients" (vitamins, minerals and enzymes) and drink *good* water (at least 1/2 gallon per day). A healthy diet is really inexpensive when you consider the cost of sickness and the things most people spend their money on. A study done in 1995 showed that the top 10 items purchased in grocery stores, ranked by dollar volume, were: 1) Marlboro™ cigarettes; 2) Coke Classic™; 3) Pepsi Cola™; 4) Kraft™ processed cheese; 5) Diet Coke™; 6) Campbell's™ soup; 7) Budweiser™ beer; 8) Tide™ detergent; 9) Folger's™ coffee and 10) Winston™ cigarettes. Not one nutritionally balanced food in the top ten! These are the things that are really *expensive* (to your health as well as your pocketbook). You're getting worse than "nothing for your money"—you're getting poison! Drop the non-foods and there will be plenty of money for the essentials, the ingredients of a good **Peace Soup**.

Finally, it's important to keep *under*-eating as a basic rule. Always leave the table a little hungry. Our society is notoriously overweight. It's been said that "we dig our graves with our forks!" Remember the basic exercise in dieting: *pushing away from the table*. Never eat that second helping—it's not *helping* (even if it's Mama's cooking). In a study of 2,000 people who lived over 100 years, the only thing that was common in all of them was moderation in the quantity of food. It's actually much better to eat five or six *small* meals a day than three *big* meals. The body digests the food more easily and you will actually lose weight! Learn to *eat to live,* instead of *living to eat!* Stick to the recipe and live life fully, without ever getting full!

Always leave the table a little hungry.

"The Truth Detector"
How to Always Know What's Right!

I mentioned earlier in this chapter that there is a way you can always determine what's right for your body, and that *your body* will tell you. This is one of the most valuable tools you can learn, not just for nutrition, but for all of life's decisions. It's known as *muscle testing* or, more scientifically, *applied kinesiology*. It has been used for years by health care professionals such as chiropractors, naturopaths, nutritionists and sports doctors.

Kinesiology taps into the innate intelligence of the body.

Kinesiology taps into the innate intelligence of the body and works with the muscular system, as well as the electrical and nervous systems. It bypasses the thinking process, so the answers are always true and without input from our belief system (b.s.). It's very simple and easy to learn, and with a little practice can give you an exact answer every time.

Traditionally, it takes two people to perform the muscle testing. One acts as the test subject by holding out one arm laterally, parallel to the ground. The second person then presses down with two fingers on the wrist of the extended arm, and says, "Resist." The subject then resists the downward pressure with all his or her strength. A question is then asked in the form of a statement that can be answered by a simple "yes" or "no." For example, "This artificial sweetener is good for the body of the test subject." The test subject, holding the sweetener on their solar plexus with their other hand, will not be able to resist the downward pressure. Another example might involve an *organic* apple. The arm would remain strong and be able to resist the downward pressure.

This testing technique is the one recommended by Dr. J. Diamond in his books BEHAVIORAL KINESIOLOGY and YOUR BODY DOESN'T LIE, both published in 1979. It has withstood the test of time and is more widely used now than ever before. I recommend that you learn it and use it to test all your foods and non-foods, especially your vitamins and minerals, to make sure they're natural and fresh and right for your body. When the arm goes down, it indicates the food or substance being tested will cause stress and is *not* good for the body being tested. When the arm stays strong, it indicates the substance will strengthen or be beneficial for the body.

Be specific and keep the statements simple. If you're getting inconsistent results, the test subject may need more water in their system. The electrical system is involved in this process and it works best when there is adequate water in the body, so have them drink a glass of water. If the test subject is physically weak, it may help to have them "thump the thymus," hitting the upper chest several times, saying, "Ha… ha…ha…" each time. Adjust the amount of pressure you use according to whom you're testing; for example, you don't need to use much pressure when testing children. This is not a test of muscle strength, but muscle *integrity*. Be sure to relax the testing arm between tests. (For more information on kinesiology, you may want to read the books POWER VS. FORCE by David Hawkins, M.D., PhD. and DON'T HAVE A COW by Janeson Rayne.)

Rule 3: Elimination

Thus far, we have explored two of the *four* rules of the body… *relaxation* and *nutrition*. The third rule is equally important. It has been said that "death begins in the colon!" The waste products from the foods and micro-organisms, and the toxins from the non-foods, are causing our eliminatory systems to be over-worked, or to not work at all, and build-up occurs.

The Flow Bowl says that there cannot be peace where there is blockage. There cannot be health in a *clogged* body. Dr. Richard Schultz, famous medical herbalist, says, "All disease, all illness, all sickness of any kind is caused by some type of physical, emotional or spiritual blockage. It could be blocked blood flow, blocked nerve impulses, blocked lymphatics, blocked nutrition, blocked colon, blocked attitude….When an area of your body is sick, it is cut off from some type of circulation, and when you free the blockage and get the circulation back, your body will heal itself."

So, elimination is a part of circulation, the natural flow of the universe, and it's essential that we detoxify, or cleanse, the body on a regular basis. Healthy elimination requires a bowel movement for every meal we consume, three or more times a day, not the "normal" once a day, or the

Elimination is a part of circulation, the natural flow of the universe.

"chronic" once every three days! We live in a constipated society, and the blockages take place not only in the colon, but also on a cellular level. Each cell is surrounded by a thin, porous membrane that's designed to process *good food*. The indigestible toxins from non-food clog the pores of the membrane, causing the cell to become sluggish and tired. Tired cells produce a tired body—stale soup stock! The **Peace Soup** recipe requires that we keep the body cleansed, both externally and internally.

Commercial laxatives are *not* the way to *go!* They are very harsh on the system and throw the natural rhythm off. So "X" the laxatives and go with a gentle herbal program on a daily basis, with a special detox once a season. There are many good colon programs available at your health food store. Just be sure the one you select includes the maintenance of healthy flora (bacteria) in your colon.

The Quarterly Detox

The following detoxification program has proven effective as a general cleansing regimen for the change of seasons. It also has the added benefit of developing more control over what you eat, even after the seven-day period of cleansing. It's simple and easy to follow. Just remember, you can do anything for seven days. What you'll find is that you'll feel so good you won't want to go back to the old heavy diet. This program will also help the body establish the proper alkaline/acid balance and flush the toxins from the system. I thank Chef Ruth (Jarrett) for providing me with this diet.

The Seven-Day Detox

First: Take an *herbal* or *vegetable* laxative (from the health food store, not the drug store) 24 hours before starting, and repeat this three or four days throughout the week.

Second: Take a warm bath every night, adding Epsom salts or, for sensitive skin, apple cider vinegar, to the water. Be sure to shower after the bath to wash off the salts or vinegar and toxins.

Third: Pick a seven-day period in which it will be fairly easy to stick to the diet.

During the seven days, you *will not* eat:
Starches (bread, cereal, rice, potatoes, etc.)
Proteins (meat, fish, eggs, cheese, milk, etc.)
Sugars ("sweeteners," dried fruits, honey, etc.)
Fats (butter, creams, oils, etc.)
During the seven-day diet, you *will* eat:
All fresh fruits (except bananas,
which are slightly mucus-forming)
All fresh vegetables, raw or slightly steamed
Lemon juice on your salads and vegetables
Mineral broth, made as follows:

Cut up one bunch each of celery and parsley, one pound of greens (turnip, collard, etc.), a bunch of carrots, and any other mineral-rich vegetables (squash, radishes, spinach, etc.). Place them in a large cooking pot, cover the vegetables with pure water and boil gently for 3–4 hours. Pour off and save the liquid, and discard the pulp (all the minerals are now in the liquid). Add two quarts of unsalted tomato juice and a minimum of one cup of Bragg's Liquid Aminos™ (available in your health food store) to the liquid. (Season to taste with the liquid aminos.) Keep in the refrigerator and drink either hot or cold throughout the seven days.

Start each day with a glass of pure water with the juice of one lemon…this helps cleanse and alkalize the system.

Breakfast will consist of fruit (berries, cantaloupe, citrus) and unsweetened juice.

Mid-morning: a large glass of tomato juice or a serving of fruit.

Lunch: vegetable broth, large salad (with lemon juice for dressing), one steamed vegetable.

Mid-afternoon: vegetable broth or tomato juice or fresh fruit.

> *Dinner:* vegetable broth, plate of three steamed vegetables, salad with lemon juice dressing, berries or melon for dessert.

You may vary the combinations to suit your taste. If you get hungry, eat! But stick with fruits and vegetables. Seven days will pass quickly and the results will make it worth the effort. You will feel so good. Your skin will clear up. You will be thrilled with the weight loss. (You won't lose weight unless you need to.) The toxins will be gone, the soup stock will be healthy and light, and you'll be anticipating the next season, so you can do it again!

Rule 4: Movement

The human body is designed to move—every part of it! The expression "move it or lose it" is true of your body. If you've ever had

"Move it or lose it." a broken limb and had it in a cast for any length of time, you know how difficult it was to move it when the cast came off. The body gets "stove up" when you don't move it.

There are many good forms of exercise, including walking, jogging, running, swimming, yoga, aerobics, weight-lifting and tai ch'i. Yoga and tai ch'i are especially beneficial because of the stretching that the muscles and tendons need. Probably one of the most effective forms of exercise, and one of the easiest, is *rebounding*. Rebounding makes use of a small trampoline and has the benefit of exercising every cell in the body at the same time—and anyone can do it, no matter what the physical condition.

The Miracle of Rebounding

Al Carter, the world's greatest authority on rebounding, says in his book, REBOUND TO BETTER HEALTH, "Rebounding is by far the most efficient, the most effective form of exercise yet devised by man." The data presented in the book has been confirmed by NASA, the U.S. Air

Force, Dr. Kenneth Cooper's Institute of Aerobics Research, and the Hong Kong University in China, where Chef Al taught the benefits of rebounding to 35,000 members of the police and fire departments.

Jumping is a simple contest between the jumper and gravity, a willing and constant opponent. At the top of the jump, your body is weightless, and at the bottom, you're exerting more pressure than normal, depending on the height of the jump. This process is expanding and contracting the cells of every tendon, ligament, gland, organ and system of the body. The benefits are awesome!

Gravity provides opposition to our muscles; moving against gravity develops strength. A weightlifter adds weight to gravity for more resistance, to develop more strength. Running and jogging are also ways of using gravity to develop strength and stamina, but weight-lifting, running and jogging can cause injury through straining or pounding. Rebounding not only gives you a soft landing, but increases the effect of gravity, giving you more resistance and thus more strength.

There are many exercises that have been developed for the rebounder, including those for better eyesight and hearing, but the three *basic* exercises are: 1) the *Jump;* 2) the *Bounce;* and 3) the *Jog.*

1) *The Jump* takes your feet off the rebounder and increases the resistance to gravity. This strengthens the large muscles of the body. The higher the jump, the more resistance; just be sure to maintain your balance. After only 5 to 10 minutes of jumping, you'll feel the effects.

2) *The Bounce* is the single most effective exercise ever developed! It's especially effective for maintaining health in the vital organs and glands and for keeping everything flowing. The bounce takes the body as high as possible without letting the feet come off the surface of the rebounder. Fifteen to 20 minutes of bouncing each day will keep your soup stock flowing nicely.

3) *The Jog* provides the aerobic exercise that gets you winded, without the wind, and the rain, and the cold or the heat, and the cars and the dogs of out-of-doors. You can jog five miles and never leave your bedroom!

You can jog five miles and never leave your bedroom!

Just put your rebounder where you'll stumble on to it when you get out of bed and you'll remember to do your exercises every day. Rebounding and other forms of movement will stir your soup and keep the fat from settling to the *bottom*. Just do it!

One more word on gravity...and aging. Why do you think yogis stand on their heads? It reverses the effects of gravity! Gravity is pulling down on us from the moment we're conceived, and as we age we begin to sag. It is very helpful to turn ourselves upside-down for a few minutes every day to stop the sagging. The headstand is a good exercise, but it can be stressful if not done properly, and can even cause injury.

An alternative that is easy, simple and equally effective in reversing gravity is a *slant board*. The slant boards that are used for sit-ups are ideal. If you can't find one of these, just get a board

Hanging down is very up-lifting.

and slant it. Lie on your back with your head down for a few minutes, then turn over on your stomach for a few minutes. Hanging down is very up-lifting.

You may want to include one other exercise in your daily routine—the tummy lift—to reverse the pull of gravity on your vital organs. The tummy lift is simple and easy and can be done several times throughout the day. Pull your abdomen in as far as possible, counting to 10...then draw the abdomen inward even more, counting to 10 again...and then, instead of relaxing, start a third count of 10, pulling in more and more, breathing very shallowly with the upper part of your lungs, then completely let go! It takes only 30 seconds and, doing it a few times a day, before you know it, your tummy will begin to firm, and not only look better, but also provide essential support for your abdominal organs and glands.

"The Electric Body"

The entire universe is a magnetic force field and your body is exposed to this invisible power from the moment of conception. The

Earth is a magnet and the human body, being of the earth, is designed to be close to the earth. For most of our existence, mankind has slept on the ground and walked barefoot on the ground, but in the modern world we're not *grounded* any more. We sleep high off the ground in houses, we wear shoes and walk on concrete, so the subtle flows of energy in the body in relation to the earth are not balanced—and our bodies are feeling the effect.

Not only are we not grounding ourselves, our modern technologies are bombarding our bodies with electromagnetic radiation. Since most electromagnetic energy cannot be detected without instruments, we don't realize how drastically and how abruptly we've changed our magnetic environment. Dr. Robert Becker, in his book, THE BODY ELECTRIC, says, "In 1892, Nikola Tesla lit up the Chicago World's Fair with the first A.C. power system. Now over 500,000 miles of high volume power lines crisscross the United States. There are over 10,000 commercial radio and TV stations in the U.S. and 7 million private transmitters, not counting the high power 'secret' transmissions of the military."

Microwave beams and other electromagnetic contamination are cutting through our electro-chemical bodies and disturbing the natural balance. EMFs (electromagnetic fields) interfere with the biological cycles; stress and impaired cellular growth are the result, increasing cancer rates and producing serious reproductive problems. Dr. Andrew Weil, author of EIGHT WEEKS TO OPTIMAL HEALTH and NATURAL HEALTH, NATURAL MEDICINE, says, "Electromagnetic pollution (EMF) may be the most significant form of pollution human activity has produced in this century. All the more dangerous because it is invisible and insensible." A magnetically balanced body requires a balanced magnetic environment. Much of the pain we feel in the body comes from the sensitive electro-chemical nervous system. Much research is being done around the world using magnetic therapy in relieving pain.

A magnetically balanced body requires a balanced magnetic environment.

Dr. N. Nakagawa, chief of Tokyo's Isuzu

Hospital, has used magnetic therapy on thousands of patients, successfully freeing *90%* of these patients from pain! Many golfers, tennis players, football and baseball players now use magnets to eliminate pain. What they're really eliminating is stress, the stress caused by injury to the healthy balance in the electro-magnetic body. Using magnets and *controlled* electrical stimulation machines can help keep the body in its natural, balanced pain-free state. I sleep on a magnetic mattress, sit on a magnetic seat in my car, use magnetic insoles in my shoes and wear a tiny copper coil (EMF) necklace. If I'm injured or stressed, I get a healthy dose of controlled electrical stimulation from my health-oriented doctor. Magnetic balance is essential for your "electric body" to function properly. The **Peace Soup** recipe produces this electrical balance and provides you with a *magnetic personality!*

This concludes our overview of the rules of the body and the creation of a healthy soup stock. With this basic information in mind, we're now ready to complete Step 2 of the recipe by folding in these ingredients, using the technique which I call...

The Laboratory of the Mind

You have now explored the essentials for creating a perfect soup stock (physical body). Next comes the practical integration of these ingredients into your life, pouring them slowly into your kettle (consciousness). This is done easily and gently, using the mental exercise I mentioned earlier in this chapter—turning on the television, the imagination of your own mind. This exercise builds upon the autogenic exercise from Step 1 of the recipe.

Psychologists tell us that most of us don't learn well under pressure. If you were thrown into a raging river with the idea that it would teach you to swim, you might avoid drowning, but your method would be fear-motivated and it would be unlikely that you would then become a championship swimmer. You would always have that fear stroke that was locked in under pressure.

It is much more effective, in the learning process, to practice in a relaxed, non-stressful atmosphere; you can use the power of the imagination to create this atmosphere. Remember, the subconscious mind cannot distinguish between what's real and what's imagined, so you can create anything you want by imagining it into reality. I find it helpful to visualize a large television screen in my imaginary laboratory and see the images as they play on my screen. If you don't visualize well, you may want

You can create anything you want by imagining it into reality.

to just *think* about a television screen, or just think about the images without a screen. Whatever you do, be sure to incorporate the other "senses." Make it in surround-sound, using aromas and a taste test. You might like to "feel" yourself relaxed in a soft, warm, comfortable easy chair.

You will enter your laboratory of the mind by descending a flight of stairs with ten steps leading down. This stair-step technique is a favorite of self-hypnosis and you begin it immediately after completing the autogenic exercise. You already have this experience under your belt from your practice in Step 1 of the recipe.

You can use this laboratory of the mind to imagine anything you want, and through the power of your creative, sub-conscious mind, bring it into existence in your life. It works, but keep in mind that the motive must be pure and always in the best interest of all concerned. Otherwise, you'll mess up the recipe and create a bitter, poisonous soup. The power of the mind is awesome, and it works equally well in creating good or not so good. Keep your vision the way you want your soup to be…perfect…wholesome…heavenly…peaceful…serene…

The autogenic exercise that we learned in Step One has gotten you completely relaxed and poised on step ten, ready to move down into your laboratory. As you step down, in your mind, to nine you will become *twice* as relaxed as you were on step ten…and then again, *twice* as relaxed as you step down to eight. Deeper and deeper now as you step down to seven…

twice as relaxed now, as you step down to six...even more relaxed as you step down to five...so, very relaxed now as you step down to four...twice as relaxed as you step down to three...deeper and deeper now as you step down to two...very, very relaxed now as you step down to one...completely and totally relaxed now as you step down to zero....

You're now in your laboratory, relaxed in your easy chair...warm...comfortable...serene. In this deep, relaxed state, you begin to visualize yourself on your life-size television screen...being the way you want to be...looking the way you want to look...being your perfect weight and in perfect health...doing the things you want to do...being with the people you love to be with...living the vital, abundant lifestyle you want to live...gently saying "no" to the things you *don't* want and supplanting them with the things you *do* want.

An example of how you might use this technique is if you're in the presence of someone daily whom you can't stand to be around, but must, because of work. This person rubs you the wrong way, pushes all your buttons, irritates you to no end. There *is* an end! In your laboratory, in your relaxed state of mind, visualize yourself being with this person, seeing them doing what irritates you, and see yourself responding in peace, smiling, happy, undisturbed, just letting them be. When you've practiced this auto-suggestion for several days in the relaxed privacy of your sanctuary, you'll begin to find that when you're around this person in real life, they don't seem to bother you as much and, ultimately, not at all. Then, very often, a strange thing will happen. This person will either change the way they act, or leave your environment. They were there as your teacher and you've learned your lesson. If they do stay and continue doing what they do, it won't bother you any more, so it won't *matter*. You've learned peace, practiced peace, and you're free!

It Doesn't Matter

You'll discover that you have ultimate control over what matters in your life—what you experience *in matter* or manifestation. When something is bothering you, don't your friends ask, "What's the matter with you?" What they're really saying is, "What are you making into matter in your life?" As we've seen, your beliefs control what you create, and your belief system is always under your control. You can believe anything you want to, and make it matter. I say, "It doesn't matter what you believe, it's what you believe that matters." Choose your beliefs carefully. False beliefs create Stress Soup. Formulate peaceful images in the laboratory of the mind and *peace* will be what *matters* in your life.

> **"It doesn't matter what you believe, it's what you believe that matters."**

Your life is like a movie. You are the scriptwriter, the casting director, the set decorator and the main character. If your movie is not turning out the way you want it to, rewrite the script, get a new cast of characters, redecorate the set and put a new face and attitude on the main character. You can create anything you can imagine on your own private sound stage, the laboratory of your mind.

You can also recreate the *past*. Where does the past exist, anyway? Only in your mind. So if you have some unpleasant memories, you can go back, record over the old video, and create a new, more pleasant, past on your TV screen. The old hurts don't matter any more. You've erased them and recorded a new, peaceful, joyful, loveful picture in their place.

A General Practice Session

Let's continue this step of the recipe by moving on through the practice session in your laboratory. Since I don't know exactly what you're working on in your life, we will be using very general images, but you can "plug in" whatever it is that you want to create in your private sessions. I will continue this in the first person and in the present tense, as you will do when you practice alone.

I'm in my easy chair now, watching myself on the screen. It's as if I'm reading my own mind. I realize that I have complete and total control over my physical body, and, as I realize that I have complete and total control over my physical body, I realize that I have complete and total control over my mind. It feels so good to relax, and I use this relaxation technique often...each time becoming more and more relaxed, each time gaining more and more control over my physical and mental self.

I feel myself developing the attitude that no matter what happens to me in my life, I can handle it. No matter what happens, I can handle it...and I can handle it in a relaxed, calm, easy manner. I am in control of my life. I have perfect confidence in myself and I know I can accomplish anything I want to, by seeing it done. I see myself at my perfect weight, wearing beautiful clothes, driving my dream car, living in my dream home, living with the family I love, having all the money I could possibly use, traveling to exotic places, giving, sharing, being happy...peaceful. I see my mind and body as perfect in every way, no dis-ease, no malfunctioning, only perfection... only peace.

I am in control of my emotions. I see myself responding to all situations lovingly, joyfully. I love everyone unconditionally, including myself. I see myself in perfect relationship with everyone in my life, especially the *difficult* ones, realizing they are my greatest teachers and the taste-testers for my **Peace Soup.** I am open-minded and non-judgmental...giving of myself in every way, light-hearted, happy, joyous, having fun in my life.

I see myself taking care of my body, following the rules, exercising with vim and vigor, eating only live and vital foods, saying "no" to the temptations of sweet desserts, coffee, colas, drugs, cigarettes, alcohol, or other non-foods that poison the soup. I see myself performing perfectly in the things I do for recreation...accomplished, coordinated, flowing easily, totally relaxed and in joy. Every area of my life is in balance.

I am my own best friend. I see a close up of myself on the screen and I say to myself, "I love you!" This gives me a warm, glowing feeling. I love myself just the way I am, knowing that every day, in every way, I am getting better and better, healthier and healthier, happier and happier, more and more in control of my life.

Any time I feel stress in my life, I use this as a trigger to relax. I replace stress with relaxation. When the phone rings, I relax. When someone pulls out in front of me in traffic, I relax. When someone criticizes me, or yells at me, *I relax*. I see myself relaxing in *all* situations. I develop the byline: *I relax and I let go*. Whenever I feel stress, I relax and I let go. I no longer *re-act* to life—I respond! I have a great "response" *ability*. I respond in love and in trust...peacefully. I speak only words of peace, positive words, creating peaceful images. I am at peace, everything is easy, everything is good. I am gentle, I am relaxed, I relax and I let go...

My whole body feels warm, heavy, comfortable...my mind is quiet and at ease. I allow the vision on the screen to slowly fade away and I mentally move back up the stairs 1...2...3...4...5...6...7...8...9...10...and into the sunlight of a new life. As I allow my eyes to drift open, very, very slowly, I carry with me the images that I developed in the laboratory of my mind. As I stretch and move into my new positive, peaceful life, I realize how good it feels to be alive!

This exercise is ideally done later in the day, after work or before bedtime, just after the autogenic exercise. This is relaxation and is a release *from* activity. As you practice the autogenic exercise more and more, relaxation will become automatic, and soon you will be able to move into the laboratory of the mind very quickly. To help facilitate this, I would like to share...

Chef Wally's Shortcut (to the Lab)

Chef Wally (Minto) is one of the most aware teachers I know, and he shares his expertise willingly through his course, *Alpha Truth Awareness*. Chef Wally likes to use what he calls a "triggering mechanism," which is simply a programmed response to anything you decide to use as a trigger. You'll remember we used this technique in the stress replacement technique in Step 1. When we have a stress-causing event, we use it as a trigger to relax.

In the shortcut to the laboratory of the mind, you are able to bypass the autogenic exercise (once you've learned it thoroughly and practiced it diligently) and the stair-step technique, and you're able to move immediately to your easy chair in front of the television screen. Here is Chef Wally's shortcut:

---

1) Take a deep breath and, as you exhale, repeat the word "relax" several times.

2) Take another deep breath and, as you exhale, repeat the magical words "I am" several times.

3) Take a third deep breath and, as you exhale, repeat the word "within" several times.

This trigger will get you into the lab very quickly, and when you have learned your relaxation through the long method (autogenic exercise), you will be just as relaxed with this shortcut. When you have gained the ability to relax and are practicing the rules of the body, your soup stock will be clear and free of stress and dis-ease, and you'll be ready to add the next ingredient to your soup. You'll be ready for...

Step 3

The Secret Ingredient:
Developing the Peaceful Mind

Simmering the Boiling Pot

In the first two steps of the recipe, we have peeled back the outer layers of the onion by learning to relax the physical body and follow the rules that make for a smooth and flowing soup stock. Now we're ready to put some real meat into the soup. We're ready to add the *secret ingredient* that is both essential and elemental for **Peace Soup**.

This ingredient is not called "secret" because no one knows about it. In fact, all the great master chefs used it in their recipes and insisted that their disciples include it in their soup. It is called "secret" because of where it takes place. This secret place is even more private than your *Laboratory of the Mind*. The ancients called it "the secret place of the most high." Master Chef Jesus, in instructing His disciples, called it "the closet." He said, "…when you pray, enter into your closet, and when you have shut the door, pray to your Father, which is *in secret;* and your Father, which sees in secret, shall reward you openly." (Matt 6:6, rev.)

The *secret place* is in the deep recesses of your heart, and the secret ingredient of **Peace Soup**, the process that moves you to this place, is *meditation*. Meditation is not a religious activity, although most religions teach meditation. Meditation is not the same as prayer. Prayer is *active* participation in accessing your spir-

> **The secret ingredient of Peace Soup is meditation.**

itual nature (spirit…God), while meditation is *passive*. Prayer is using thought, word or deed to contact a higher power, while meditation eliminates thoughts, words and deeds. Chef Charles (Fillmore) called this secret place "the silence." It is the absence of all thought, all movement, every *thing,* while experiencing no-thing—the pure essence of being…God…Spirit.

Notice I said that meditation is a process. This is important to keep in mind as we prepare the recipe. The secret ingredient for **Peace Soup** is not the secret place itself, but the *process* of getting there. My meditation teacher, Chef James (Gattuso, Jr.), gave me this working definition and it's the one we will use in preparing the soup:

**Meditation is a mental process of introspection
that leads one to a greater sense of self-awareness,
and ultimately to a greater sense of universal awareness.**

The master chefs say, "Know thyself," and meditation allows you to lay aside the outer *trappings* and move within, to know your true self—your spiritual self. Jesus said, "The kingdom of God is within you" (Luke 17:21), and *meditation* allows you to move into that kingdom and to ultimately know "the truth that sets you free"…free from stress, free from bondage and suffering, free from the *sins of the flesh* (the world). A sin, as we discussed earlier, is an error belief, and meditation helps you to release error beliefs and experience *True Peace*, the essence of **Peace Soup**.

The Maharishi Mahesh Yogi, founder of the Society for Transcendental Meditation, describes meditation as "diving within." The Maharishi says there are three phases in the meditation process:

1) Intellect is phased out, increasing the feeling of serenity and inner peace.
2) The feelings of serenity—love, joy and contentment—fade way.
3) Selflessness is experienced—a deep feeling of unity—union with the universe and everything in it.

The meditative process has been likened to dropping a steel ball into a pan of oil. It settles slowly to the bottom and reaches its resting place gently and effortlessly, with no friction, no noise, no excitement. There is no trying—no pushing. "Don't push the river," the Zen master says. "Row, row, row your boat, gently *down* the stream."

Meditation not only relieves tension and reduces anxiety, but it builds self-confidence, gives you a clearer self-image, and helps you tap resources and talents that you never knew you had. It is the key to achieving serenity, that "last lesson of culture" described by Chef James (Allen) in As A Man Thinketh. It brings *pure joy* into expression. Those who meditate regularly tend to be cheerful, optimistic and excited about life.

Meditation brings pure joy into expression.

Until recently, meditation has been practiced mostly in Eastern society. It seems that Western civilization has tended to venture *outward,* while Eastern man has ventured *inward*. From the days of early explorers, Western man has preferred to discover new lands and explore outer space, while Eastern man has delved deeply into the world of inner space and the riches to be found there. Both are important in our growth and development, and the **Peace Soup** recipe is designed to bring the outer and inner worlds into a perfectly peaceful balance.

Dropping the Tail of Ignorance

The Indian mystic, Ramakrishna, likened man to a frog who, in his youth, lives in water as a tadpole. "Later," he says, "when the tail of ignorance drops off, he needs both land and water to attain his fullest potential." We need both the outer (worldly) and the inner (spiritual) life to reach our potential as accomplished chefs and *realized* (real-I-zed) human beings.

The dropping off of the "tail of ignorance" is the process of re-forming the belief system and changing the qualities in your personality that are undesirable. This recipe helps you transform these undesirables into something useful, admirable and dynamic. This is an exciting adventure, and meditation is the key to self-mastery and true happiness.

Meditation cannot be taught…only *experienced*. Techniques can be taught, but peace and enlightenment come from practice. The practice

Meditation cannot be taught…only experienced.

of meditation allows you to grow beyond your old conditioned beliefs. You transcend much of what you once thought was *real* as you "*know* the truth." Again, no one can tell you the truth…you can only know it in your own heart. Meditation is *self*-taught through practice. You don't need a guru. As the

comedian Swami Beyondananda says, "How do you spell guru? Gee! You Are You!" The only true teacher is the spirit of truth that dwells within you!

There are certain stages in your spiritual growth when it may be helpful to have a teacher or guide. When these stages arise, the teacher will appear, and the *true* teacher will always tell you that it's not him or her who's doing the teaching, but that they're only with you to help draw out that which is already within you.

One who doesn't practice meditation and experience the truth from within, misses out on the *true* life, for they have no *true* knowledge, only second-hand knowledge. What you hear and what you read, even from so-called "holy" men or "holy" books, is still second hand. True

True knowledge comes only to you, through you.

knowledge comes only *to* you, *through you*. Meditation is first learned, then practiced, and finally real-"I"-zed! Self real-I-zation and *in*-lightenment are the ultimate rewards.

Self-realization requires self-discipline. Meditation, especially in its beginning phases, while usually deeply satisfying, is still *work*, often frustrating, with much resistance from ego. The rewards, however, are definitely worth the effort. In meditation, you are tuning and training your mind, much as an athlete tunes and trains his or her body. The Control Bowl is an essential element in this step of the recipe. Practicing the techniques fills up this bowl so you'll always have a full bowl of control to draw from.

Patanjali, the legendary founder of Yoga, described the *Seven Stages to Enlightenment* through meditation:

1) Deeply and sincerely seek the Truth.
2) Use proper meditation methods.
3) Phase out ego and intellect
   (all previous conditioning).
4) Purify mind and body to be worthy
   of further Truth.
5) Achieve serenity in the face of the
   distractions of everyday life.
6) Perceive the world and its ways as unreal
   and know that it will pass away.
7) See the eternal spirit, the mystic unity,
   the universal consciousness in everyone
   and everything.

This is basically the process that you will follow in blending the secret ingredient into your soup.

In this recipe, we incorporate two basic schools of meditation—Zen and Yoga. There are other meditative disciplines, such as the Hebrew tradition and the Christian monastic tradition, but these others tend to take more time and effort, and are more intellectual and emotional, while Zen and Yoga techniques utilize the simple *mental process of introspection* that I defined earlier. All the meditative disciplines ultimately lead to the secret place, but Zen and Yoga seem to be the easiest for our busy minds to fold into our soup. If the techniques we use here don't seem to work for you, then by all means "seek until you find" what does work.

One of the reasons meditators drop away from their practice is that they have been taught that there is only one *right* way to meditate for everyone. The **Peace Soup** recipe recognizes that there are many ways and, if based in Truth, they're *all right*. It's up to you to discover what's best for you, but first give this recipe a chance to be absorbed and digested. It has worked for thousands of people and the techniques we use have been around for thousands of years. They *do* work for almost everybody, because we *do* use more than one technique, each one accomplishing a certain purpose and each one building on the previous steps.

I use both Zen and Yoga because they each focus on different aspects of being. Zen techniques deal mostly with an awareness of internal breathing, while Yoga connects with the outer by utilizing physical movement and/or other external stimuli, such as a "mantra" (sound) or a "yantra" (picture, mandala). You may have seen someone meditating while looking at a candle...this is a yogic technique.

Yoga, because of this outer connection, seems to be easiest for most people to incorporate into their daily routine and, for this reason, the mantra was chosen by the Maharishi Mahesh Yogi as *the* technique for Transcendental Meditation (T.M.).

This recipe will utilize the basic Yoga technique (the mantra) as an alternative to the basic Zen technique (breath counting). We will explore *both*, since some people relate more to one or the other, depending on their background and personality. Both are equally effective in achieving the control (discipline) we are seeking in the first phase of the meditative process.

Meditation, as I continue to emphasize, is a *process*...a process of leaving the outer world and moving within, "losing your senses." You will not have a true meditative experience until the senses are left behind, and this takes practice. In the meditative process, which moves through several phases, you will gain awareness, control, balance and flow from your mixing bowls and stir them into your soup until all stress and tension are gone from body and mind. You are then free from "the world." In the process, you will overcome (come up over) the world and its tribulation.

You will not have a true meditative experience until the senses are left behind.

Chef Jesus said, "In the world you shall have tribulation, but be of good cheer, for I have overcome the world." (John 16:33) Meditation is the secret ingredient in *overcoming*...in making **Peace Soup**.

I emphasize again that meditation is not a *religious* activity, but has been proven scientifically to be of great value in achieving our goal of a physiological and psychological state of peace. Meditation can be practiced by the atheist as well as the religiously inclined, to explore the hidden aspects of mind and to discover the essence of True Peace.

Physiological Benefits

Meditation has become more accepted in our Western society, since the results are now measurable, scientifically, through the use of bio-feedback devices. The data on the benefits for both mind and body is impressive. Studies have shown the physiological benefits to include:

1) a lower metabolic rate, allowing the body to rest and heal itself
2) a slower and more balanced brain wave activity
3) a lower heart rate (as much as 25% lower)
4) a balancing of blood pressure
5) a reduction of blood lactate levels, indicating a lessening of stress
6) a stronger immune system
7) a lowered rate of using oxygen and producing carbon dioxide
8) a more balanced interaction between the left and right hemispheres of the brain
9) a faster reaction time and a more *centered* response.

This ninth benefit is one reason many athletes and athletic teams meditate before a game—not to become "gurus," but to become more balanced and centered, and thus more effective in their performance.

The physical control developed by long practice in meditation can be phenomenal! You may have seen or heard of examples of yogis being buried alive for hours, even days, with only the air contained in a sealed coffin, and coming out alive and well. Perhaps you have seen

Chef Jack (Schwartz) pierce his arm with a *rusty* spike and then heal the wound immediately, without pain or bleeding.

Pain control is possible through the use of meditation. Pain control is possible through the practice of meditation. Pain is not bad…it's good! It's a warning from your body telling you that something is out of balance and needs to be corrected. Once you know what's out of balance, you don't need the pain anymore, and you can learn to release it! You may even have known people who can go to the dentist and let the dentist drill without using a pain killer! These people have the same nerves as everyone else, but they've learned to release the pain immediately, just like Jack Schwartz does. Chef Jack says, "Pain is man's servant…an alarm clock that wakes you when something goes wrong in the body that you should know about. But if you're doing something to the body of your own free will, something that you know is not really going to hurt you, then there is no reason for the alarm to go off, is there?"

The startling results of those who have developed exceptional control are an example of what is possible through long practice of meditation, but these phenomenal results are not the aim of this recipe. Sufficient for our soup are the nine benefits listed above.

One of the other physiological benefits deserves more elaboration, as it is a definite measure of the effectiveness of meditation: the second benefit…"slower and more balanced brain wave activity." The human brain is continually emitting electrical impulses that vibrate in "energy cycles per second" (cps). In 1929 a German scientist, Hans Berger, developed the electroencephalogram (EEG), a very sensitive device that measures these electrical brain emissions (brain waves). They are measured in microvolts (one millionth of a volt), so you're not likely to shock anyone with your brain power.

Hans Berger discovered that there are basically four brain wave frequencies: *beta, alpha, theta* and *delta.* (See Figure 2.) They were named in the order in which they were discovered, *alpha* being the first. Alpha

Beta . . . .above 13 cps . . . . .outer conscious awareness
Alpha . . . . . 8–13 cps . . . . .inner conscious awareness
Theta . . . . . . 4–7 cps . . . . .deep reverie (dream state)
Delta . . . . . . .1–3 cps . . . . .sleep...unconscious

Figure 2

is the relaxed state and takes place when the body (including the brain) relaxes and the brain waves slow down below 13 cycles per second. Beta is a more active state, the thinking, doing state—or normal life activity. Beta extends upward from 13 cps, and is associated with outer conscious levels of mental activity—physical activity, working, exercising and mental problem solving. High beta is stress-related—hypertension, hyperactivity, neurotic and psychotic conditions occur in high beta. Meditation brings the "hyper" levels down to a more manageable frequency of beta and then into the slower vibration of alpha. Alpha is associated with those processes that take place in the *inner* dimensions of mind, and requires that we become *in*-trospective, looking within to the secret place, the "closet." *In*-spiration, *in*-tuition, *in*-lightenment and creativity come from these inner conscious levels of mental activity.

The great inventor and soup chef Thomas Edison had one of the most creative minds of anyone in history, and it's said that he developed his own way of accessing the creative alpha state. When he had a problem to solve, Mr. Edison would lie down on his bench for one of his famous "cat naps," but he didn't go to sleep. He held a weight in his hand and when he was so relaxed that the weight would fall out, the sound of it hitting the floor signaled him to stay in *that* level of consciousness. That level was probably deep alpha... bordering on theta. This *alpha-theta* state is the most creative level of consciousness, and Chef Thomas, in this receptive, creative/intuitive state of mind, would receive the inspiration for solv-

The alpha-theta state is the most creative level of consciousness.

ing his problem.

Theta occurs when the brain wave slows down below 8 cps, but remains above 4 cps. Theta is the dream state, a state of deep reverie. It is the deepest *in*-trospective level of consciousness you can reach. It is in theta that you tap into what is known as "universal consciousness" or "divine consciousness." When you slow the brain wave below 4 cps, you enter delta, which is sleep…dreamless sleep…total *un*-consciousness. As you approach 0 cps, of course, you approach the *flatline*—no more life!

The "normal" daily routine for many people living on Stress Soup is to move quickly from delta into beta when the alarm (bell) rings in the morning. They then *rush* through breakfast (breaking a fast with ham, bacon or sausage, eggs, waffles or pancakes, sugared donuts, cereal and coffee), *rush* to work (during *rush* hour), build up stress in the pressure of the work day, take coffee *breaks,* smoke *breaks,* lunch *breaks, rush* home (another *rush* hour), have a drink or a pill to relax, rush through a toxic T.V. dinner, get a dose of "toxic T.V." and then *crash*—back down into delta—tossing and turning in restless or night-marish sleep, or taking a drug to wipe them out completely! This life of rushing totally bypasses any contact with the beneficial levels of alpha and theta, except for the restless dreams or nightmares.

Dreaming is nature's way of relieving stress, and your dreams indi-cate to you how much stress you're *under.* Peaceful dreams mean you're

Bad dreams indicate dis-stress and show that you're out of control. pretty much in control of your stress. Bad dreams indicate dis-stress and show that you're out of con-trol…breaking down. When you dream, you're bouncing from sleep (delta), up into theta, and you're releasing *some* of the stress you've built up during the rush, but you're coming at it from an *unconscious* level, so you don't release all the stress and you carry the residue into the next day. You then add that day's stress, and the next, day after day, adding stress until you finally *break down!* You have a *nervous* breakdown, or a *mental* breakdown, or a *physical* breakdown…you get sick, dis-eased, and are *forced* to rest, at home or in an *institution*, a hospital, or a cemetery!

It's much better to follow the **Peace Soup** recipe for rest and relaxation and stay mentally, physically and emotionally fit, never breaking down, never getting sick. It's been proven that you actually get more rest during meditation than you do during sleep! Meditation acts like the release valve on a pressure cooker. It allows you to release the stress gradually and gently, so you don't "blow your top!" You don't need to "medicate" when you *meditate*. No more sleeping pills, no more tranquilizers…

You don't need to "medicate" when you meditate.

One who meditates needs less sleep and has more awake time to accomplish his or her goals in life. One study has shown that 20 minutes in deep meditation gives the body the same beneficial rest as two hours of sleep. Some scientists even believe that sleep is not absolutely necessary, but it is a carry-over from our "caveman" era. When the sun was down, there was no light to see how to do anything, so man learned to sleep. Now it's a habit! You will cut your sleep needs with the secret ingredient of **Peace Soup**, but you will still need your sleep, just not as much.

The process of meditation trains you to move into alpha and theta, at will, from a *conscious* level. After learning and practicing the techniques, you will be able to slow down and absorb the shocks of a busy day so you're not "bouncing off the walls" in high beta. The meditative techniques help you develop *shock absorbers*. You learn to release stress immediately and automatically as it enters your awareness. The daily practice of meditation, the secret ingredient, keeps the soup fresh, wholesome and palatable.

Psychological Benefits

The psychological benefits of meditation may be even more impressive than the physiological. Psycho-logical in this recipe means that trying to be *logical* can make you a *psycho!* Thinking can be very valuable when it's under control, but for most people it's out of control. Most people have dozens of unrelated and confusing thoughts going around in their heads at the same time: fear thoughts; thoughts of anger, jealousy and guilt; worry and anxiety about relationships, finances, sickness—mental chaos! No awareness…no control…no balance…no flow. You want to clear your mind of the chaotic thoughts. As the Zen master says, "You cannot see a jewel in a muddy pool."

As we discussed earlier, one of the benefits of meditation is that it tunes and trains the mind. Alan Watts, great soup chef and teacher of meditation, once said, "If we look deeply into such ways of life as Buddhism and Taoism, Vedanta and Yoga, we do not find either philosophy or religion as these are understood in the West. We find something much more resembling *psychotherapy.*" Meditation is a healing process for the mind as well as the body.

Meditation allows the natural tendencies of healing to take place.

As Chef Alan indicated, meditation in itself is not "mystical" or "religious." It is simply the process of letting go and allowing the natural tendencies of self-healing to take place…letting go of the *thinking* and *doing* parts of life for a while, so that you can balance and integrate your true nature—your spiritual nature—into the overall expression of life.

Meditation allows you to see life from a different perspective—a higher perspective—and express with greater efficiency in every area: spiritual; mental; physical; social; emotional; financial; and sexual. It gives you a way of relating to the world with a serenity and an inner peace that remains stable, even in the presence of turmoil and tribulation. Meditation shows you what is superficial and what is important, allowing you to face life calmly and wisely.

We've all witnessed the seeming dichotomy that from the exact same circumstances, some people become miserable and depressed, while others achieve serenity and inward strength. Obviously there is a quality that allows one to overcome that can be learned by the other. The problem is ignor-ance—ignoring the truth and buying into harmful images and emotions which bring about chaotic thoughts, wrong speech and destructive actions, causing endless suffering and pain. There is a way beyond suffering and pain, and meditation is an important step along that way. One who meditates regularly develops the capacity to transcend the painful and negative aspects of everyday life and to live with an inner peace, a greater joy and an unlimited ability to love.

Meditation is not an *escape* from pressing problems or the challenges of life; it simply enables you to be more creative and successful in *overcoming* the problems and challenges. When you meditate regularly, you will find it easier to concentrate on projects and relationships, becoming more productive and more highly functional. Children who learn to meditate improve their study habits and become

Meditation enables you to be more creative and successful in overcoming problems and challenges.

calmer…their grades improve and they get along better with adults and peers. Executives who meditate have less stress; salespeople gain self-discipline and more confidence; musicians and artists deepen their *feelings* and gain more *in*-sight.

Meditation can also help with addictions of all kinds, and many find that when they begin to meditate, they gain the control necessary to choose wise behavior and renounce unwise behavior without painful withdrawal symptoms or involvement in expensive and time-consuming "programs." Harmful addictions are entered into with the hope of somehow changing life, causing it to be more pleasurable and less painful, but the side effects cause just the *opposite* results—life becomes *less pleasurable* and *more painful*. Meditation gives you all the benefits of more pleasure and less pain, without harmful side effects.

The mind awakened by meditation is capable of much more than average intelligence. In meditation, you are tapping into a wisdom that is beyond the rational mind…beyond the intellect. Meditation brings you to a state of awareness of realities that lie beyond "sense" experience. In deep meditation, one does not know *about* Truth—one *knows*

Truth! This is the "Truth that sets you free"—free from the world and all its agents of bondage. Through meditation, one knows the essential harmony of the universe, and all life becomes sacred.

Meditation brings you to a sense of humor at the seriousness with which people take themselves and life, yet it also gives you a sense of caring, of pure love for all people and all belief systems. The pure beauty of meditation cannot be described in words…it is beyond words, beyond thought. (Truth cannot be spoken!)

Meditation brings more life to life! Everything is more vivid and vital, more clear. Colors are more brilliant, tastes more poignant, feelings more sublime, sounds more pleasing and soothing. It brings out the best in you in every possible way, and helps you realize your unlimited potential. It keeps you growing, expanding, reaching ever higher. One of the great medieval chefs, Meister Eckhart, wrote: "There is no stopping place in this life—no, nor was there ever for any man no matter how far along his way he'd gone. This, above all, then, be ready at all times for the gifts of God, and always for new ones."

Meditation helps you move out of your head and into your heart.

Meditation keeps you ready, awake, and open to these "greater gifts" that are coming to you. Meditation helps move you out of your head, out of your ego, out of your emotions—and *into your heart*. It increases your sensitivity to your own feelings and to the feelings of others. We are all "sensitives" and as you learn to tune in to the subtle energies of the universe, you increase your ability to tune in to the minds and hearts of those around you and to help them in *their* quest in overcoming.

The True "Psychic Connection"

William James, sometimes known as the "father of modern psychology," in his book, THE VARIETIES OF RELIGIOUS EXPERIENCE, says, "Our normal waking consciousness, rational consciousness as we call it, is but one special type of consciousness, while all about it, parted from it by the filmiest of screens, there lie potential forms of consciousness entirely different….We may go through life without expecting their existence, yet no account of the universe in its totality can be final which leaves these other forms of consciousness disregarded."

We've all heard the statistic that even a so-called *genius* uses less than 10% of his or her potential. The mind has been called the "next frontier." There is much unknown territory to be explored and much more potential for all of us to express (press out from within). We have only just begun to tap the powers of the mind, and meditation is, so far as we know, the safest and most effective method of opening up this new frontier.

Meditation is not like hypnosis, or even self-hypnosis. Biofeedback shows us that in hypnotic trance, the alpha rhythms remain the same as in a normal waking state, unless *suggested* otherwise by the hypnotist. In hypnosis, there is also no change in metabolism, as occurs in meditation. The physiological and psychological patterns are different and, while both are valuable in their own right, they serve different purposes. Hypnosis is *trance* that is highly focused, while meditation leads to un-focused, expanded awareness.

Meditation is quite natural and not a trance. There is no loss of consciousness and the mind is fully under control at all times during practice. The *whole* mind is awake, alert, alive and working in unity. Hypnotism (clinical, not stage) is effective because a part of the mind is put to sleep, leaving another part free to work.

Meditation is quite natural and not a trance.

It makes the free part stronger, since it is not fighting against itself. Still, there is only a portion of the mind at work when a person is hypnotized. The hypnotic state is not a clear-conscious state and cannot result in transformation through expanded spiritual awareness. It can be helpful in clearing the subconscious mind, but that's as far as it goes.

Meditation is also different from *contemplation*. Contemplation is actively thinking *about* something (words, an idea, a physical object, a project) with the goal of problem solving by re-arranging data that is already known consciously or subconsciously. Meditation expands the range of consciousness beyond what is known. It opens you up to "super-conscious" awareness—*without thinking*. Again, both are valuable, they just serve different purposes.

Meditation is not a way to channeling or mediumship; in fact, it's a way *from* it. It can be a temptation to be fascinated with the *different,* the *super-natural* and the *mysterious,* but to do so only takes you away from the path to freedom. It's best to stay away from illusory practices that give power to other "entities." Clear your mind—completely!

Some of the early pioneers of mind exploration tried psychedelic drugs to get them into altered states of consciousness, but they found the side effects not worth the trip! Many of them later discovered that with meditation they could reach the same states, and even expanded ones, without the side effects associated with drugs. Studies show that it's very difficult (I believe it's impossible) to meditate properly while taking drugs. They alter the central nervous system and prevent the effectiveness of meditation. Transcendental Meditation (T.M.) requires that one abstain from recreational drugs for 15 days before taking the course.

It's very difficult to meditate properly while taking drugs.

The objective of the meditative techniques of **Peace Soup** is not to take psychedelic trips—it's just the opposite. Mind trips "sidetrack" the benefits of true meditation and sour the soup. You want to sidestep the sidetracks, but you also want to allow your natural psychic abilities to surface.

We're All Psychic!

Up to this point in our human development, we have looked at "psychics" or "intuitives" as a phenomenon, yet all the great masters used their God-given psychic abilities all the time. The prophets in the Judeo-Christian tradition used their psychic abilities in fore-telling what was going to happen. John the Baptist, Jesus, Mary, Peter, Paul, and John the Beloved of the New Testament were all "seers." Buddha,

Krishna, Confucius, Lao-Tzu, Mohammed were all *tuned in* to universal consciousness…universal intelligence…divine mind.

They all talked to God and to angels, and they all came to teach us that we can do it, too! There is nothing "weird" or "supernatural" about psychic ability. It's perfectly natural, except to the ignorant—those ignoring the true nature, the *divine* nature of all mankind, and our connection with the all-knowing Mind of God (spirit).

We're all sensitive to the leadings of spirit, if we'll just be still and listen! We all have the same "intuitive" abilities as the master chefs—the prophets of all ages—and meditation, the secret ingredient of **Peace Soup**, will help you develop yourself into a master of your own life. *Mastery* is the goal, and it's no mystery, when you are *aware, in control, balanced* and *flowing*. Our secret ingredient keeps the soup fresh, alive and vital. It keeps us *awake* and sensitive to *all* of life, visible and invisible.

> **We're all sensitive to the leadings of spirit, if we'll just be still and listen!**

Dungeons and Dragons

You will probably encounter resistance to some of the things we explore in this recipe and the resistance may cause hesitancy in following through with the process. This resistance comes from your ego, your old conditioned belief system…*past* conditioning. The resistance is perfectly normal, and it's *good*. It's a protective mechanism that keeps you from destructive beliefs. But if you allow it to prevail, it puts a *drag* on your ability to grow. When you stay awake (aware), you will not allow any *de*-structive beliefs into your consciousness, and you *will* allow *con*-structive beliefs. It's when you're asleep (in your un-awares) that the drag-ons gain their power and put you in the dark dungeons of doubt and fear.

The resistance (the drag-ons) will be appearing throughout the process. It's part of the process! In fact, it's so much of a factor that we will devote one full step of the recipe (Step 4) to becoming familiar with ego and learning how to spoil the spoiler of the soup. For this third step, it's only necessary that you know that the dungeons and drag-ons exist, and that they're a natural part of *you*. The Master Chef, Jesus, called the resistance "the adversary." He said, "Your foes are of your own household (a part of you)." (Matt 10:36, rev. ver.) "Agree with the adversary quickly, while you're in the way with him." (Matt 5:25, rev. ver.) In other words, "Don't resist the resister!"

"Don't resist the resister!"

As you allow the soup to boil gently, applying just a little bit of fire, you'll see that the *dregs* and *drags* boil to the top, so they can be spooned off and discarded. What you've been taught to believe may have been beneficial to you in the past, but some of it shuts you down and keeps you from growing. This is what you want to spoon off.

Ego is not bad. It's the tester, the teacher, and like all good teachers, it gives pop quizzes. You'll be tested (tempted) throughout your meditative experiences, and at times the temptation may be to drop out of school! Don't do it! This is a required course for your *Master's degree*. If you drop out now, you'll just have to take it later, after much more pain and suffering. Just do it—just meditate. The techniques in this recipe are designed to pull you through the resistance…to help you slay the drag-ons and pass every test with flying colors!

Using meditation to strengthen your spiritual/mental muscles is like lifting a weight to strengthen your arm muscles. As you're lifting the weight, you may be saying, "I can't do this! This is not working. It's boring. It's not doing me any good. I'll never get muscles!" But if you keep lifting the weight, what's going to happen? You'll get muscles! Keep practicing the techniques, preparing your soup, and you *will* learn to meditate. It just happens…*shift happens*…naturally, gently and easily. As the soup continues to boil, the aroma gets sweeter, the texture gets smoother, the taste more delightful! Let go—*leggo the ego*—the old beliefs.

Let go—leggo the ego—the old beliefs.

Now you know the benefits of the secret ingredient, you have the desire to learn how to meditate, and you know you'll be experiencing some resistance along the way. So you're ready to add the next ingredient, a helpful ingredient that you can refer to when you encounter resistance and/or difficulty in the learning process.

The Basic Guidelines for Meditation
Guideline #1
It is extremely misleading to strive toward
any particular state of mind while meditating.

Strive means *try*, and you know what that means—you can't *do* it! Meditation is a natural, spontaneous process in which one's consciousness flows in the direction of pure, inner awareness. Trying to get somewhere, to some state of mind that you've heard about, or read about, or even been in before, will keep you from going where you need to go this time—this moment! You want the mind to be led from within, from an awareness that's beyond your conscious mind. Let it happen, whatever happens, even if it's nothing—*especially* if it's nothing!

Guideline #2
Thoughts are not to be prevented,
but allowed to pass through without elaboration!

Thinking is a habit, especially in our Western culture where we worship the intellect. We are encouraged to get good grades, have a high I.Q., think, be smart, and this *is* good. Thinking is a very helpful tool in functioning in the *outer* world, but thoughts are not helpful in functioning in the *inner* world, and they can thwart your meditation and destroy your peace if you allow them to run wild. Even in the outer world, thoughts are like wild stallions that need to be trained and controlled if they are to be of any use. In meditation, you learn to first control your thoughts, and then to let them go, not by force, but by not giving them any power. Remember the alligator? Try not to think about him and he'll eat you up!

In meditation, let thoughts pass by without thinking. I liken it to watching a moving "marquee" with the words scrolling across the screen. You see the words moving by, but you don't read them. They pass, without your thinking about them. Ultimately you can tune out thoughts much as you might tune a radio station to a frequency where there's no station on the air. You develop a tranquil state of mind during meditation where no thought really *matters*.

Guideline #3

Do not try to prevent mental or physical distractions.
If a distraction occurs, patiently bring your
attention back again to the meditation technique.

There will be sounds, thoughts, physical sensations, etc. that can pull you out of your meditation...if you let them. The key here is *attention*...concentration on the meditative technique. Each technique progressively trains and disciplines the mind. Just be patient and gentle with yourself and you *will* learn perfect control—keep practicing.

Guideline #4

Never try to do a good job meditating.

There's the *try* again. "The harder you try, the more stress you apply." Meditation is a natural process, and it must be approached knowing that you *will* be successful. It just happens...as you practice...you don't have to be *good* at it. You don't have to *do* anything special. In fact, meditation is not *doing*, it's *being*. Being something special, which you are!

Guideline #5

Don't approach meditation with a negative attitude.

If you've *tried* to meditate before and not seen results, let it go. Keep practicing and you *will* receive the benefits. Remember, you are getting stronger each time you practice. Keep lifting the weight, it has to work! It's the law (the measure)!

Guideline #6

Don't approach meditation with a positive attitude.

The attitude is neutral—it's simply meditation. It's not the greatest thing since sliced bread. If you get *high,* you always go *low* to balance it. To most people, life is a roller coaster ride of highs and lows. Keep the Balance Bowl ready. You want to be high, but not *emotionally* high. It's a *blissful* high—peaceful, tranquil and serene. Accept all experiences, whether pleasant or uncomfortable, with the same peaceful *in-*difference.

Guideline #7

Don't interpret your meditations.

Interpretation requires thinking. Thinking is not meditating. There will be times when you seem to be receiving a message, but it's usually just a part of the releasing process...old beliefs (drag-ons) bubbling up from the dungeons (subconscious mind) to be released. Don't get caught in the game of dungeons and drag-ons. If you *try* to figure them out, you're playing into their hands and keeping them fed. Don't give them power...let them go! If you need to remember something, you will, later...not *during* the meditation. Let everything go, and it will be gone—for good.

These guidelines were given to me by my meditation teachers, James Gattuso, Jr., and Dr. Victor Zarley. They have been helpful for many in getting a *feel* for meditation. It is to be an easy, flowing process with no parameters, no boundaries, no shoulds, have to's, musts. These make life "musty," and it's designed to be clear and light...easy...flowing...relaxing...satisfying, like a good soup...**Peace Soup.** Peace is all that matters when you add your secret ingredient, so let's learn *how* to meditate!

The Process

Meditation, like life, always begins with the breath. Breath is life! You can live for a long time without food, quite a while without water, but not very long without breath. How you breathe tells a lot about your life. If your breath is irregular, if you sigh a lot, yawn, catch your breath or hyperventilate, you are reflecting stress and/or emotional imbalance.

Most of us have never had formal lessons in how to breathe. We began, suddenly, when the doctor spanked us on the bottom, and we took a quick, shallow breath. We've been breathing that way ever since—in the chest, using only a portion of our lungs.

A balanced, flowing life requires a balanced, flowing breath. A balanced, flowing life requires a balanced, flowing breath, utilizing the entire lung. This is known as *deep* or *diaphragmatic* breathing.

Breathing deep in the diaphragm feels almost like breathing in the stomach. As you inhale, the diaphragm fills and the abdomen rises. As you exhale, the diaphragm empties and the abdomen falls. The rising...falling motion of the abdomen is the key to a balanced, flowing breath. Only a normal breath is necessary. The breath is not, in any way, to be forced or voluntarily suspended or held. It's an easy, natural flow. The breath will slow down as you practice, but you don't need to slow it down—it will happen on its own.

The Zen Exercise

The first exercise in our meditative process comes from the discipline called Zen. Zen means meditation. It's not a religion, it's the discipline of meditation. It involves the deep, diaphragmatic breathing we've been describing, so you begin by feeling the breath moving in, with the abdomen rising, and moving out as the abdomen falls.

I like to think of the breath as being a semi-circular motion, beginning at the nose (Yogi says, "Nose is for breathing, mouth is for eating"), with the air moving through the nostrils, down the throat, through the chest, and into the solar plexus (diaphragm) as the abdomen rises. The exhale reverses the process; the abdomen falls as the air moves from the diaphragm, back up through the chest, through the throat, and out through the nostrils. This inhale and exhale is one full breath.

In the beginning, it may be helpful to place your hand on your stomach so you can better feel the rising…falling motion. You may also need to force the abdomen to rise for a few breaths as the air comes in, and pull it in as it leaves. Do whatever it takes for you to begin to *see* the breath in your mind, and *feel* the movement in your body.

Again, I emphasize that it's important not to overdo the breath. Inhale only as much air as you require and don't draw the air in—let it come to you. When you exhale, comfortably let all the air out. There is very little movement in the chest area; only the abdomen rises. It's a normal breath, not a heavy breath. Practice this for a few minutes. Mentally follow the breath down inside to a spot just below the rib cage, the solar plexus, and then back out again.

Now we'll add a second step to this exercise…concentration. Most of us know we need some work on concentration. Our thoughts are scattered and our minds wander in different directions. This Zen exercise allows you to work on your breathing and your concentration at the same time by *concentrating on the breath*. This is a discipline exercise. We learn to concentrate on the breath to the exclusion of everything else, and then, finally, we can let the breath go and think about nothing!

The "discipline" is developed by counting the breaths. As you visualize the breath flowing in and out in the semi-circular motion, and the rising and falling of the abdomen, you don't think about anything but the breath. Then you

The "discipline" is developed by counting the breaths.

take your second full breath…inhale…exhale…a normal flowing breath, deep in the diaphragm, still thinking only of the breath. The objective is to count from 1 to 10 breaths, without thinking of anything but your breathing. If you let your mind wander to anything besides your breath, you must go back and start over again *at 1*.

This sounds simple, and it is, but for an undisciplined mind, it's not so easy. I've had students who couldn't get past *1* for days, their minds wandering incessantly, but as they persisted and kept practicing, they finally made it to *10*. Once you reach 10, without thinking of anything but your breath, you begin again with another set of 10 breaths.

If you were to go to a Zen temple to learn to meditate, this would be the first exercise you would be given, and the Zen master would tell you that until you can do 10 sets of 10 breaths (100 breaths) without thinking of anything but the breath, you're not even beginning to concentrate! Don't go beyond the count of 10. We've been counting to 10 throughout our lives, so we don't have to think about it anymore. A count to more than 10 breaths diverts attention from breath to counting and breaks concentration. You may think you're concentrating, but there's a difference between mere intellectual concentration and the higher concentration necessary for meditation. A person succeeding in the higher concentration is not in a state of mental bondage, but is free from attachment and worldly considerations. The concentration of meditation is *extra* ordinary. In ordinary concentration, the mind still holds on to the un-whole-some aspects of its own creation. In meditation, you let go of these un-whole-some aspects.

The concentration of meditation is extra ordinary.

As you practice, you develop purity of thought and calmness of mind, continually bringing the wandering mind back under control. Each practice session builds discipline, and all future conduct is illumined by each meditative experience.

When you have distracting thoughts of business, family, sickness, fear or worry, don't resist them, but let them pass without elaboration (Guideline 2). Let them be *fleeting* thoughts. Look at them as if they don't concern you. When they arise, allow them to pass through on the marquee and on into nothingness. If you tie on to them, you've broken concentration and you start the count again—*at 1*.

Your goal for this step of the recipe is to practice this breath counting exercise for about 20 minutes twice a day until you can complete the 20 minutes without thinking of anything but your breathing (or nothing at all). When you can do this easily, without effort, you'll be ready to move on to:

The Zen Technique

The exercise of breath counting shows you a lot about yourself and your ability to concentrate. Some of us have great ability, some not so good, but as you get this exercise under your belt (so to speak), concentration becomes easier, and meditation becomes easier. In fact, the breath counting exercise is the most difficult for most people, and all the techniques from here on get progressively easier and easier. Mindfulness (the ultimate technique in this recipe) is the easiest of all, but it cannot be effectively

The techniques get progressively easier and easier.

utilized if *tried* out of progression, before the basic techniques are mastered. So stick to the recipe and learn each technique in order as you pro-gress.

The Zen *technique* is the Zen exercise with one added dimension. We are trained by the world to be top heavy. Everything takes place in our heads. We see in our heads, hear in our heads, think, taste and smell in our heads. Everything is going on *out there*, and we're continually falling on our faces. The center of your being is in the solar plexus, and you want to begin to bring your awareness more *in here*, into the center. This is what is meant by the phrase "getting centered"—getting away from the top-heaviness and becoming balanced and poised, ready to handle anything that comes your way, easily and peacefully.

The way you do this is instead of simply counting numbers, you actually visualize the numbers (1 through 10) and allow them, one by one, to flow down, with the breath, into the abdomen where you leave them. Begin with the vision of the number "1" in front of your face and as you breathe in, bring the number in with your breath. Allow it to flow through the nostrils, down the throat, through the chest and into the stomach where you place it and leave it. Then allow the breath to move back out to pick up number 2. Inhale the number 2 and place it in your stomach next to the 1, leaving it there, and again moving out with the exhale to pick up number 3, and so on through number 10.

Keep the numbers small. I've had students say, "I feel like the num-

bers get stuck in my throat," or "I'm getting fat, stuffing all these numbers into my stomach!" Ego will come up with all kinds of resistance.
You'll learn more about how to handle the resistance in Step 4. For
now, just see the numbers as etheric...they dissolve into nothingness,
and there are no calories in them! The whole idea of taking the numbers down is to bring your awareness to center as you concentrate on
your breath. These are the three aims of this technique: 1) breathe properly; 2) concentrate; 3) center.

It's a wonderful technique, and I've seen miracles happen in a very
short time with just this one part of the process. This is the first step,
the *baby step,* that leads to the giant step—*pure peace*—so practice. ***It
will work for you only if you practice.*** In the beginning stages, meditation requires some effort...maybe even some force to overcome the
inertia of past conditioning. The desire for self-mastery must be greater
than the desire to continue life in the known, safe, *stressful* way—the
way of the world. To simply read this book and nod at the points you
agree with won't get you anywhere. You'll remain locked in your old
mind set. As every soup chef learns, if you don't change your direction,
you'll end up where you're headed. To change your life, you must
change your *mind,* and change requires effort—practice.

Twenty minutes twice a day is all it takes—20 minutes in the morning and 20 minutes in the late afternoon or early evening. Occasional
practice of meditation doesn't accomplish much. You're integrating the
benefits into every part of your life and without *regular* practice, this
cannot be accomplished. Reading is no substitute for practice. Reading
is easy when compared to meditation. Remember, it's a peaceful *life* that
you're cooking up with the **Peace Soup** recipe, not *occasional* peace.

When, Why, Where, Who and What

It's not essential that your meditation time be in the morning and
afternoon or early evening. Just keep in mind that meditation is "a
preparation for activity." If you meditate before bedtime, it will wake
you up and you won't want to sleep. Early morning is best, when you

first wake up, and in the beginning, you may find yourself falling back to sleep. Your body is trained to believe, "When the eyes are closed, it's time to sleep!" You're re-training yourself, but it may take a little time. If you find yourself falling asleep, let your eyes open slightly. If that doesn't do it, do your physical exercises first, or take a bath or shower to wake you up, then complete your meditation.

It's best, also, to meditate before eating and not for at least an hour afterward, so that the body is not involved in digesting food. Digest your *spiritual food* first and it will actually help in the physical digestion process.

Meditate alone during your "regular" meditation time. When close friends or relatives, even spouses, join you, their presence will affect your meditation and keep you from your Self. Pray together, yes, but be in solitude during your regular **Be in solitude during your regular daily meditation.** daily meditation. Chef Schopenhauer once said, "Solitude has two advantages; firstly that one is with oneself, and secondly that one is not together with others." The one person you'll always be with, throughout eternity, is *you!* "Know thyself!"

It is useful for compatible people to meditate together at times, and group meditation can make great changes in group consciousness and contribute to the general well-being of the community (common unity), but it is through our *individually* transformed lives that the more effective and lasting impact is made upon the world. (We'll explore this more fully in Step 7 of the recipe.)

It is important to sit up when meditating, to allow energy to flow properly, but a full lotus position is not necessary. Most of us are used to sitting in chairs, so a chair is fine, as long as it has a straight back. We want to keep the energy centers in the spinal column open and flowing. Your position will fulfill these three conditions: 1) comfort; 2) a straight back; and 3) easy breathing. Be resolved to sit motionless with your head balanced on your shoulders so that all the forces can flow inward.

It is usually helpful to meditate in the same room during your regular meditation time. Do not become dependent on the room, but memories of previous meditation successes in that room may assist you, and the environment will be charged with love, peace and joy…this will support you even more. "Close the door" to the room (as Jesus instructed) and, for Heaven's sake, disconnect the telephone!

You won't need a clock. You have one built in and you'll know when approximately 20 minutes are up. It doesn't have to be exact, but you'll find that it's always pretty close. (We'll discuss *time* more fully in Step 4 of the recipe.) At first it may seem like more time has elapsed, later it will seem like less. Ultimately, when it doesn't matter, your timing will be exact! Choose a time that will always be disturbance-free (quite early if you have children) and can always be adhered to, unless something very unusual comes up.

If you don't feel like meditating, do it anyway. If you don't feel like meditating, do it anyway. Remember the Control Bowl. We're working on discipline, learning to overcome the habit of "ego resisting your good!" You will feel better about yourself for having mastered your subconscious resistance. Your confidence will increase and enable you to master other situations in your life.

Meditate in silence—no music, no tapes of guided meditation. Listening takes the edge off your concentration and keeps you on the surface. You cannot give full attention to the inner process if anything demands the attention of the senses. There are two schools of thought on this and I agree that there is a time for music, candles, guided meditation, incense, etc., but for your daily meditation it is better to keep the senses quiet, or you may be *incensed* by your lack of pro-gress. You will get out of meditation, just as with all of life, only what you put into it. Input equals output, until you totally let go—then you will actually get *more* than you put in!

Sometimes beginners *try* to concentrate too much. They try to speed up the process and become frustrated, impatient and bored. They may also feel physical sensations that are not altogether pleasant. It's not uncommon for beginning meditators to report a feeling of pressure, especially between the eyebrows or at the crown of the head. This will subside so long as one is relaxed and not straining to concentrate. Don't strain; let the process be gentle.

Some may experience episodes of mild confusion and even emotional unrest due to the release of suppressed emotions and unpleasant memories. This indicates that a clearing is taking place as old material in the subconscious mind is being released. During this process, it's important to remember Guideline 7 (Don't interpret your meditations). If you try to figure out what's being released, it won't be released. If you *think* about it or try to psychoanalyze yourself, you stop the process and *stuff* the "stuff" even deeper! Let go and let the recipe do its work. The release of suppressed emotions and unpleasant memories is an important part of preparing **Peace Soup**. The sub-

Let go and let the recipe do its work.

conscious mind and, along with it, the physical body and its nervous system, are actually being re-fined and re-structured. Even muscular "twitching" is a good sign, as it signals the releasing of tension.

Do not compare your progress, or seeming lack of progress, with that of others. We all move at our own rate, depending on what we've experienced and stored in our computer that needs to be released or restructured. You will pro-gress at *your* perfect pace and, as you practice regularly, you will experience breakthrough many times, as you reach new plateaus of peace and joy.

Approach your practice of meditation with sincerity, openness, and a genuine desire to learn. Make up your mind that whatever is worth doing, is worth doing right. The rewards come from study, self-discipline and practice. There is no easy road and no end to growth and discovery—it is eternal. As you practice more and more, you find yourself more and more at home in the world and in the universe, better able to function peacefully and handle the "tribulation" of life efficiently and effectively. You solve problems easily and quickly by getting to the origin of the problem. Meditation doesn't treat the symptoms (give the symptoms a treat) as do worldly techniques. It gets you to the core of your being and to the core of any problem by tuning you in to an intelligence greater than your own.

Do – Be – Do – Be – Do – Be!

In closing this section on the practice of meditation, I would like to emphasize how important it is to come out of your meditation slowly and gently, so as to maintain and carry over the benefits you have gained. As meditation has been described as "diving within," coming

Coming out of meditation may be likened to "swimming (or floating) back to the surface." out of meditation may be likened to "swimming (or floating) back to the surface," un-folding with a sense of being rested and tranquil. This unfolding connects the serenity of the meditation with your outer world and allows you to integrate the benefits into your life, not only through the rest of the day, but through the rest of your life! It all becomes a *rest*-full experience.

So again we say, "Don't push the river." Be gentle, let it flow, and go with the flow. Don't *do* your meditation, just *be* in meditation. Chef Lao-Tzu said, "It's like cooking a small fish—one must be careful not to over-*do* it." Chef William (Shakespeare) said, "To be or not to be, that is the question." He might have said, "To be or to *do*, that is the question," or simply, "Do? Be? Do? Be? Do?" Whatever the question, the answer is do *be*. The rewards come from your *being,* and they come when they're ready to come, at their own speed, in their own good time. They cannot be hurried, they cannot be ordered or scheduled. The Zen master says, "When the apple is ripe, it will drop from the tree of its own weight." Be patient and allow changes to occur naturally.

You now know what to do and how to be. All that's left is for you to enter your room, shut the door, assume the proper position and breathe. Breathe in and out the sweetness…the serenity…the joy…the love…the peace. Your **Peace Soup** now contains the *secret ingredient.*

A Few Words of
Caution...and Assurance

Caution: People with histories of serious psychological problems or mental illness may want to seek responsible supervision in the beginning stages of meditation.

In the meditative process, as with all processes of dramatic change, there is a time of transition or chemicalization, where one may get worse before he or she gets better. Someone with serious mental disease may need a trained professional to guide them through the transition. After the initial period of release and trans-formation, they will be free to practice on their own.

There are no negative side effects to meditation for anyone of normal and sound mind, since it is quite a natural process. It is, nevertheless, a powerful mental process of release and, as the old thoughts and emotions "bubble" to the surface, a few of them may seem fearful or dis-quieting. This is perfectly natural, and if a feeling of fear or anxiety does arise, simply allow your eyes to open slightly and look around reassuringly to see that everything is secure, then gently allow your eyes to fall shut again. This doesn't happen often, but if it does, just know that it's good—you're bringing that old stuff that you "stuffed" long ago, up for release, and you don't even have to know what it is, or what caused it. You're releasing it and letting it go by not thinking about it! Don't get dragged into the dungeons with the drag-ons. Just let it all go, don't think about it, and the drag-ons will go *poof*—like the *magic dragon!*

You're bringing that old stuff that you "stuffed" long ago, up for release.

"The Mantra"
An Alternative Technique from Yoga

As we discussed earlier, the **Peace Soup** recipe draws from two schools of meditation, Yoga and Zen. Each of these disciplines has a beginning or basic technique and both of the techniques are valuable and effective, ultimately taking you to the secret place. Some people relate better to one than the other and I suggest that you give them both a chance, so you can see which one best suits you. Remember, there is no one best technique for everyone.

I recommend that you practice the Zen technique of breath counting first, for at least seven days (14 sessions), before you use this alternative. Then use the mantra for a week. Give them both a chance to do their magical work before you decide which one you prefer. Ultimately you will probably use both techniques, not at the same time, but to perform different functions.

There may be times when you're really wrapped up in the physical body and the mantra may be more effective in shaking you loose, since it is more of a *vibration*. Some people find that the mantra is more effective in slowing down the brain waves, and the mantra I'll be suggesting is a two-syllable word, so the rhythm can be altered, to slow down the vibration. Before getting into the actual sound, I want to explore the technique, where it comes from and how it works.

The mantra is literally as old as sound itself.

The mantra is literally as old as sound itself, at least the sound of the human voice. Primitive man began making sounds by forcing air through the voice box, and the most basic sound is made by simply opening the mouth and saying, "Ah." As you empty your lungs and begin closing your mouth, at about midpoint, the sound changes to "oo." Finally, with the lips together, there is "mm," which seems to vibrate through the whole body. The complete sound is "Ah-oo-mm...Aum...Om." This sound, "aum" or "om," is known as the *universal mantra*.

Since the beginning of consciousness, this basic sound has been sacred—the sound of God. It is a word-bridge between the mind of man and the mind of God, and also between the mind of man and his body. "Om" or "aum" blends mind and body, unifies them, transcends them and reaches out to the mystical unity of the universe.

Since he began making sound, man has experimented and created other mystical sounds. The early Sanskrit from India has an alphabet of sounds, and the Sanskrit words have been used by many disciplines, including Yoga and Buddhism, in expressing the mystic unity. Sanskrit was instrumental in the origin and development of comparative Indo-European linguistics.

Chanting is popular in Western as well as Eastern religions. The monks in the Christian monasteries chant, and the cantors in the Jewish and Catholic traditions are really the "chanters," the ones who lead the voice sounds in the church. The psalms of THE BIBLE were originally sung or chanted in a sing-song mode of speaking. In the mystical Judaic tradition, the secret names of God were sometimes chanted (Yahweh, Jehovah, etc.). The Whirling Dervish sect of the Sufis use a mantra while they're whirling, saying, "Yahhaadi!" ("o guide") faster and faster as they dance.

The mantra can have a religious meaning, as we've described, or it can be used simply as a vibration without any understanding of the meaning of the sound or word. This is how we use the mantra in the **Peace Soup** recipe. The mantra we use does have a meaning, but you don't need to know what it is. It's actually better if you don't know, so there will be no mental or emotional charge on the meaning.

Any voice sound can be used as a mantra. In Transcendental Meditation (T.M.), you are given what is known as "your personal mantra" and are not to share it with anyone else. The T.M. teacher will select your personal mantra from a list of choices and will usually match it to your personality. In actuality, you may select any sound that feels right to you—just make sure it doesn't have that mental or emotional charge that can interfere with the meditation.

I heard a story several years ago about a woman who didn't like the mantra she received in T.M., so she went searching for her own. She decided she had found the perfect mantra when she began to chant, "Paul Newman, Paul Newman, Paul Newman!" This is definitely *not* the choice of image you want; in fact, you want *no* image, just a sound, a vibration.

The sound I suggest for the **Peace Soup** recipe, as I said earlier, is a two-syllable word from Sanskrit…"Ihgah," pronounced "ing gah." (For proper pronunciation, listen to the CD.) This sound may be said aloud to get a feel for the vibration, but in your practice sessions it's repeated silently within your own mind, instead of *out* loud. Keeping it quiet internalizes the vibration and brings you to that inner stillness.

You begin it at a fairly rapid pace and then allow it to slow down. Don't try to control it, such as timing it with the breath, but allow it to flow and slow down of its own accord. The goal is letting go of conscious thought by first concentrating on one thing, the mantra, and finally *no*-thing, just as we did with the breath counting exercise of Zen. Whichever technique you decide is best for you, remember that they both lead to the same place, the "secret place of the most high"…the silence…no thought…no movement…no sound…just peace…pure peace…

Now that you have the secret ingredient stirred into your soup and are beginning to feel the strength and vitality that come from tasting the soup, you're ready to get a better understanding of the resistance, the *adversary,* that may show up at any time to spoil the soup! This "spoiler" is lurking in the dark shadows of the dungeons, ready to sneak into the soup whenever your Awareness and/or Control Bowl/s run low.

The next step of the recipe is designed to shine light into the darkness, to en-lighten…

Step 4

The Spoiler!
The Resistance to Peace

The spoiler has carried many names throughout his-story. It's been called: "the serpent"…"the enemy"…"a fallen angel"…"Lucifer"… "Beelzebub"…"Mara"…"the tempter"…"the tester"…"the adversary"… "the prince of the world"…"the devil"…"Satan"…"alter-ego"… and just plain "ego!" No matter what you call it, it's up to no good, trying to foil every plan, ruin every life, spoil every soup. I love the insight of Chef Pogo when he said, "We have met the enemy and he is *us!*"

The devil by any other name is still a part of us, each one of us, no matter how evolved we may be. Chef Jesus was tempted in the wilderness, not by some "being with pitchfork and horns," but by His own personal ego. He was hungry. He had been fasting for forty days and forty nights and His body was **The devil by any other name is still a part of us.** crying out for food. He knew how powerful He was. He knew He could turn water to wine, stones to bread, but He also knew that His mission in life required that He not give in to His body's demand for food. He had to *give up* the physical demands and live "by the word of God."

He also knew if He were to cast Himself off the pinnacle of the temple that "the angels would bear Him up." He would be able to fly (levitate), to walk on air, as he would later walk on water—but that would amount to *tempting* God. He knew He had the power to take over all the kingdoms of the world, but that would require falling down and worshipping a power-hungry ego. And what was His statement? "Get thee behind me…." This is where the ego belongs, behind—in the past!

I like to define ego as "the old, conditioned belief system." I repeat,

Ego is the old, conditioned belief system.

Ego is a scapegoat (that's why the devil has horns). "It wasn't *me* that did it, it was that other guy, the one in the red suit, he made me do it!"

We don't want to take the responsibility for our questionable actions, so we invent a *fall guy.* The *fall* began way back with Adam and Eve. "The serpent said I should eat the fruit." Yeah, right, Eve…like snakes can talk! Your power-hungry ego told you to do it. The spoiler (ego) ate "the fruit of the tree of the knowledge of good and evil" and started judging—good *and* bad, right *and* wrong. Ego sees *two*. Duality! Two gods—a good God and a bad God, warring against each other. And the war continues unto this day. Where? On the battlefield within each one of us. It's the past warring against the present and the future. The resistance comes from the past…past conditioning, what's behind us— *the old, conditioned belief system.*

The Legend Unfolds

There's a story from long, long ago in ancient India. It's a story about a prince who was born to a very wealthy king and queen. Prior to the birth, the king and queen began having visions and dreams that were unusual and disturbing to them. They called upon their wise men to interpret these unusual dreams and visions, and the wise men agreed that the dreams concerned the child. He was to be a very special being, a great leader even beyond the present kingdom.

He was to be a very special being, a great leader.

This pleased the king and queen and they seemed satisfied, but just as the advisors were about to leave, the "wisest of the wise" paused for a moment, and added, "Yes, he will be a great leader, but it's undecided as to whether it will be in the *material* realm or the *spiritual* realm. If he sees only abundance, opulence and lavishness as he grows up, he will become a leader, like his father, in the material world. On the other hand, if he sees anything of suffering, pain, poverty or hardship before he is grown, his great compassion will cause a shift, and he will become a leader in the spiritual realm."

"I'm not going to raise some religious fanatic!" the king shouted defiantly. "I'll see to it that he sees no suffering before he's grown."

When the child was born, the king instructed all the old, crippled, sick and poor to leave the palace area. All the guards were instructed in how to keep the prince lavishly supplied at all times. If any one of the palace personnel were to become sick or hurt, they were to leave immediately, avoiding the prince at all costs. He was to be given anything he wanted, anytime he wanted it, and was never to experience suffering in any form. This was a sublime up-bringing, and—it worked!

He was never to experience suffering in any form.

For sixteen years, the boy grew in this sheltered environment until he was almost a man. He hardly noticed that there were no old people in his life, except for his father and mother. The fact that they were aging bothered him a little, since he had tutors who had schooled him in the idea that he would one day inherit the kingdom and assume the duties and the station of the king.

He had wondered where his father would go. The prince had never been outside the palace compound, with its immense grounds and surrounding forest, and he was curious about what lay beyond the forest. He had learned something about "villages" and "other kingdoms" and had been told that he would see them "at the right time."

"I'm sixteen," he thought. "I should be old enough now." He went to his father and said, "Father, I know that I will one day inherit this kingdom, and I feel I need to know more about what it's like beyond the forest. I want to visit the villages and meet the people there."

"Yes," the king replied, "I understand how you feel, and there will be a time for that, but for now, your mother and I have planned something more important. We have arranged for you to be married, and a princess from a neighboring kingdom is on her way here, at this very moment, to become your bride!"

All thoughts of travel immediately left the prince's mind; his father's timing was impeccable. He was so excited about being married, and he fell so head-over-heels in love with his beautiful princess, that for the next several years he was totally absorbed, first with his bride, and later with both her and their own son.

It was a wonderful life, a blissful life, and the king and queen had given a sigh of relief when their grandson was born with an easy birth. They believed that their son had made it to manhood without experiencing suffering and would now maintain the materialistic mode of living. They were to find themselves sadly mistaken.

It was not until well into his 29th year when the prince began to again feel unrest and curiosity, and, for the second time, he approached his father with the idea of seeing the villages and the rest of the kingdom. "I've been expecting this," the king replied, "and I feel that with your life as solid as it is right now, this *is* a good time for you to see more of the world. I will make the arrangements."

That evening the king very carefully instructed his trusted charioteer to go the next day into the villages and prepare a parade route for the prince to follow. The charioteer and his men were to remove all the sick, poor, old and lame from the route and instruct the villagers that there were to be only happy, cheering, smiling faces to greet the prince as he came through on the following day.

There were to be only happy, cheering, smiling faces to greet the prince.

On the morning of the adventure the prince was the first one at the stable. He was so excited he hadn't slept a wink the night before, but he was still full of energy for this momentous occasion. He rode on the chariot with his father's driver and, as they made their way through the forest and into the first village, he was greeted by hundreds of healthy, happy, cheering people. They, too, were excited to see the prince they had heard about for so many years, but had never seen.

The morning hours went quickly as they travelled from village to village, greeted always by throngs of the well-to-do villagers. By early afternoon, the prince began to become a little bored with the sameness of activity, and as they approached the largest village in the kingdom, he decided to look around a bit more. "I'd like to turn down one of these side streets," he shouted to the charioteer. "No, we can't do that," the driver replied. "I've been instructed to stay on the main route through the villages."

"I'm the prince and I say turn down this side street!" he demanded. He "pulled rank," and his voice was so commanding that the chariot seemed to almost automatically turn, as it began moving down the side street. The scenery was definitely different. The street was not nearly as well kept as the main route, and there seemed to be people everywhere, strange-looking people, the likes of which the prince had never seen before.

They had travelled less than 100 yards when the driver had to stop the chariot to avoid running over an old man, with long, un-cut white hair and beard. He was bent over and walking very slowly, using a stick for support. "What's the matter with that man?" the prince asked. "Why does he look so grotesque? Why can't he walk upright like a normal person?"

The charioteer's face turned ashen gray at that question. He feared he had made a fatal mistake in getting off the main route. "That man's old," he replied in a soft voice. "He's crippled and he can't walk upright." "I don't understand," the prince said in a quizzical tone, "I've never seen anyone like that!"

> "That man's old. He's crippled and he can't walk upright."

As the old man made it out of their way, the chariot again started to move down the street, slowly making its way through the crowd. Several beggars came up to the chariot, cups in hands, asking for money. They were so dirty, grimy, pitiful-looking, that the prince almost immediately felt his heart leap in compassion. Their rags of clothing were literally falling off their bodies, and the bodies themselves seemed to be falling apart, being riddled with disease. "Why don't these people dress like us?" the prince asked. "Why are their bodies so ugly? Why are they asking us for money?" "They're hungry, they're sick, they're poor," explained the driver, resigned to his new role as teacher. Sick? Poor? Hungry? These words had no meaning to the prince. He couldn't relate.

A little further along, they met a band of monks, holy men dressed in flowing robes, their heads shaved clean. "Stop!" the prince shouted, "I want to talk to these men." The charioteer pulled to a halt and the prince jumped down and went over to the monks. He explained who he was, and they began asking him questions about his soul, about his spiritual nature, things he had never even considered

His head was spinning, his mind was in a whirl!

before. He had no earthly idea what they were talking about, his head was spinning, his mind was in a whirl! He returned to the chariot and they headed back to the parade route, the charioteer relieved, the prince in a daze.

Late that afternoon, they made their way back to the palace. The prince had not spoken since the encounters on the side street. He felt totally lost. He was realizing that he knew nothing about the world, that his whole life, up to that point, had been a lie! He felt betrayed, but more than that, he felt he had to find out more.

When they reached the palace, the prince asked to be dropped off, and he went immediately to his father. He was angry, but he didn't really blame the king. He respected his father and he knew he must have had his reasons for what he had done. He also knew he had much to learn and he had to do it on his own. He told his father what he was feeling, about his experiences of the day, that he had to know more, and that he was planning to go back out into the villages the next day, alone! Interestingly, the king did not object. He somehow knew this had to happen and he gave his son his blessing.

The prince didn't say much to his wife that evening. He did tell her the events of the day and she knew he was going through some deep soul-searching. She offered her support, but she, too, somehow knew it was something he had to work out on his own. She was up with him early the next morning, after he had had another sleepless night, and she kissed him, knowingly, as he mounted his white stallion and rode off into the dawn of that day, and what proved to be the dawn of a new life for both of them.

It was something he had to work out on his own.

That day he rode through many villages. He talked with people from all walks of life. He visited with families in their homes, he saw sick people, old people, poor people, suffering people. The most traumatic experience for him that day was when he went into a home where someone had just died. There was the corpse laid out in front of him, and people were mourning, crying, wailing. This really stirred something deep inside of him.

At the end of that day he was totally drained. As he quietly made his way through the forest and he approached the palace, he could hear the sounds of music, singing and laughter. His father knew what he was going through, and had decided to throw a party to try to cheer him up. Everyone was singing and drinking and dancing, having a good time, but the prince was quiet. He just stood in the background and watched. "This is not real," he thought. "What's real is out there in the world, and I don't know anything about it. I've got to find out more."

"I've got to find out more."

That night after everything had settled down and everyone else was asleep, he made the most difficult decision of his life. He decided he must leave. He didn't tell anyone. He quietly went into his little son's room and saw him sleeping sweetly in the moonlight. With tears in his eyes and a heaviness in his heart, he said goodbye to his son, not knowing when, if ever, he would see him again. He did the same in his wife's room. Kneeling beside her bed, he silently told her how much he loved her. When he saw how beautiful she was, as the light of the full moon glistened in her hair, it was almost too much for him to bear. He assured her that what he was doing was beyond his mortal power to control. He had to be true to his destiny, whatever that turned out to be. He was being guided solely by his heart. He loved her more than words could express and he knew his heart would break if he tarried even a moment more. "Goodbye my love," he whispered as he stole quickly into the darkness.

He didn't take anything with him, only the clothes on his back and a few coins in his pockets. He started out on horseback, on his own white stallion, but soon realized he had to leave all contact with the past behind, so he dismounted and released his horse to return to the stable. He continued on foot. It was a long walk to the nearest village, and it was almost dawn when he approached the outskirts. He was walking gingerly in the dawn's early light, surprised that he had so much energy after three sleepless nights, when he heard a voice from the shadows under a tree. "Can you spare a coin for a poor beggar?" As the prince approached the tree, he could barely make out the image of a man, about his size, dressed in rags and obviously having not quite slept off the drunken night before.

"Can you spare a few coins?" the man asked again. "Here, take these," the prince said, emptying his pockets. "No, wait! Change clothes with me. You take my clothes, I'll take yours!"

The beggar immediately snapped to attention. "Yes, sir!" he said, eyeing the beautiful clothes of the prince as he slipped out of his rags. They very quickly changed clothes and when the exchange was complete they both burst out laughing. What an unlikely sight they made—the handsome prince in rags, the poor dirty beggar in princely garb! The prince felt lighter in every way. It was as if the weight of the world had been lifted from his shoulders as he released the last vestige of his *past*.

He released the last vestige of his past.

For the next six years, he travelled throughout India. He learned of many cultures and many different belief systems as he experienced a world he had not known about in his childhood. Without prior conditioning to poverty and sickness, he was able to see the stark contrast between the suffering world and the world of plenty he had known in his earlier life.

He joined with a band of travelling monks and spent much of his time developing his understanding of spiritual things, renouncing the material world. He took on the ways of asceticism and the practice of denying the body. He shaved his head, slept on stones and went on long fasts. During one of these fasts he overdid it and almost starved to death! Someone found him just in time and nursed him back to health.

He realized during the ordeal that this torturing of the body couldn't be the way God meant for one to become enlightened. There must be an easier way, and he was determined to find it. He decided to go directly to God, so he just sat under a tree and waited for God to enlighten him. He sat there, in meditation, for 49 days (we're working on 20 minutes)! During this time he could feel himself becoming lighter and lighter as he emptied his mind of thought and opened the way for wisdom. On the 49th day (seven times seven) the process was completed—he *was* enlightened!

He sat there in meditation for 49 days!

At this point he knew he had a choice to make. He could continue to work alone, on himself, and experience perpetual *nirvana,* or he could begin to teach others what he had learned. It wasn't such an easy choice since he thought no one could understand what he had to teach, but, through his enlightenment, he knew his role was to be that of teacher. He also knew that if he must go back into the world, he would go with his eyes open.

After a light meal and a bath, he donned a new robe and went searching for the band of monks he had been travelling with for so many years. He learned where they were, and as he approached their group, they saw him wearing the new robe and feared he must be lost again, back in the material world. When he came into their midst and began speaking, however, they immediately knew something had changed. He was speaking of things they had not even dreamed of, and the more they heard, the more they realized he was not like them anymore.

They began asking him, "What are you? Are you a god?" "No," he

Buddha means to awake and to know!

answered. "An angel?" "No." "A saint?" "No." "Then what are you?" "I am awake!" he said. His answer became his title—*Buddha* means to awake and to know!

The Significance

This is the legend of the prince, Siddhartha (Gautama), who lived a charmed life as a child, with his ego conditioning sheltered from the hardness of the world. There are as many versions of this legend as there are story-tellers, but the key to understanding the significance is that he had no taste of suffering, sickness, death or poverty in his *formative* years, so when he was faced with suffering in later life, he was able to see it more clearly, possibly, than anyone ever has, before or since. This clear vision, without pre-conditioning or prejudice, allowed him to formulate what he called:

"The Four Noble Truths"
The First Noble Truth
"Life is a suffering experience for most people."

Not all life is suffering, just *unregenerate* life—life asleep. Most people live in a series of traumatic experiences, beginning with the trauma associated with birth, progressing through injury, illness, poverty, challenging relationships, and into old age, with its decrepitude and the fear of approaching death. Life, for the most part, and for most people, is being separated from what one loves, and being saddled with what one hates.

The Second Noble Truth
"The cause of all suffering is 'attachment.'"

We become emotionally attached to things—the demands of ego.

We become emotionally attached to people, places, to ideas and beliefs, to time frames, to *things*—the demands of ego. We seek fulfillment in trying to satiate ego, our old conditioned belief system. We seek approval *from* others and control *over* others. We think we cannot be happy without the things we're attached to, and we're eternally trying to hold onto them and to get more. Desires and attachments make us tense, frustrated, disappointed, insecure and fearful. We are constantly at the mercy of *things* and *people,* trying desperately to make them conform to our ego demands.

Master Chef Ken Keyes, in his master-piece THE HANDBOOK TO HIGHER CONSCIOUSNESS, has taken the Buddha's teaching and put it into Western terminology. He has interpreted the word "attachment" as "addiction." He says we become *addicted* to people, places, things, ideas and time frames, and we think they must meet our programming. If they don't, we cause ourselves to suffer. Ken Keyes defines an addiction as "an emotion-backed demand." Emotion is the cause of all suffering (emotional attachment...addiction), and all emotion comes from ego—the spoiler.

Chef Huston Smith, in his essay on Buddhism, says, "Can we not see that 'tis self by which we suffer? Far from being the door to abundant life, the ego is a strangulated hernia; the more it swells, the tighter it shuts off the free-flowing circulation on which health depends, and pain increases." 'Tis ego, the programmed belief system, that is the cause of all suffering!

> "Tis ego, the programmed belief system, that is the cause of all suffering!

The Third Noble Truth
"There is a way beyond suffering!"

We don't have to suffer. As the great soup chefs Chad and Lyte (O'Shea) say, "Misery *is* optional!" When we are released from the narrow limits of self-interest (ego-fulfillment), we will enter a new realm of being, the vastness of universal awareness.

The Fourth Noble Truth
"The Way"

The Buddha's way is what he called *The Eight-Fold Path.* It is basically the way of right living. There are many ways to enlightenment.

Jesus had His "Kingdom of Heaven" way. Lao-Tzu taught "The Way of the Tao." They all have the function of spoiling the spoiler...of overcoming the control of ego...re-training the belief system.

What we want to do is enlighten the ego.

Ken Keyes says, "We don't want to *kill* the ego, just retire it for lack of work." I believe what we want to do is *enlighten* the ego. All the great master chefs had large egos...enlightened egos. Their old conditioned belief systems said that they were masters, that they knew the truth and were free! They believed this, and they followed the way of a master. They cooked up the peaceful life of a master chef, and shared their peace with the world.

This recipe is designed to help you master *your* life, clear *your* senses, spoil the spoiler, so *you* can be "in"-lightened. You become enlightened not by what's written in these pages, or in any book, but by what's written in your heart, by the spirit of truth, the truth that cannot be written or spoken, only known. When your ego is open to mastery, you will be able to train yourself in the way of a master, the way of peace, love, joy, wisdom and understanding. A lofty goal and a "noble truth!"

His Story

As we alluded to earlier in this step of the recipe, ego, the spoiler, has been around for a long, long time—actually since man took on the consciousness of judgment, the consciousness of right *and* wrong, good *and* bad. Early man lived mostly by instinct and had only a primative brain that was highly sensitive to the dangers of a pre-historic world. He lived mostly alone with a small family, or in small tribes, so he could depend on his instincts to guide him away from trouble. When man began to become more civilized and joined in colonies, his instincts became confused and harder to read. There were others who were equally evolved, and competition arose, causing one to possibly do harm to another. Communication was necessary and, as language developed, there also developed a need for a mechanism to *judge* what was the best way to do things. A new brain began to develop, a brain where the language was sorted out and *thinking* began to take place. This is what some scientists now call "the left brain." This is the mechanism that allows us to function rationally. At this point, mankind took a giant leap out of pri-mative existence and into the evolved state of so-called "intelligent" human beings.

A new brain began to develop.

The Things That You're Liable to Read in The Bible

Biblically speaking, the early existence of man was what is described as the "Garden of Eden" consciousness, and the *fall* came when the new brain developed, and *judgment* became a way of life. Mankind "ate of the fruit of the tree of the knowledge of good *and* evil," God *and* ego, and we began to think of ourselves as separate from God. We began to think for ourselves and judge for ourselves. We began to judge *outwardly,* by appearances, and put together a belief system. Ego was born with the development of the left brain, the rational thinking part of the brain, and it includes the intellect. In actuality, the creation of ego was not the

We began to think of ourselves as separate from God.

fall of man, but a giant leap *upward.* The development of the intellect has been responsible for much of the progress that mankind has made, but, like all progressive developments, it's a two-edged sword! It can be used for good or for evil...for God or for ego!

When under control of the true Self, the divine Self, intellect can lead to the uncovering of truth (dis-covery) which leads us, as individuals and as a society, into greater spiritual awakening. When under control of ego—the old conditioned beliefs (superstitions) involving fear, hatred, anger, jealousy, envy and guilt—intellect can lead us down the road to suffering, hardship, war, famine, greed, crime and destruction! The so-called "criminal mind" is highly intellectual and ego-centered.

We have been given the ability to choose. We can choose peace or suffering, life or death. All the great master chefs have given us instruc-

We can choose peace or suffering, life or death.

tions in choosing life, choosing peace, and it always requires that we overcome the temptations of ego. It requires letting go of past conditioning that holds us in bondage. "Become as a little child," Master Chef Jesus instructed—have no past! Where does the past exist, anyway? Only in our heads, in our memory, our intellect. History (his story) books can be altered (they *have* been altered) and when this happens, the belief system changes.

Your old conditioned belief system (ego) is a history book, herstory book, *your story book.* It's a recording of your past and if you don't like some part of it, you can record over it—you can change it! The prince wiped his slate clean when he gave up his princely garb and took on the beggar's rags. That was his choice, his destiny. He changed his life completely and you can too!

Just like taking a magnetic imprint off a magnetic tape, you can take the emotional charge off the recordings you have in your ego. All the old stuff that is buried in your subconscious mind, that has caused you to

You can get a new lease on life—a "re-lease!"

suffer all these years, can be released. You can get a new lease on life—a "re-lease!" The process of making **Peace Soup** is designed to help you do this. This *fourth step,* "spoiling the spoiler," is essential in understanding how to clear the old belief system (b.s.).

It's All B.S.

The process of evolution I described above, the development of consciousness from primitive man to intelligent human being, is not *the* truth, it's just *my* belief system (my b.s.). There are belief systems that say man was created from clay and woman (womb man...whoa man) came from his rib. They're just "ribbin' ya." That's not true, either. *It's all b.s.!* Some belief systems have become very popular and have become known as "religions." All religions are ego driven and can be detrimental to your spiritual health and well-being.

None of the great master chefs started out with the idea of forming a religion and none of them taught with that in mind. The religions came *after* they were gone; they were formed *about* them. True Buddhism is not *about* Buddha—it's the living "of" his teachings. True Christianity is not *about* Jesus—it's living the life of Christ. True Taoism is not *about* the

Religion can be detrimental to your spiritual health and well-being.

Tao—it's living the Tao (the way). True spirituality is the *way* of the masters—the *way* to enlightenment.

Lao-Tzu probably did the best job of taking the focus off himself and putting it on "the way." The Tao (pronounced *dow*) actually means "The Way."

Taoism says:

> *There is a being, wonderful, perfect;*
> *It existed before heaven and earth.*
> > *How quiet it is!*
> > *How spiritual it is!*
> *It stands alone and it does not change.*
> > *It moves around and around.*
> > *But it does not on this account suffer.*
> > *All of life comes from it.*
> *It wraps everything in its love as in a garment.*
> *It claims no honor, for it does not demand to be lord.*
> *I do not know its name, and so I call it Tao, the way,*
> > *And I rejoice in its power.*

Lao-Tzu was born in China around 600 B.C. He was the keeper of the archives in his native western state. He was also a great teacher and philosopher. Each day he would teach for a time in the town center and people would come from all over China to hear him. In his later years, the government of his province became corrupt (as all governments do—self-government is the only true government), and he decided to leave the country before an insurrection occurred. He was about to cross the mountains into what is now Tibet,

Self-government is the only true government.

when he was stopped by a gate keeper who was guarding the border. The gate keeper recognized Lao-Tzu, as he was one who had come to hear him teach. Lao-Tzu had always said that he would not write down his teachings because he knew that if he did, his followers would make a religion out of them, and he knew the nature of religion!

The gate keeper, however, insisted that he take time to write the teachings down, or he would have him arrested for trying to leave the country. Lao-Tzu decided it would be nicer in Tibet than in jail, so he relented…and consented to write. He retired for three days and returned with a slim volume of 5,000 characters (81 verses) titled TAO TE CHING, or "The Way and its Power."

In the first verse of the TAO TE CHING, Lao-Tzu gives this disclaimer: "The Tao that can be named is not the eternal Tao." The way that can be *talked about* is not the true way. What he was really saying was, "All that I say from this point forward is not 'the truth.'" In a later verse he says, "He who speaks does not know…he who knows does not speak." As we learned in Step 2 of the recipe, no one can speak the truth. It can only be *known* in the heart.

The Philosophy of the Tao

The word "ch'i" comes from the Taoist teachings and it literally means "breath" (spirit), "vital energy." It is the life force that the Jedi knights learned to work with in STAR WARS. "The Force is with you," said Ben (Oh, Be One) Kanobe to Luke Skywalker. This life force (spirit) flows freely, unless it is blocked by the "dark invader" (Darth Vader)—the ego.

Get in the flow, and stay in the flow.

The objective of Taoism is to align one's daily life to *The Tao,* to get in the flow, and stay in the flow. Chef Jesus put it this way: "God is a spirit (breath, vital energy) and they that worship Him, must worship Him in spirit and in truth." (John 4:24, rev. ver.) "Seek first the kingdom of God (spirit) and His rightness, and you can do anything." (Matt 6:33, rev. ver.) You can hit any target you choose when you allow ch'i, Tao, God, spirit, *the force* to flow, uninterrupted by emotion, attachment, ego, the dark invader—the spoiler.

The Taoists say, "wei wu wie," which means "supreme action, without action." Chef Deepak (Chopra) calls it "the law of least effort" in his book SEVEN SPIRITUAL LAWS OF SUCCESS. You can accomplish much more by being still than by running around *doing*. We are human *beings,* not human *doings,* and our true nature, expressed, will accomplish infi-

> **We are human beings, not human doings.**

nitely more than all the *stuff* ego can come up with. Ego says, "Do...do" and that's what it gets us into—deep do-do! Spirit says "be"—may the force *be* with you. Jesus gave us the "Be" attitudes. When one lives freely, fed by a force that is unimpeded, life is serene and graceful, rising above excess and tension.

Putting ego in its place is sometimes known as humility. "The meek shall inherit the earth," Jesus said in His "Be" attitudes. The TAO TE CHING says, "He who stands on tiptoe does not stand firm," and it adds that "the ax falls first on the tallest tree." The Taoist says, "He who feels punctured must once have been a bubble."

Be humble, yet be Self-assured, not by the ego self, the little "s" self, but by the big "S" self, the *true* Self, the *divine* Self, the "image and likeness of God" Self! Jesus said, "I of myself can do nothing, it is the spirit of God, flowing through me, that does the perfect work." (John 5:30) Jesus lived 600 years after Buddha and Lao-Tzu and many believe He had the benefit of their teachings. I believe He was both Buddhist and Taoist in many ways.

The "Non" Ingredients of Chef Jesus

In His great Sermon on the Mount, Jesus gave us many of the ingredients of His recipe. Two of the most important I call the "non" ingredients, because He said to leave them *out* of the soup. The first "non" ingredient is judgment. "Judge not that you be not judged," He said.

(Matt 7:1) "Judge not according to the appearance, but judge righteous judgment." (John 7:24) Our judgments come from ego, and much of our ego conditioning comes from our parents. He might even have said, "Judge not according to (what) a parent sees." If you were born into a Jewish home, you "grew up" as a Jew. If your parents were Catholic, you're probably Catholic. If you come from the South (southern U.S.),

**Everybody's right...
and nobody's right!**

your parents were likely Southern Baptists, and you are too! If you were born in India, you're probably Hindu; in Japan, Buddhist; in Iran, Muslim. Who's right? Everybody's right, and nobody's right! It's *all* right. It's *all* good. It's *all* God!

If you judge others as *wrong,* you're letting ego spoil the soup. You're adding a "non" ingredient that Master Chef Jesus instructed us to leave out. The ones who sin (miss the mark) most, and make batches of Stress Soup, are those who judge all others as wrong, saying, "My way is the *only* way. What *I* believe is *right* and everybody else is *wrong.*" That's ego in all its glory! That's the way religious fundamentalists in *any* religion think, and it breeds anger, fear, pride, prejudice and hatred. It's the cause of all religious arguments and wars!

Jesus gave us a living example of Truth when He encountered the woman at the well in Samaria. According to the Jewish fundamentalists, He was not even supposed to be talking with a Samaritan woman. Her religion and His religion were at odds (at war) about many things. One of the arguments was *where* God was to be worshiped. "In the mountain," as the Samaritans believed, or "in the temple," as His sect of the Jews believed. The woman saw Him as a prophet and asked Him, "Who's right?"

Jesus answered this way, indicating that *neither* was right, and *both* were right: "God is a spirit," He said, "and they that worship Him must worship Him in spirit and in truth." (John 4:24) God is not only in the mountain and in the temple, he's everywhere, in spirit, and there's no right or wrong *place*, or right or wrong *way*, to worship, no matter what a religious belief system says. Follow Jesus' example, and His recipe, and leave judgment out of your soup!

There's no right or wrong place, or right or wrong way, to worship.

Keep in mind that there is a difference between judgment and *discernment*, and the difference is *emotion*. Judgment has an emotional charge; discernment is seeing the events of life and making decisions *without emotion*. We'll be covering the difference in depth in Step 5 of the recipe, keeping in mind that there's a difference also between emotion and feeling.

The second "non" ingredient in Chef Jesus' recipe is the one that deprives ego of nourishment. Ego is fed by *resistance*. There's great wisdom in the saying, "What you re-sist, per-sists." Resistance keeps ego alive! Jesus' recipe says, "Resist *not* evil! Agree with the adversary. Love your enemies!"

Resistance keeps ego alive!

How many people who *think* they follow Jesus, abide by this teaching? How much of the religious world is out there—*fighting evil?* Jesus' key ingredient in His recipe is *love*—His "one commandment"—and love cannot express in judgment or resistance, just as ego cannot express without them.

If your religion or your belief system (b.s.) contains judgment and/or resistance of any kind, you may want to look more closely and question, in your own Self, your true Self (without asking your parents), which belief system will be most helpful in achieving your true goal of peace? Will it contain judgment or *non*-judgment, resistance or *non*-resistance?

The recipes of all the master chefs require a *stirring* of the soup. They realize that it's necessary to *shake up* the ego (the old conditioned beliefs) in order to grow spiritually, to see if there's any judgment or resistance lurking in the kettle. If it's stuck to the bottom, it's very difficult to dis-lodge. It takes some deep soul searching to overcome some of the deep-seated ego beliefs that have been emotionally or religious-

It's necessary to shake up the ego.

ly ingrained, but it's necessary, in order to clear the soup and keep it free flowing. If you have an emotional attachment or addiction that's causing you unrest, it's ego stuff and you'll not be at peace as long as *it* controls *you*. Check out your resistance to *anything*—it's spoiling your soup!

In exposing the spoiler, shining light on the dark invader, you're taking the charge off of your ego reactions. You're learning to *respond* and see beyond the appearances, beyond your *parent-ces* and *grand-parent-ces*, beyond judgment, to the rightness—the goodness of all life. Your old beliefs were well-intentioned and even helpful, but they're behind you now. Non-judgment and non-resistance pull the plug on ego, and leave you at peace—in joy!

"The Farmer Whose Horse Ran Away"

There's another little story that I've found helpful in seeing beyond appearances, not judging, not resisting. It's about a farmer who had a small spread in a rural community where he lived with his wife and son. They owned only one horse, and one day the horse ran away. The horse was a very important part of running the farm and when the farmer's neighbor heard about his misfortune, he came to commiserate. The farmer, however, had only one thing to say, "Could be bad, could be good."

The farmer had only one thing to say, "Could be bad, could be good."

In a few days the horse returned, but it was not alone. It had taken up with a drove of wild horses and had brought the whole herd home to the farmer's corral. This time the neighbor arrived with congratulations! "How lucky you are to have all these horses." "Could be good, could be bad," was the farmer's only reply.

The next day, as the farmer's son tried to mount one of the wild horses, he was thrown and broke both legs in several places so he was unable to walk. Again, here comes the neighbor. "What a horrible misfortune," he said again. "Could be bad, could be good," said the farmer.

A few days later, soldiers came to the farm commandeering young men for the war that was raging and killing many. The broken legs made the farmer's son ineligible for conscription and he couldn't go to war! "How wonderful," said the neighbor. "Could be good, could be bad," said the farmer, and on and on and on. Ultimately it all works together for good and, when your belief system is trained to see beyond appearances, you can remain peaceful and poised, without emotion, in joy, in love, no matter what's going on (and on and on).

Ultimately it all works together for good.

The Taoists say, "Before enlightenment, life is chopping wood and carrying water. After enlightenment, life is chopping wood and carrying water." Life doesn't change with enlightenment. The way we *see* life changes, our *perception* changes, and we stop judging by appearances...we stop judging altogether, stop resisting evil (ego) and remain "calm, steadfast, serene."

Too Smart for Your Own Good

In all my years of teaching meditation, the students who have had the most difficulty in getting balanced, being still and in control, in the flow, were the intellectuals. The highly developed intellect, while being a valuable tool, can block the ability to achieve peace. The intellect is continually trying to analyze things, looking *out* instead of looking *in*. The intellect is not bad, but when it's under the control of the spoiler, it blocks

Intellect can block the ability to achieve peace.

spiritual growth. It thinks, it resists, it argues, it analyzes, it questions, it keeps us in stress, away from peace, out of heaven. Chef Wayne (Dyer) says, "Analyzing is intellectual violence! When you analyze something, you have to break it apart, tear it apart, break it open, find out every little piece of it."

In the great recipe book, THE BIBLE, John the Baptist, Jesus' cousin, metaphysically represents the illumined intellect. He was the fore-runner of the Christ and a great teacher in preparing the way, but as great as he was, he couldn't make the grade into the peaceful consciousness Jesus called "heaven." Jesus said of his cousin John, "Among them that are born of woman, there hath not risen a greater than John the Baptist; notwithstanding, he that is *least* in the kingdom of heaven, is greater

"You can't get to heaven in the intellect!"

than he." (Matt 11:11, rev. ver.) John resisted evil (ego) in the form of Herod until finally his intellect was severed—he lost his head! This is what we must do, too! Not literally, as John did, but figuratively. "You can't get to heaven in the intellect!"

Intellectuals are so thoroughly trained to think, that their conditioning (ego) won't allow them *not to think!* Many times, their personalities are rigid, even frigid, but, while it's initially more difficult for them to let go, to break through the old conditioning and stop thinking, when they finally *get it* (through their thick skulls), they can be some of the most accomplished meditators.

I believe that the resistance of the intellectual actually comes from emotional attachment—it comes from fear, the fear of being wrong. They have been trained to *know* all the answers—intellectually. Fear, ego's greatest tool, keeps them in bondage, in the dungeon with John the Baptist. The intellect is afraid of being shut down, being quiet (it might lose its life), so it just keeps on thinking.

The intellect keeps judging and resisting. As the great metaphysician, Chef William (Shakespeare) said, "There is nothing either right or wrong, but thinking makes it so." We, in the **Peace Soup** recipe, want to convert the ego into a tool for progress. Thinking "can be good, can be bad" (not so good), depending on the programming, the conditioning. We can train the intellect to think only good thoughts, if we can get

We can train the intellect to think only good thoughts.

it to shut up long enough to listen! It likes to chatter, keeping itself fed by reaffirming the old stuff, the b.s. The technique you'll be learning in this step of the recipe is designed to *shut up* the intellect, the thinking process. "Off with her head!" said the "Queen of *Hearts.*" Stop the chatter, the questioning, the judging, the resistance. Stop this un-disciplined little child (ego) from messing up wonderland. Stop the spoiler from spoiling the soup!

It's About Time

Before we get into the technique for spoiling the spoiler, we want to discuss one more important belief that keeps us bound to ego, bound up in the past and the future and out of the now moment. It's the belief in *time!* Time does not exist in truth. It's a concept invented by man. The early intellectual watched the sun come up regularly and called the interval "a day." (Some call it "a day" when the sun goes *down.)* When the seasons continued to roll around on a regular basis, the complete cycle was named "a year." The years were divided into months according to some intellectual concept, then the months were broken into weeks, the weeks into days, days into hours, then minutes and seconds, and recently nano-seconds!

The concept of time has progressively bound us more and more closely with ego—so closely, in fact, that we all now have a built-in clock! The clock is always ticking and it keeps us locked up, in bondage—limited, by the minutes in an hour, the hours in a day, the days in a year, the years of our lives! How often do we wish for more hours in a day, more days in the week, more years in our lives? We limit life with our belief in time, a belief we invented in the first place! There is no time—life is eternal and unlimited, but with our belief in a concept that doesn't exist, we limit eternity and believe in death. The belief in time causes death—the *belief* in death! Thinking about time, believing in time, keeps us in the dead past or the imagined future, and neither of these exist! They *seem* real because we believe in them, but they have no basis in truth. We keep coming apart at the *seems.* Past and future are a construct of intellect—of ego—to keep us fighting the drag-ons in the dark dungeons of the mind (intellect).

We limit life with our belief in time.

The Subtle Master

Time is the most subtle of ego's tools, and is the most ingrained in our belief system. We are slaves to time! The belief in sickness is ingrained, too, but not so deeply as time. If you're experiencing sickness and I say to you, "Sickness is an illusion and you can be healed in the 'twinkling of an eye'" (no time), there is something inside of you that says, "Yes, I can believe that," but when I say, "Time is an illusion, it does not exist," there is a reaction of *dis*-belief. The instruction of Jesus to "take no thought for tomorrow" (Matt 6:34) is truly a scary thought for ego. Ego thinks that with no thought beyond the moment, it will surely die—and it will! Actually, it will be transformed... enlightened!

"Time is an illusion, it does not exist."

The enlightened ego knows that any thought beyond this moment, past or future, is what causes death. It's about time that the ego is enlightened! It's about time to stop the *thinking* process. The activity of thinking can only happen with prior experience, and prior experience is what makes up ego (the old conditioned belief system). Ego takes thoughts of the past, of prior experience, and projects them forward, creating what it calls "the future." Neither the past nor the future exist—it's all mental activity that keeps us *thinking,* keeps us off base, out of control, out of the flow, away from peace.

The past, present and future are all a part of man's consciousness—race consciousness, social consciousness—the dirty kettle of Stress Soup. Only the present belongs in the **Peace Soup** kettle. The present is awareness, being aware, being *in*-lightened. Why do you suppose the now moment is called "the present?" It's a gift from the universe, an *eternal* gift, and ego (the spoiler) is determined to spoil the party, and the present, by keeping us *on time.*

Only the present belongs in the Peace Soup kettle.

Draw from your Awareness Bowl and see how little of your thinking is about the present. Most thinking is *spent* in the past and the future. The idea of *spending* time, or *wasting* time, keeps ego in control of your life and how long (how much time) you have to live. "Time's so short," we say. "I have to hurry, I have so little time." "I'm late, I'm late, for a very important date," said the Rabbit through the looking glass! Everything in the "looking glass" is just the opposite of truth—it's the *world,* and everything in the world (the appearances), is all backward! You'll never get *there* any way. You'll always be *here*—and now! *Here* is where heaven is, *there* is hell! The only difference between "here" and "there" is the "t"—*time.*

You'll never get there. You'll always be here— and now!

The belief in time literally keeps you from living. You do not live in the future. You do not live in the past. You do not even *exist* in the past or the future, so thinking about them puts you out of existence—out of life!

If you want your soup to taste heavenly, if you want your life to be peaceful, harmonious, joyful, free, eternal, creative, spontaneous, loving and holy (whole), you will have to eliminate, or at least strictly limit, the belief in time as a part of your life. Begin now to bring your life into this moment. Embrace the gift...the present. Give no thought for tomorrow, or yesterday. Be here now! Begin *now* to welcome and experience eternity.

Tick Tock...Tick Tock

As I mentioned, we have been so conditioned to the illusion of time that we each have established a built-in clock. We can program ourselves to wake up at a certain time. We can estimate pretty closely how much time has passed (past) during an activity. Sometimes, however, we lose track of time. Why does this happen? The activity is so interesting, so engrossing, so much fun to us that it keeps our attention in the now moment. "Time flies when you're having fun," we say, or as the Zen master frog said to his disciple frog sitting on a neighbor-

As the Zen master frog said, "Time's fun when you're having flies!"

ing lily pad, "Time's *fun* when you're having *flies!*"

Time "stands still" or "speeds up," based on your perception. As you get older, time seems to move faster. Time is relative, and different relatives experience time differently. To a baby, 6 weeks of age, a day is eternity, since it's a great percentage of his or her life. For a 6-year-old, a day is shorter, since it's a lesser percentage of their prior experience. By the *time* you're 60 years of age (60 years young), a day is nothing, and it's over in a flash!

Time, as we've created it, is based on movement—it's a measurement of change. We measure the movement of the earth and the sun and call it "time." The age we experience is determined by how much movement we've measured, how much change has taken place in our lives. When you stop measuring, stop thinking about it, the aging process has less effect on you, and you literally stay younger, longer! When you combine this with abiding by the rules of the body from Step 2 of the recipe, you can live a long, long time—in this body! You may have a "bio-*logical* clock" as some scientists believe, but you can re-set the clock with the **Peace Soup** recipe.

Watch Out...Watch Off

Watch out for the time traps. Ego sets them everywhere. Time pieces are set, everywhere. Speaking of "*watch*-ing out," we wear time on our wrists! Ego uses the watch to drag us around by our wrists! "Watch out!" says ego. "Look in," says spirit. Which are you going to follow?

Ego uses the watch to drag us around by our wrists!

I'm not saying you should get rid of your wrist watch, but you probably *will,* sooner or later. I used to have a beautiful watch that I had won in a golf tournament. I really loved that watch and I would take it off when I played golf and put it in my pants pocket. When I started learning the truth about time, and teaching and practicing meditation, I was playing golf one day and the watch disappeared—the golf gods got it back! Since then I've never worn a watch and I've never been late!

Some people may have *thought* I was late, but I've always been *where* I needed to be, *when* I needed to be.

Do you think you have to meet dead-lines? That's where time leads you—in a line to death! Living in the now moment gives you a *life-line*, a gift, the present, that will bring peace and tranquility, and what you'll notice is that everything gets done *in no time*. Being in the now moment gets you out of the rat race and into the *master race* of enlightened egos.

> **Living in the now moment gives you a life-line, a gift, the present.**

As you practice meditation, as you practice not thinking, as you practice being in the *now,* ego will lose its stranglehold, and the tools of the spoiler will begin to drop away, including the belief in time. Without time, you have eternity—heaven. As my teacher, Chef Dennis (Neagle) says, "The coordinates of the kingdom of heaven are *here* and *now.*" *There* doesn't exist anymore, nor do the past or the future. They were only tricks of the mind, the intellect, the thinking nature—keeping ego active, spoiling the soup.

So now, you're out of time, and you're out of luck, so you are ready to enter heaven, the consciousness of peace and tranquility. All it takes *now* is learning the technique, and a little practice, and you will overcome the bondage of ego and the world. When Master Chef Jesus said, "Be of good cheer, for I have overcome the world" (John 16:33), He was assuring us that we can do it, too! When a storm came up in His life, He simply said, "Peace, be still!" and the storm subsided. You, too, have storms coming up in your life, and with the **Peace Soup** recipe you can calm them quickly. The spoiler thrives on storms and it will cause resistance if you fall asleep (in the boat), so the technique for this step of the recipe is designed to keep you awake and to shut down the ego—the spoiler. Here's how it works:

This Technique is Non-Sense!

As I said earlier, you don't want to *kill* the ego—it's you (your belief system)! You want to re-train it, *in*-lighten it, bring it into alignment with your *true Self*. True peace resides "within," as Jesus said, in the *secret place*. The poet Robert Frost put it this way: "We all sit around in a circle and *suppose*, while the secret sits in the center, and *knows*."

We have to stop the chatter of the outer world, the incessant activity of the intellect. Stilling the intellect has been a problem ever since thinking became a part of us. Since the beginning of recorded history, the wise chefs have taught that we must *still* the thinking mind (intellect) in order to "know the truth that sets us free."

The doorway to heaven is stillness.

You cannot get into heaven, here and now, by thinking. The doorway to heaven is *stillness*. "Be still and know," the psalmist says. Still the body…still the mind…still the ego…still the emotions.

You've learned to control and still the body with the relaxation technique in Step 1 of the recipe. You've learned to control and still your thoughts, to center, to concentrate and to breathe, with the Zen breathing technique and the mantra in Step 3. Now you're ready to rein in the ego—the questioning, tempting, rational mind that blocks your progress by keeping you off balance, re-membering the b.s. of the past, and anticipating and fearing what *might* happen in the future.

The technique you'll be using to still the ego has roots going back at least 5,000 years. It works! In the Hindu (Yogic) tradition, it's known as a "koan." It's essentially a non-sense phrase. It doesn't make any logical sense, but it has an underlying meaning, a hidden meaning, that can be *felt,* but not figured out. Probably the most widely known koan is:

What is the sound of one hand clapping?

You know the sound made by two hands clapping—the sound of resistance—collision! One hand cannot clap; there is no sound. It doesn't make sense to the rational mind. When you say the phrase to yourself, over and over, the thinking mind gets tired

"This is silly. I'm not playing anymore!"

of it. It gets bored and quits—it shuts down. "This is silly," it says, "I'm not playing anymore!" Good! Now there's stillness, silence, no thinking. Now you're meditating.

The underlying *feeling* that is produced by this phrase is that of non-resistance. One hand clapping is the flow—peace. It puts you in the Flow Bowl and your soup begins to take on that soft, velvety texture…tranquil, serene, smooth, peaceful.

This *feeling* puts you in touch with your inner Self and in contact with higher levels of being. You begin to experience what some call "True Self awareness." This experience, this awareness, cannot be taught, it cannot be talked about or even thought about. Thoughts and words cannot lead you to this state of *knowing*—only practice…experience.

Before getting to the actual practice of the technique, I would like to give you an alternative to the koan stated above. While it is popular and it does give the valuable image of non-resistance, it does not necessarily resonate with everyone. The following phrase has been very effective in our classes and it comes from Zoto Zen, which practices what is known as Zazen. Zazen simply means "sitting meditation." The word "Zen" means meditation. The philosophy of Zen states: "One who stills the mind realizes the 'True Self'; the 'True Self' realizes the nature of love; he who knows the nature of love is eternal." In Zen, the technique is called a Zenrin, instead of koan, but the results are the same. The alternative phrase is:

There is no place to seek the mind,
it is like the footprints of the birds in the sky.

Using the Koan or Zenrin

What is the sound of one hand clapping?

or

There is no place to seek the mind,
it is like the footprints of the birds in the sky.

Begin by sitting quietly with your eyes closed, head upright and balanced on your shoulders, paying close attention to your breathing, watching the rise and fall of the abdomen. With this technique, you do not count the breaths or draw them down with numbers, you simply concentrate on the diaphragm area and the rising, falling motion of the abdomen.

When you feel quite peaceful, begin to contemplate the phrase, saying it over and over to yourself. Do not analyze it or try to interpret it, simply let it rest upon your mind like a leaf on a calm, still pond. Repeat it over and over until you find yourself *not thinking*. The intellect has shut down and you are now in the silence. If a distraction occurs—a thought, a sound, a vision—gently begin repeating the phrase until you're back in the silence again. Continue this process for 20–30 minutes.

This is a much softer exercise than the discipline exercises in Step 3 of the recipe, and without the control they produce, it is not likely you will receive the full benefit of the koan or zenrin. Each step of the recipe, each technique, builds on the previous steps, so it's important to learn and practice them, in order, in the beginning. You will then have them "under your belt" and be ready for the next step, and you will always be able to refer back to them when you need them.

This Fourth Step exercise (koan or zenrin) is much simpler than the previous exercises, but it's not so easy without the physical relaxation and control produced by the autogenic training in Steps 1 and 2, and the mental discipline and control developed through the practice of the breath counting and/or mantra in Step 3. If you find, in using the koan or zenrin, that there is still an abundance of mental or physical distractions, you will want to continue with the previous discipline techniques for a while longer. Be patient, let go of your ego demands to "hurry up" and you'll learn in *no time!*

The stillness produced by the first *four steps* of the recipe is preparing you for the greatest challenge of all—that of overcoming the emotions! When you truly feel the softness, the serenity, the "peace that passes understanding," that is beyond thinking, beyond questioning, "beneath the waves, beyond the tempests, in the eternal calm"—then you're ready for...

Step 5

Sifting Out the Emotions!
The End of Suffering

As we discovered in Step 4 of the recipe, emotion is the cause of all suffering, and all emotion comes from ego...the old conditioned belief system. We become addicted to our beliefs and, when life doesn't meet our demands, we act like an addict! We get anxious and upset, fearful, angry, guilty, envious, resentful, hateful, jealous...and *peace* is destroyed. Emotions have a *charge* on them, and our goal in this step of the recipe is to take the charge off. We will learn to put out the raging, devilish fire that causes our emotions to boil over, create a stink, and spoil the soup!

Emotions vs. Feelings

In this **Peace Soup** recipe, we make a distinction between feelings and emotions. It's really just semantics; we could call them "positive emotions" and "negative emotions," but I find it much easier and clearer to separate them completely, since they come from different places. Emotions come from ego, the "prince of the world," and they keep us in bondage, locked up in a reactionary condition which causes turmoil and tribulation. Master Chef Jesus said, "The prince of the world comes and hath nothing in me...." (John 14:20, rev. ver.) No emotion, no resistance, no judgment! Jesus was coming from a different place—He was at peace! He had overcome His emo-

Emotions come from ego and keep us in bondage.

tions, and was allowing His feelings—love, joy, peace, oneness—to express. In this recipe we are saying that emotions come from ego, the little "s" self, and that feelings come from the big "S" Self, the true Self, the enlightened Self.

When boiled down to their essence, there is really only *one* emotion—FEAR—and only *one* feeling—LOVE. That's it! Emotions vs. feelings, is simply fear vs. love and, as Chef Jesus put it in A COURSE IN MIRACLES:

"Love is letting go of fear."

The next two steps of the recipe are designed to help you learn to let go of fear and establish ever-lasting love in every area of your life. This seems like a tall order, but our recipe makes it fun, and even *easy*. We learn to let the fears gently boil to the top, so we can spoon them off, leaving only pure **Peace Soup**.

The Ghosts of Fear

Fear is nothing, no-thing, a ghost! The mind, however, with its potent imaging ability, can create an image of what we fear that's so *real* we can actually manifest it in our lives. There are people who have actually seen the devil, red suit, pitchfork, horns and all! As we discovered in Step 2 of the recipe, the imagination is a two-edged sword. It can be used to dream up good *or* evil. Our work is to train the imagination to see only good, then the evil (d-evil), the ghost, the fear, the *nothing*, will dis-appear!

Our work is to train the imagination to see only good.

In 1908, Chef Napoleon Hill was commissioned by Andrew Carnegie to conduct a study of people who were successful in life, and also of those who were unsuccessful. His goal was to determine what caused the difference and then write a book about success. Chef Napoleon spent 20 years interviewing hundreds of America's most successful people, including Carnegie, Ford, Wrigley, Eastman, Rockefeller, Edison, Woolworth, Morgan, and Firestone, as well as three United States presidents! He also interviewed hundreds of people who were considered failures and, in 1928, published the first interpretation of THE PHILOSOPHY OF INDIVIDUAL ACHIEVEMENT. During the Great Depression of the 1930s, Dr. Hill became an advisor to President Roosevelt. It was Napoleon Hill who wrote the speech for President Roosevelt in which he uttered his most famous line, "We have nothing to fear, but fear itself!"

Chef Napoleon had discovered, in his study of human nature, that the only thing that separates those who are successful in life from those who are failures is the *nothing* we call *fear*. In 1937, Dr. Hill wrote his book entitled THINK AND GROW RICH. In the section, "Fear Is Only A State of Mind," he says:

> *There are six basic fears, with some combination of which every human suffers at one time or another. Most people are fortunate if they do not suffer from the entire six! Named in the order of their most common appearance, they are:*
>
> 1) *Poverty*
> 2) *Criticism*
> 3) *Ill health*
> 4) *Lost love*
> 5) *Old age*
> 6) *Death*

These basic fears remain pretty much the same today—the possible exception being that the first and second, Poverty and Criticism, may be reversed, *Criticism* being the #1 fear!

All fear is learned. A new-born baby has no fear. The psychologists say they have two—the fear of falling and the fear of loud noises—but I believe those were *learned* during the birth experience. We fear only the unknown—what we think *might* happen. It's all imagined. There is no-thing to fear here and now. We *know* what's here and now. The un-known is in the

We fear only the unknown— what we think might happen.

future—the next moment, the next day, the next year. We take the learned fears of the past—the conditioned beliefs of ego—and project them into the future, bypassing the present (the gift)—the now moment—where there is no-thing to fear. In the *now* there is only experience, actuality, truth!

As an example, if you were in the front of a room full of people and a giant monster came into the back of the room and began gobbling up people, you and the others in the front of the room would try to run away from the monster, afraid of being eaten, too! Would the people in the back of the room be afraid? No, they're already gobbled up! When something is actually happening, there is no fear of that experience. The fear is of what we imagine might happen next, in the future. As you'll remember from Step 2 of the recipe, the subconscious mind cannot distinguish between the *real* and the *imagined*. When we learn to be here and now, experiencing fully what's happening, life becomes a fear-less *ad*-venture. We're *add*-ing one peaceful *venture* to another.

Another example of fearing (the ghost) might be if you're married and you're afraid your spouse is stepping out on you. Then you find out it's true—he or she is! Are you *afraid* they are? No, now you *know* it's true, but you now become afraid he or she might leave you. Then they do leave. Are you *afraid* they're going to leave? No, he or she's left! There is no fear of them leaving, but then you become afraid of not finding anyone else, afraid of being alone. When you do find someone else, your past experience then becomes the new fear of the future ("He or she might leave me, too"), so your peaceful experience of a secure relationship is destroyed, and on and on and on it goes, one fear begetting another...all for *nothing*. We have nothing to fear, but *nothing!*

We have nothing to fear, but nothing!

Understanding eliminates fear. Some people are afraid of snakes, other people handle snakes for a living. They understand snakes, they know about snakes. Some people are afraid of heights, other people wash windows 60 stories up, or do construction on skyscrapers. They know how to handle themselves in high places. It may *seem* that some of us are born with certain phobias, but they're all learned, somewhere in the past, and they can all be *unlearned,* erased from the belief system. Handling snakes or washing windows may not be your thing, but being at peace in the face of fear *is* what this recipe is about, so we're going to look at the basic fears that hold us back from experiencing the fullness of life here and now. We'll look at the easier ones first.

Six Ghosts of Fear

Ghost #1: Death

Death, "The Grim Reaper," is nothing. There is no death—life is eternal! You can believe in death or you can believe in eternal life…it's your choice. Most people believe in death because it *looks* so real, but we know "looks can be deceiving." We believe in death because of appearances, but it's becoming much easier "now-a-days" to see that death is not final, because of so many accounts of near-death experiences. According to Dr. Raymond Moody, who has made a study of this phenomenon, after a near-death experience, the person no longer fears death. I'm not recommending a near-death experience as a means of overcoming the fear; just change your *belief* about death—it's not final! Death is just another experience in eternal life, moving us into another state of being.

Death is just another experience in eternal life.

Jesus said, "In my father's house are many mansions (many states of being). I'm moving on up to prepare a place for you, and when you're ready, I'll bring you up there with me." (John 14:2, rev. ver.) I believe that Jesus went through crucifixion and resurrection to prove to us that death is no-thing. He *died* to save us from the sin (error) of believing in death. God is eternal and we, as his children, created in His image and likeness, are eternal, too! "God is a spirit," not a ghost! Death is a ghost, the devil is a ghost (no-thing), the "grim reaper" is a ghost. We're learning to be "ghost busters." With **Peace Soup**, we can say, "I ain't afraid of no ghost!"

Ghost #2: Old Age

I say, "Age is a matter of mind—if you don't mind, it doesn't matter!" We all know people in their 90s, or higher, who are full of vim and vigor, full of life, going, doing, and being pretty much as they have always been. And then we all know people in their 50s and 60s who act like they're death warmed over. The **Peace Soup** recipe says, "Let's live fully, with a positive 'upbeat' attitude, until we decide to move on up to a new 'mansion.'" I love the attitude of Chef Charles (Fillmore) who, at age 93, affirmed this statement every morning: "I fairly sizzle with zeal and enthusiasm and spring forth with a mighty faith to do the things that ought to be done by me."

Age is a matter of mind—if you don't mind, it doesn't matter.

Old age, like death, doesn't exist anywhere but in our belief system (b.s.). We see people in a nursing home unable to care for themselves and we judge that as bad, we resist it, we worry about it, we fear it, and we *create it*. As Job said on his way to becoming a chef, "The things I have feared the most have come upon me." (Job 3:25) We feed the things we fear with anxiety and worry, and then wonder why they grow to be so strong and healthy. We say, "This is just what happens as you get 'old.' You lose your sight, lose your hearing, lose your memory." Stop saying it. *Stop believing it!* It's a ghost, it's nothing…don't give it any emotional energy. Think young, act young, speak young, and guess what—you'll *be* young! The body may lose some resiliency, but as we learned in Steps 2 and 4, when you obey the rules of the body and stop thinking about aging, you can stay young forever—in every now moment.

Ghost #3: Lost Love

Now we're beginning to get into some really emotional stuff! It's very easy to get attached to other people, and not so easy to get detached. Psychologists tell us that the most traumatic experience you can have in life…the most *stressful* event…is the *death* of a spouse. It's as if a part of *you* has died. The same is true in the death of a child, a sibling, or a close friend. An adjustment has to be made; a mourning process must take place. A great change is happening, and your emotions are running wild!

Any situation that leads to a major loss—be it divorce, death, injury, natural disaster or loss of a job—stirs up the emotions, and the process of *grief* must take place. Understanding the grief process can help you, as can knowing that *everyone* grieves at times like these...it's a natural and *essential* process. Even Chef Jesus went through the process, and His example shows that it can be a **The process of grief must take place.**

quick process. He was very upset when He heard that His friend, Lazarus, had died. He felt a "groaning in the spirit" and..."Jesus wept." (John 11:35) This is the shortest verse in THE BIBLE. He wept...He processed the emotion...and then went on about His business. He knew the truth, that His friend had not really died, only moved to another state (of being). He also knew that an adjustment had to take place in *His* life, so He wept, He released, He let go! *Good grief,* it was easy— and quick!

Death of a spouse is the most stressful event (according to the psychologists); the second is a divorce and the third is a legal separation. All of the top three have to do with the ghost of *lost love,* or seemingly lost love. Again, we come apart at the *seems.* Love, true love, can never be lost! When the life situation changes, an adjustment has to be made, and it can be made quickly and easily, in love, or slowly and painfully—in emotion. How many divorces end peacefully? Not many. How long do most people carry the memory of that experience—the **True love can never be lost.**

anger, resentment, hatred, guilt? A lo-o-ong time! Jesus described the slow, painful adjustments, with *ego's* emotional input, as "the wailing and gnashing of teeth!" I've not found a more vivid description of this bitter process.

Chef Elisabeth (Kübler-Ross) has devoted her recipe to the grieving process, and I've found it helpful, for anyone recovering from loss of any kind, to be aware of her *Five Stages:*

1) **Denial**…The "This cannot be happening to me" feeling. One cannot "face the facts" of what is actually happening.

2) **Anger**…The sense of disbelief turns toward blaming oneself or others. Anger (the emotion) usually comes unexpectedly and is not easy to control.

3) **Bargaining**…Involves "If only" thoughts. "If only she would move back in, I'd make it up to her. This time I'll do the right thing." A superficial sense of hope may develop.

4) **Depression**…The recognition that a loss has occurred and nothing can be done about it. In this phase (without **Peace Soup**), the feeling of hopelessness and powerlessness to change any thing can be overwhelming. (It's easy to get stuck to the bottom of the kettle in this stage.)

5) **Acceptance**…Involves submission to the new reality. This is a state of emotional *balance* reached after the tumult of a major change. One is able to deal realistically with his or her new status in life.

The techniques in this step of the recipe will help you learn to move through these five stages quickly and easily, peacefully, in love and trust, without the "wailing and gnashing"…but the adjustments still need to be made.

Ghost #4: Ill Health

"Ill health" is an oxy-moron, but *oxy* or not, it can still put *more on* us than any of the other fears! We began busting this ghost in Step 2 of the recipe, where we discovered that when we abide by the rules of the body, we need never get sick. We are, however, still a part of the "collective unconscious," as Carl Jung called it. Social consciousness or race consciousness is the sum total of everyone's consciousness on this planet, and most people have been conditioned to believe in sickness. It all comes from fear. In fact, fear itself is a sickness—and it's contagious! We can *catch* fear from others. One person panics and the herd follows. Fear destroys our defenses and our ability to see clearly, so we're left wide open to other emotions and *dis*-ease!

The world and its image makers are forever creating images of new diseases and spreading the fear of catching them. They've created a "cold" season, a "flu" season and a myriad of *new* diseases, unheard of only a few years ago. Then we're bombarded with "remedies" and "cures." Fear is what keeps illness alive, and the things we fear, we create. We give e-motion (energy in motion) to the idea of *ill health*—we create stress, which lowers the natural defenses, the immune system, and we get sick. It all comes from *nothing*, the ghost of ill health. Sickness is psycho-somatic, and perfect health can be psycho-somatic, too! Relax, eat right, eliminate, exercise, think right, stop resisting, and the ghost has nothing to keep it alive—it just *dis*-appears!

> **Sickness is psycho-somatic, and perfect health can be psycho-somatic!**

Ghost #5: Poverty

In this abundant universe, poverty can only exist if we create it. Mankind (and womankind) lived and evolved on this planet long before money (and the lack of it) was developed. We lived off the land, hunting and foraging for food, until we became civilized and began trading and bartering. We then used our talents to create wealth. We traded our talents for food and other goods until someone (the intellect) came up with the idea of *money* as a means of exchange. This is a good idea, when we keep in mind that it's still our talents that create wealth.

Talents are God-given, but it's up to us to develop them and share them. We are *"co-*creators" with God, and if we *do* nothing, nothing happens! Fear, the ghost, the *nothing* causes us to do nothing, and more nothing comes to us. The talents and the energy (inner "G"…God) we waste through fear and worry, keep us from experiencing the abundance we would otherwise have through developing and sharing them.

Prosperity and self-development come not from hard work, but from knowledge—knowing the Truth…knowing the *Law*. In the **Peace Soup** recipe, we call this law "The Measure." Jesus put it this way: "Give and it shall be given unto you; *good measure,* pressed down, and shaken together, and running over…with the same measure you give, it shall be measured to you again." (Luke 6:38, rev. ver.)

The quickest way out of a poverty consciousness, dispelling the ghost of poverty—and I believe the *only* way—is through giving. "Give" to *God,* "give" to *yourself,* "give" to *others,* "give" to the *world.*

The more you give, the more you receive— that's the law!

The more you give, the more you receive—that's the law! What do you give? Give *yourself*—your talents, your energy, your time, your love, your money! Chef Deepak (Chopra) says in his SEVEN SPIRITUAL LAWS OF SUCCESS, "Everyone has a purpose in life, a unique gift or a special talent to give others. Expressing your talents to fulfill the needs of others creates unlimited wealth and abundance!"

The richest people in the world are the ones who give the most. Do they give the most *be-cause* they are rich, or are they rich *be-cause* they give the most? They *be* the *cause*. Giving always comes first, sowing *before* reaping! They gave, then they received. Those who try to get without giving will *all ways* end up in poverty. The more you develop your talents, your "inner G," the more you will be able to give, and the more you will be able to receive. Be the best you can, at whatever you do. Give of your Self, and you will receive abundantly.

What you *do* with what you receive is important, too. You must learn to be a good "stew-ard" in order to cook up a full-filling stew. I believe that the best policy is to follow what Chef Catherine (Ponder) calls *"The* Prosperity Secret" in her book THE PROSPERITY SECRETS OF THE AGES. Give the first seed (the best seed), as every good farmer does, to the planting for the next harvest. Give the *first* 10% (the tithe) to the person or organization from whom you receive your spiritual food. This keeps you in tune with, and in the flow of, the universe. Tithing has proven itself to the wealthy throughout his-story and it will prove itself to you, too! In the Great Recipe Book, God said, "Bring ye all the tithes into the storehouse…and prove me now…if I will not open the windows of heaven and pour you out a blessing, that there shall not be room enough to receive it." (Mal 3:10, rev. ver.) That's the Truth!

The second 10% (or more) goes to your Self. *You* are the connection between universal abundance and your abundant life! In his delightful and truth-full book, THE RICHEST MAN IN BABYLON, Chef George (Clason) tells us the "secret" that the richest man discovered: "A part of everything you earn is yours to keep (and invest)."

You are the connection between universal abundance and your abundant life!

Sir John Templeton, one of the richest men in our modern world and one of the greatest soup chefs I've ever had the pleasure of meeting, tells the story of his beginnings in a flat near Wall Street in New York City. He earned very little and lived a meager life, but he always saved and invested 50% of everything he earned. How much control (discipline) did that take? Plenty. Did it pay off? The proof is in his soup. If Sir John could save and invest 50%, can you not do 10%? or 20%? I say you *can,* and you will, if you want the best soup possible.

One other little tidbit for the best soup: Invest the part that you give to yourself, using what I say is "the greatest economic tool ever devised." It's called *dollar cost averaging.* Here's how it works: Using a good quality, growth-oriented mutual fund (for diversification and safety), invest the same dollar amount each time you invest, whether it be weekly, monthly, quarterly or annually. When you do this, it doesn't matter if the stock market and the fund go up or down over a long period. In fact, you will have *more* if it goes down for awhile, as long as it rebounds at some point. The reason for this is that your dollars are buying more shares at the lower price, and when they rebound, you have more shares at the higher price! It works, and it works even better when you remember to re-invest the capital gains and dividends.

Chef George says in THE RICHEST MAN IN BABYLON, "Let your investments have children...and don't *eat* the children!" Allow the earnings of your investments to grow and flourish on their own and they will increase your wealth astronomically, instead of gastronomically! Follow this recipe and the fear of poverty won't have a ghost of a chance with you.

Ghost #6: Criticism

Do you live your life based on what other people think of you and what you do? We all have a tendency to do this, and it's a *hell* of a way to live! "What you think of me is none of my business," says Chef Terry (Cole-Whittaker) in her book of the same title. You may want to use the criticisms of others as feedback, and this can be helpful at times, as long as there's *no emotion involved.* Again, the cause of all suffering is emotion. If you are saddened, depressed, guilty, angry or resentful because of what another person has said about you, you're allowing ego to have the upper hand, and it leads you down the road to *de*-struction. You're allowing someone else's ego (conditioned b.s.) to influence your little "s" self-image. Even a so-called "compliment" may only feed your ego if you let it. Vanity is another of ego's effective tools.

Allow your true Self, your big "S" self, to control your image.

Allow your true Self, your big "S" self, to control your image. Know who you are, *in truth,* and you will be able to stand strong under the attack of other people's opinions! Their opinions come from their belief system, and they're all wrong—and they're alright! Chef Jesus said, "Agree with the adversary quickly, while you're in the way with him." Don't resist the criticism, just accept it for what it's worth—

nothing! It's a ghost! Know the truth and be free. You are good the way you are and "gettin' gooder" every moment of every day.

The Children of Fear

We've seen the six basic fears for what they are—ghosts, apparitions, nothing—but their offspring can seem more real than the fears, and affect us even more strongly! These children are like *demons* and can cause all kinds of sickness, pain and suffering. The **Peace Soup** recipe is designed to help us demonstrate the truth and set the *demons straight!*

The 1st-Born Child of Fear: Anger

Anger has been called "the vice of saints." Even the saints experience anger. Jesus got angry! He chased the money-changers out of the temple, and where did it get Him? It got Him crucified! Anger always has re-percussions, or just plain "cuss-ions!" It's the law—the measure.

Master Chef Jesus understood the law, maybe better than anyone ever has, and He knew that if He was perfectly loving all the time, He would never be crucified. He *had* to die—so He could fulfill the prophecy, so He could resurrect and save us from the sin (error) of believing in death—so he set it up with Child #1, anger. He let His ego, His judgment of the religious men ("vipers" and "hypocrites," He called them), do the job for Him, and it worked! It always does. Anger sets up an energy that is de-structive and it must be dissipated or it *will* destruct! If you let it build up, you will explode, and your soup will be splattered all over the kitchen!

Anger is the fire-iest child of fear, and the fire is born of self-righteousness. "I'm right, and you're doing something that doesn't meet my rules, so you're wrong and I'm getting mad!" Mad means crazy! Anger is mental illness. When you lose your temper, you lose your mind, your *cool*. Your mixing bowls are empty. You're out of awareness, out of control, out of balance and out of the flow.

Anger is mental illness.

Some psychologists say we must get our anger out by expressing it—beat a pillow, or a rubber chicken, scream and shout, rant and rave! Get it out, we must, or we will cause the repercussions, but I believe there is a better way, an easier way, a softer and gentler way to process the anger—to deal it out. We'll be exploring the "how to" in a little bit, but first let's look at the other children of fear.

The 2nd-Born Child of Fear: Hatred

The color of hate is *red,* the same as anger! Anger and hatred are born (and live) very close together. Some people believe that hatred is the opposite of love, but it's really just another child of fear, a child of nothing. Love has no opposite, but it does have *opposition.* Fear and its children exist only as apparitions, but they can block love. Hatred can cause war in people, in families, in nations!

Love has no opposite, but it does have opposition.

Hate implies great dis-like. "You're not *like* me. You're a different color, a different nationality, have a different heritage, a different belief system, so my ego says I should *hate* you! You're breaking my rules." Ego rules. When ego rules, it creates tribulation and spoils the soup, but be of good cheer, we will overcome hatred as we sift out the emotions.

The 3rd-Born Child of Fear: Guilt

Guilt is the most cunning and, in some cases, the most deadly and destructive of fear's offspring. The image that the word "guilty" brings up from ego is the heavy hammer of the judge, as he or she slams shut any hope of escape! As we've discovered, judgment is the greatest tool of ego, and the idea of guilt comes from self-judgment. We judge ourselves as guilty and then sentence ourselves to prison! We're back into dungeons and drag-ons, ghosts of the past projected into the future, causing us to self-de-struct.

Chef Louise (Hay), in her book, YOU CAN HEAL YOUR LIFE, says, "Guilt is a totally useless emotion. It never makes anyone feel better, nor does it change a situation." It's a ghost, an apparition, but the appearances can be excruciating! Chef Louise says, "Pain of any sort is an indication of guilt. Guilt always seeks punishment and punishment creates pain."

Pain of any sort is an indication of guilt.

All the pain you experience in life—mental, emotional and physical—comes from guilt. Guilt comes from believing you did something wrong and you punish yourself by inflicting pain. You may even go so far as to create an accident. Accidents are a way of punishing ourselves without fault, but there is a *fault*—it's in our faulty thinking, our belief in the need for punishment. Most of us have been taught that punishment must follow a wrong act. You do something *bad* and what happens? You get punished! Ego has even gone so far as to create a God that punishes wrong, but it's always just us, punishing ourselves. That's justice, we think, just us, for all—after all.

Guilt can even lead to suicidal behavior, resulting from the belief that we sinned, did something wrong. "I'm worthless and might as well be dead!" ego says. Guilt causes shame. "Bad boy (or girl), you should be ashamed of yourself!" How devastating those words can

Guilt can even lead to suicidal behavior.

be to a sensitive little child. In shame, we hang our heads and slink away, wishing we were invisible, wishing we were dead!

Chef David (Hawkins) says in his classic work POWER VS. FORCE, "Some early life experiences, such as sexual abuse, can lead to shame and warp the personality for a lifetime, unless the issues are resolved by therapy." In his *map of consciousness,* shame is the lowest consciousness level possible, barely sustaining life, and guilt is only slightly higher.

Chef Gerald (Jampolsky), in his book GOODBYE TO GUILT, says, "It is not an exaggeration to see guilt as a self-made poison, which we administer to ourselves frequently." Guilt poisons the soup and makes it inedible. The **Peace Soup** recipe will help you to say, "Goodbye to guilt!"

The 4th-Born Child of Fear: Resentment

Resentment is sent out to others, but it's re-sent—right back to you. It's outer directed, but it eats away at your *insides*. The phrase "eaten up with resentment" is all too accurate. Chef Louise (Hay) says,

"Cancer is a disease caused by deep resentment."

"Cancer is a disease caused by deep resentment held for a long time until it literally eats away at the body."

Resentment usually begins when someone does something that destroys your sense of trust. Ego latches on to this and never lets go, and many other events are sent, and re-sent, that re-inforce the idea. It builds and builds, grows and grows, until it destroys you. We continually blame others and/or ourselves for everything that's wrong. The condition is *critical*...and *we're the critic*. Re-send resentment one more time, marked "Return to Sender!" Return it to ego, which is now behind you...in the past that doesn't exist!

The 5th- & 6th-Born Children (the Twins): Jealousy & Envy

Jealousy says, "It's mine and you can't have it!" Envy says, "It's yours and I want it!" These twins thrive on division...duality. They divide and conquer. While the color of jealousy is

Jealousy and envy thrive on division... duality.

red (hot), like anger and hatred, the color of envy is green (cool) like resentment and guilt. Jealousy mirrors the actions of the 1st-born, anger, and both are insane, out-of-control, demanding that their addictions be fed. They "fly off the handle" and spatter the soup all over the kitchen—and the chef!

Envy, guilt and resentment, on the other hand, stay below the surface and fester. They keep the soup from cooking, and peace can never come while they're around. This step of the recipe is designed to sift them out, flush them out into the open, into awareness, so they can be dissolved into the nothingness of the (ap)parent, fear, and let go—for good!

The Grandchildren of Fear

The six children of fear (666) have children of their own, generation upon generation, and the grandchildren, great grandchildren, and great, great grandchildren are so mixed up, nobody knows exactly whose children are whose, but they *all* sour the soup!

The grandchildren are led by the most energetic and first-born grandchild—pride. It's easy to see the truth in the Biblical statement, "Pride goeth before destruction." (Pr 16:18) The other siblings—sadness, self-pity, frustration, loneliness, spite, vengeance, hurt—and the lowest energy triplets—shame, victimization, depression—follow pride everywhere he goes. Even the six children of fear are influenced by the apparent strength of pride as he dresses himself up and parades as a positive emotion! National pride, ethnic pride, parental pride, look positive on the surface, but "his-story" shows that these all lead to destruction, to prejudice, to separation and war, and to the low energies of shame, victimization and depression.

Pride dresses himself up and parades as a positive emotion!

Shame comes when pride is *dis*-appointed or *dis*-pleased. "Shame on you!" The (ap)parent says, "My pride is hurt, you dis-obeyed my ego, my rules—you should be ashamed of yourself!" Shame saps all the energy and the child feels like a sap!

Injured pride also breeds victimization, and ego loves to play victim! "Innocent victim" is an oxy-moron, and it comes from piling *more on*—more emotion, more fear and its offspring on the so-called "victim." As we discovered in Step 1 of the recipe, the law, the measure, only brings back what is sown. There are no victims.

Depression is putting the pressure on even more! When you're *depressed,* guilt, sadness, shame, self-pity, loneliness, victimization, hurt, all pile on top of you at the same time. It feels like the weight of the world is pressing down on you and you can hardly move! It's like trying to swim in molasses. You're pinned under the

Depression is like trying to swim in molasses.

weight of *the nothings,* the family of ghouls that keep you about as far away from peace as you can get. It feels like hell! It's a scary place to be, and it's easy, in this state (one of the un-united states), to let the emotions pile on even more, putting more and more on, until the *more-ons* take over!

You will stay in this de-pressed condition until you decide to ex-press, to take the pressure off, break the chains that bind you! You get rid of the *more-ons* by learning the *less-ons*. With the technique you're about to learn, you'll be able to un-pile the little darlings, the emotions, the nothings, one at a time, get 'em off your back—deal 'em out! We deal them out with a process I call:

The "I Deal" Way — The "Heart Chart"

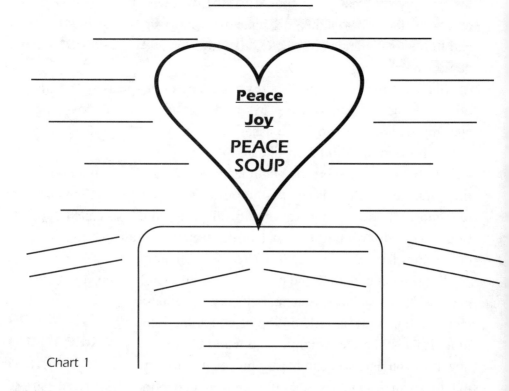

Chart 1

This unusual looking chart has been very helpful for many people over the years, and a literal life saver for some. It's designed to help deal out (sift out) the emotions and allow the feelings to predominate. You begin with the blank slate (Chart 1), filling in only the ultimate goals of Peace and Joy, the essence of **Peace Soup**. You will fill in the other blanks as you go.

Filling In Chart 2

Peace and joy are feelings and, with them in control, we *re-spond* to the events of life instead of *re-acting* in the emotions. Begin filling in the blanks in Chart 2 by writing Responses at the top of the chart and Reactions at the bottom.

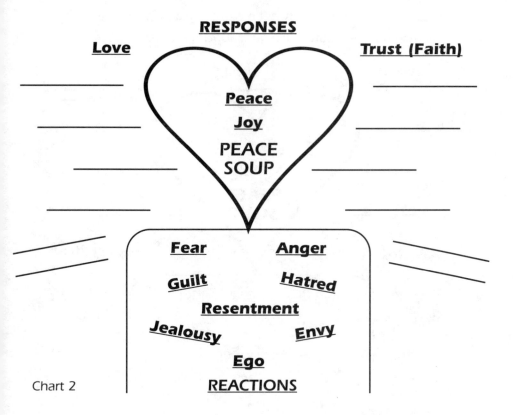

Chart 2

The reactions are the emotion-backed demands of ego, so above reactions write *Ego* and fill in the basic emotions we've just explored, Grandfather *Fear* and the children: *Anger, Hatred, Guilt, Resentment* and the twins, *Jealousy* and *Envy*. The responses at the top of *Chart 2* are *Love* and *Trust (Faith)*. In this pro-cess you are learning the less-ons of *Love* and *Trust*, which are the working tools we use to bring us into *Peace* and *Joy*. Love brings peace, trust (faith) brings joy. These then become your automatic responses to life. I like to say that your only responsibility in life is to develop your ability to respond…in love and trust (faith). In the **Peace Soup** recipe you are learning to full-fill your response-ability.

Filling In Chart 3

There are two other basic activities of ego that keep you buried in the reactionary emotions. They keep ego busy and keep you asleep to your true *responsive* nature. They are: *Judgment* and *Expectation*.

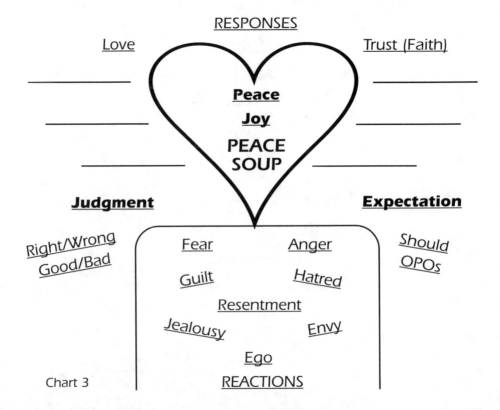

RESPONSES

Love   Trust (Faith)

Peace
Joy
PEACE
SOUP

Judgment   **Expectation**

Right/Wrong   Fear   Anger   Should
Good/Bad   OPOs
                Guilt   Hatred
                   Resentment
            Jealousy   Envy
                    Ego
Chart 3   REACTIONS

Judgment keeps you out of Love and in the reactionary state. When Jesus said, "Judge not that you be not judged" (Matt 7:1), He was saying that if you judge, if you get emotionally involved in saying something is Right or Wrong, Good or Bad, you are engaging ego and putting yourself in the reactionary state that will draw re-percussions. Judgment puts you *in* the world and *of* the world, and you're bouncing off walls, off people, off circumstances—judging and being judged! The emotions keep life *charged,* and it's a shocking experience!

I would like to emphasize at this time that there is a difference between judgment and *discernment*. The difference is in the emotion. Judgment triggers emotions; discernment is seeing *without* emotion. I can discern that something is best for me at this time, or not best for me at this time, but I don't judge it emotionally as "right" or "wrong," "good" or "bad." It just is or isn't for me at this time. That's it—no emotion. "Say yea, yea—nay, nay," Chef Jesus said, "anything beyond that is of evil (ego)." (Matt 5:37, rev. ver.)

There is a difference between judgment and discernment.

Expectation keeps you out of trust and in fear of something being *out of order.* The key word of expectation is Should! "You *should* have done it differently, and we wouldn't be in the mess we're in!" "I expect you to do it the 'right' way the next time, *my* way—ego's way!" We also think *we* should have done things differently. We expect things of ourselves as well as others. One of my favorite bumper stickers is: "The eleventh commandment—Thou shalt not should on thyself!" Should is another one of those words that we are better off without. Whatever is happening is what needs to be happening, so we can learn the less-on that's involved. Everything that happens is on purpose. Everything happens for a reason and, as we'll see in Step 6, the less-on is always the same. Knowing that keeps it simple and easy. Don't *expect* anything and you'll *get* everything! Expect something and you'll get no-thing—fear, emotion, stress! Judgment and

Everything that happens is on purpose.

Expectation keep you mired in the muck with the more-ons!

Closely allied with expectations are OPOs—Other People's Opinions. I take Chef Terry's recipe (WHAT YOU THINK OF ME IS NONE OF MY BUSINESS) one step further and say, "What you *think* is none of my business." The 12th Commandment is, "Thou shalt not should on others, or let others should on you!"

Everyone has an opinion and it's always based on their conditioned belief system (b.s.). If their opinion is based in fact, and is *educated,* it *may* be helpful. Just keep in mind that it's a limited opinion, within the limits (the box) of their education. The most valuable information (*in*-formation) comes from within you and outside their box. OPOs come from without and they usually are without…much value.

The ones who are most ready to share their opinions are your family members and friends. They are always well-meaning and have your best interest in mind while expecting you to see it *their* way. Their way always has holes (as we'll see in Step 6) and instead of taking the pressure off, it many times puts *more-on.* Again, looking within takes you out of OPOs and into the Trust that sets you free!

Filling in Chart 4…The Way Out Is "Up!"

It's not likely that you will jump from the reactionary state of ego, directly into the responsive state of **Peace Soup**. It's a process, as I've said before, and you've been preparing for this *step up* throughout this recipe.

The first step *up* to fulfilling your response-ability is essential, and you draw it from your Awareness Bowl. If you don't remember anything else about the recipe, remember this: The key that unlocks the door to Love and Trust, Peace and Joy—the first step in any growth process, but especially in this "I Deal" way—is…Observer.

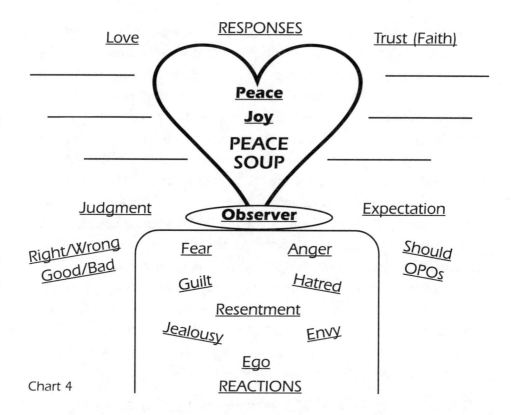

Chart 4

Observer is the point between the emotions and the feelings that takes you, the little "s" self, out of the picture. It's a place that's totally without emotion, and it's not-so-easy to go there at first. Ego is continually pulling on you to "get back down here and suffer!" It will take all the powers of relaxation, concentration and meditation that you've developed in the previous steps of the recipe to go to Observer, but when you get here, even for a moment, the feeling of freedom, of peace and joy, love and trust, will cause you to want to be here and now (in Observer) more, and for longer and longer periods, and you *will*—if you practice.

This "I Deal" way—the "Heart Chart," along with the *Mindfulness Technique* you will learn later in this step, will help you break through the chains of ego and into a new, serene and peaceful state of being. Observer is where

Observer is where hell ends and heaven begins!

hell ends and heaven begins! So remember the Observer all ways.

Being in Observer gives you a detached view of life. As we discovered in Step 4, *at*-tachment is the cause of all suffering, so *de*-tachment is the cure. To overcome your addictions, your "emotion-backed demands," as Ken Keyes calls them, you must move to neutral. I liken the Observer point to watching a stage play. You have taken yourself out of the play, and put yourself in the audience. Actually the little "s" self is still in the play and the big "S" Self is watching. The observer is you...the *true* you. You're actually seeing yourself doing the funny things you do, the serious things you do. We're all great actors, and as Chef William (Shakespeare) said, "All the world is a stage...all of us players." Observer allows you to enjoy the play, in joy, at peace.

As I said, initially you cannot stay in Observer for long, as ego and the emotions are calling you back down, so you have to choose quickly. Either move *up* into Love and Trust (heaven) or *down* into hell! Of course you want to move *up,* and there's a working phrase you can use to take the charge off and make it easier to move up.

"Here's _____(your name)_____ experiencing ___(the emotion)___ ."

You state your name and identify what's happening, from a third-person perspective...without emotion! "Here's ___(your name)___ experiencing anger." You don't say "I'm angry!" You know that using "I am" locks *in* the belief in anger, so it's "Here's _____(your name)_____ experiencing anger, or fear, or guilt"...or whatever the emotion is. Now you've identified the emotion and you choose to move into Love or Trust. If the emotion is anger, you go to Observer, say "Here's ___(your name)___ experiencing anger," and move into love.

The first step in love is... Forgiveness.

Again, it's a process. You don't move from anger into pure love, you take the first step first! The first step in love is...Forgiveness.

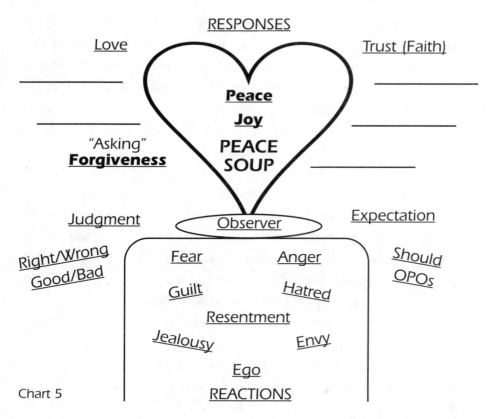

RESPONSES

Love

Trust (Faith)

Peace

Joy

"Asking"
Forgiveness

PEACE
SOUP

Judgment

Observer

Expectation

Right/Wrong
Good/Bad

Fear

Anger

Should
OPOs

Guilt

Hatred

Resentment

Jealousy

Envy

Ego

Chart 5

REACTIONS

Forgiveness is for-getting—giving for getting, giving instead of getting! It's giving up—and ego abhors it. It just *kills* ego to give up (forgive), so let's do it. Forgiveness is the first step to love—true love. Initially, forgiveness takes the form of "I forgive you." This is a baby step and it's very easy to fall back down into ego from here. In fact, the statement "I forgive you" is an ego statement—it comes from judgment. "You did something wrong and I'm going to forgive you, this time—just don't do it again!"

That's not Forgiveness! Forgiveness says, "It never even happened!" True forgiveness is *asking* forgiveness. "Forgive *me* for judging you. Forgive *me* for seeing that you did something wrong. There is no right or wrong, you just did what you did, and it's **True forgiveness is asking forgiveness.** O.K. I may not choose to do that (act that way), but it's O.K. for you. I do not judge you."

In their great recipe called THE QUEST, Chefs Richard and Mary-Alice Jafolla share the story of a couple they know, the parents of a young man who was brutally murdered. They went through the process of grief, from horror, to hatred, to bitterness, to acceptance, to forgiveness, and finally toward total release of the tragedy. They even visited the murderer in prison and expressed their forgiveness and release, which had a profound impact on him.

"It may sound impossible," the Jafollas say, "yet

"With true forgiveness, there is nothing to forgive."

the only forgiveness this remarkable couple sought was their own! They asked the man who took the life of their son to forgive them for having initially judged him as less than a child of God. This was not a matter of 'I forgive you,' but of 'Forgive me.'…With true forgiveness, there is nothing to forgive."

Forgiveness is truly being here now! The past does not exist, except in our memory. You can see why ego can't stand forgiveness. Ego, the old belief system, doesn't exist here and now. In Forgiveness there is no judgment, no emotion, no expectation, just love. Love is letting go of emotion and Forgiveness is the first step.

How many times are we to forgive? Jesus said, "Seventy times seven" (Matt 18:22), or until it's complete. Seven is the number of completion in consciousness, so seventy times seven is "completely completed," until there is absolutely no more judgment. Chef Charles (Fillmore) said, "It's helpful to spend at least thirty minutes every day consciously working on forgiveness…until every event, every person, every situation in your past is forgiven." You continue until you've asked everyone and everything to forgive you! When you've reached the level of asking forgiveness and given it all up, you're ready for the next level of love, the next step in The "I Deal" way—the "Heart Chart," known as…Compassion.

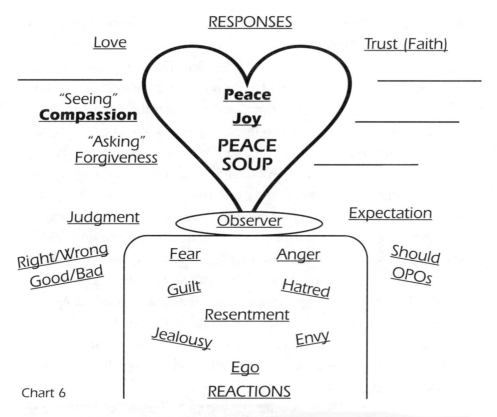

Chart 6

Compassion is seeing only goodness. It's not judging by appearances, but "judging righteous judgment" (John 7:24), as Chef Jesus instructed. The great master chefs were all known as *compassionate*. They observed the suffering, but gave it no power—they gave *love* in its place. Compassion is the ability to see that "everybody's always doing the best they can do." In the limited awareness they're experiencing, it's the best they can do, in that moment. They can, and will, learn to do better, but Compassion says that they're alright where they are, and love will free them up to do better.

Everybody's always doing the best they can do.

I believe that one of the most vivid illustrations of compassion in Jesus' recipe was in the eighth chapter of John when the religious men brought the woman who had been caught in the act of adultery to Him to see how He would handle an obvious infraction of the Jewish law. The letter of the law said, "She is to be put to death...to be stoned. Adultery is a *mortal* sin!" Jesus knew that it was the *spirit* of the law, not the *letter,* that must rule and He didn't respond right away. He took time to think out His response, even to write it out in the sand to make sure He got it right, and to allow the emotions of the Scribes and Pharisees to cool so that compassion would rule.

He finally arose and said, "Let he who is without sin cast the first stone"...and what happened? All the religious men turned and left quietly, knowing that they were guilty of error, just as she was. They saw, whether they would admit it or not, that everybody *is* always doing the best they can, in every moment. Then Jesus, the compassionate one, said to the woman, "Go and sin no more." He knew that she could do better, that she *would* do better. There was no need for forgiveness—only understanding, seeing, compassion. Jesus saw beyond the appearance, beyond the letter of the law, to the spirit, the goodness that is the true nature of everyone. He knew that it was her ego conditioning that had caused her to sin, to err, and that she could change her belief system and "sin no more."

Compassion is seeing the truth.

Compassion is *seeing* the truth, and when you truly see without judgment, without expectation, without emotion, you are boosted into the highest expression of love, to the top of the chart...Acceptance.

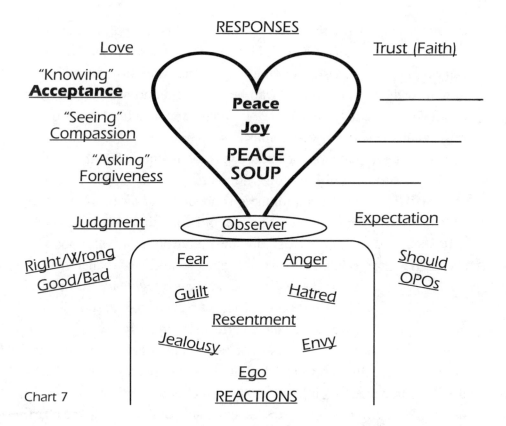

RESPONSES

Love   Trust (Faith)

"Knowing"
Acceptance
                            Peace
"Seeing"
Compassion   **Joy**

"Asking"   **PEACE**
Forgiveness   **SOUP**

Judgment   Observer   Expectation

Right/Wrong   Fear   Anger   Should
Good/Bad   OPOs

              Guilt   Hatred

              Resentment

        Jealousy   Envy

                  Ego
Chart 7   REACTIONS

Acceptance is *un*-conditional, absolute LOVE. Total acceptance is a God-like activity. God accepts all of us, all ways! "God is Love." (1 John 2:16) God does not judge. The Law (the measure) judges, in the sense that "what you sow, you reap," but absolute Love (God) accepts you no matter what the law is bringing to you.

In His compassion for the woman taken in adultery, Jesus also expressed the God-like acceptance that brought perfect peace to Himself and to a situation that could have been very ugly, if the religious men and their "letter of the law" had held sway (ego'sway). Acceptance is the expression of *mother love,* which we'll be exploring in Step 6 of the recipe. It sees and knows the innate goodness of every person, every activity, every situation.

Another Biblical example showing Acceptance was in the "Old" Testament story of Joseph when he was sold into slavery by his brothers and taken down into Egypt. Joseph knew that everything that happens is good…no matter how bad it may look. He used that knowing to carry him to the highest position in Egypt, and when his brothers came to him for help, not knowing who he was, he didn't seek revenge for their evil act. He helped them, he accepted them, and his famous quote rings with the knowing consciousness of true love: "You may have meant it for evil, but God meant it for good!" (Genesis 50:20, rev. ver.)

It's all good, no matter what the appearance may be. It's all good, no matter what the appearance may be. This awareness is about as far away from ego as you can get. Ego, the old conditioned belief system, cannot exist in the environment of goodness (Godness) and the new conditioned belief system takes over. We now have an *enlightened* ego that is enjoying pure peace. Acceptance—absolute love, absolute good—has completed the perfect **Peace Soup**, except for one thing—the grandfather, Fear, has not been totally eradicated. The children and grandchildren were sifted out by Love, but the grandfather is deeply entrenched and it takes another process to totally eliminate *the nothing*. This process completes the other side of the heart in the chart. It's the process we call Trust or Faith. The first step out of fear, the first "leap of faith," is into…Blindness!

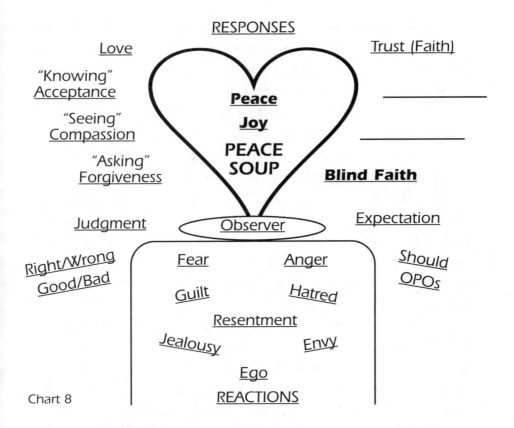

Chart 8

Blind Faith is better than no faith at all, but not much. It's trust with a little "t." It's the faith most people have when they *say* they have faith, but when "push comes to shove," when the "rubber hits the road," they fall right back down into Fear. Ego is still in control, but there's a *willingness* to get out! When Master Chef Jesus was walking on the water and He invited His disciple, Peter, to come for a walk with Him, he did. For a minute, Peter looked *within* and his big "S" Self took over. He knew he could do what Jesus was doing, then he *looked out,* saw what he was doing, and began to doubt, and fear, and sink!

Blind Faith will allow you to break out of the bondage of fear, but ego is still close by, and in the heat of battle, ego will win out. Blind Faith is also what Peter was using when he said he would never betray Jesus, never deny Him. "Never say never!"

Making promises is one of ego's favorite tricks.

Swearing—making an oath, a promise—is one of ego's favorite tricks, locking you into the past (the time the promise was made) and then using guilt and anger and fear to keep you, and those to whom you made the promise, emotionally upset!

"Promises, promises"—don't make them! They lock you into the consciousness you're in when you make them, and won't allow you to change in each now moment. Master Chef Jesus said, "Swear not at all: neither by heaven or earth or by your own head, but let your communication be yea, yea; nay, nay: for whatsoever is more than these cometh of evil (ego)." (Matt 5:34-37, rev. ver.) Making a commitment to do something in the future automatically keeps you out of the now. Let your commitment be spontaneous in each now moment, the commitment to live in love and trust. Ego wants you to be committed, to an institution—and that's crazy!

Ego says, "If you don't make promises, no one can count on you." However, if you're living the peaceful life in love and trust, they can always count on you...to be loving and trusting. Ego and blind faith deal in promises and they're easily broken. Jesus said, "I come so that those who are blind may be made to see...." (John 9:39) Blind Faith is only the first baby step in the process of Trust. The next step leads you out of blindness and into *seeing*. It's called...Understanding Faith.

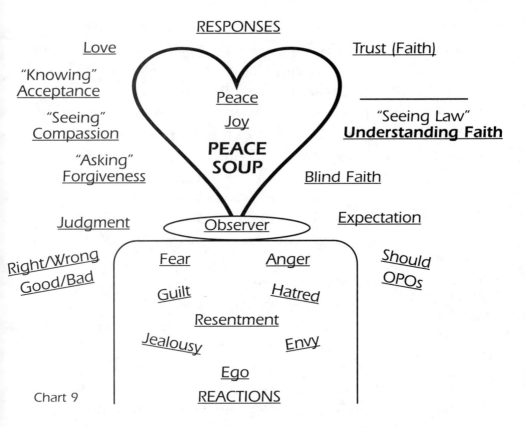

RESPONSES

Love   Trust (Faith)

"Knowing"
Acceptance

"Seeing"   Peace   "Seeing Law"
Compassion   Joy   **Understanding Faith**

PEACE
"Asking"   **SOUP**
Forgiveness   Blind Faith

Judgment   Observer   Expectation

Right/Wrong   Fear   Anger   Should
Good/Bad   OPOs
           Guilt   Hatred

Resentment
Jealousy   Envy

Ego
Chart 9   REACTIONS

Understanding Faith is *seeing* the law, the Lord, the measure, at work in every situation. "As you sow, you reap," no matter what the appearances may be. Charles Fillmore, in his REVEALING WORD says, "Understanding faith is faith that functions from principle. It is based on the knowledge of truth. To know that certain causes produce certain results gives a bedrock foundation for faith." One may seem to beat man's law, as we see in many court cases in the world's legal system, but they will always be compensated by God's law. You can trust that…it's an absolute! No matter what the appearances may be, everything's always "working together for good!"

Since fear is no-thing, it takes seeing nothing to overcome fear. The great recipe book defines faith as "the substance of things hoped for, the evidence of things *not seen.*…It brings *good*

It takes seeing nothing to overcome fear.

report." (Heb 11:1-2, rev. ver.) *Understanding Faith* sees the *nothing* for what it is, and it sees only goodness (Godness) in every person and every situation. The master chef Mother Teresa said that she saw everyone she treated as "God in the flesh!" That's how all masters see.

How many people do you know who believe that everything's good, who see everyone and every situation as working together for good (God)? Only the master chefs! "Many are called, but few are chosen," Jesus said. (Matt 22:14) "Enter in at the narrow gate; for wide is the gate that leads to destruction, and most people go that way...few enter the gate that leads to a peaceful life." (Matt 7:13-14, rev. ver.)

With *Understanding Faith*, you see things differently than the world sees things. In order to complete the recipe, you must open your spiritual eye and see only God, only good. Jesus said, "If your eye is single, your life (body) will be full of light...*See* first the kingdom of God and his goodness and an abundant life will follow!" (Matt 6:22-33, rev. ver.) In the **Peace Soup** recipe, there is a difference between *faith* and *belief*. Belief is ego-driven and can be good or bad (not so good), depending on the conditioning. Faith (understanding faith) is always good. It sees only good, reports only good!

Open your spiritual eye and see only God...only good.

"Impossible!" ego says. "There *is* evil! Just look out there and you'll see it everywhere!" "Look out!" says ego. "Look in," say the master chefs. "Be still and know that 'I am'...God (good)." *Understanding Faith* requires looking *within* to the "Kingdom of God," and when you do, you complete the Heart Chart and the process of Trust with a capital "T." The highest expression of Trust is...Acceptance.

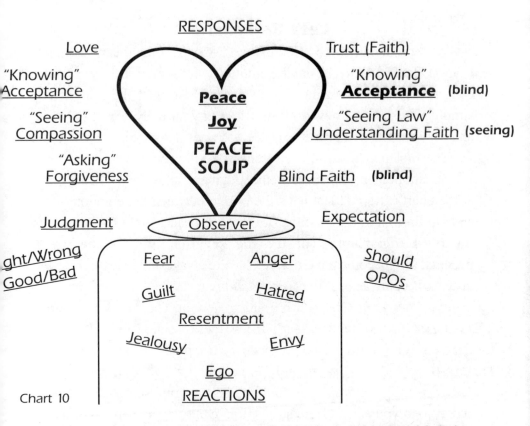

Chart 10

Acceptance (pure trust) is being blind again, but this time it's being blind to the ways of the world and its prince, ego. "The prince of the world comes and finds nothing in me," Jesus said. No-thing—no fear, no emotion, no expectation, no judgment! "For judgment I am come into this world," He said, "That they which see not (blind faith) might see (understanding faith) and that they which see, might be made *blind* (acceptance)." (John 9:39, rev. ver.)

Jesus came not to judge, but to save us from judgment (sin)! The second blindness He was talking about is *knowing!* This is unconditional acceptance of everything and everyone as a creation of God, of Good. You **The second blindness is knowing!** don't have to think about it any more, you just know! You, now, can love it all, and trust it all, and be at peace and in joy all ways! This is **Peace Soup**, the recipe you've been cooking up all along, and it's beginning to taste so-o-o-o…go-o-o-d…all good!

Let's Be Practical

We've completed the "Heart Chart" (Chart 10) and can see that it is an "I Deal" way to sift out the emotions, but it may still seem a little complicated and confusing. So, in the interest of "K.I.S.S.ing," let's simplify by showing how you can use it in your daily life. It's simple, and easy, and as you practice, peace becomes automatic.

The first step, always, is awareness. You become aware of (identify) the emotion, the expectation, the judgment, and take it where? Look at the chart (Chart 10). What's the bridge between the emotions (fear and children) and the feelings (love, trust, peace, joy)? **Observer is the most important step! It's the key that unlocks the whole process!** You become the Observer! You're awake and ready to *respond* instead of being asleep, in ego's *reactions*.

Observer is going to neutral. Observer is going to neutral. There are no emotions *or* feelings—it's the witness, seeing yourself from a third person perspective. The phrase you use is, "Here's _(your name)_ experiencing _(whatever)_ ."

Let's say you find yourself judging someone as wrong and say (to yourself), "Here's _(your name)_ experiencing judgment." From this Observer perspective you can move up into Love and Trust, or down into ego.

You choose up into Love. The first step in Love is what? (Look at the chart.) It's Forgiveness—*asking* forgiveness. "Forgive me for judging you." Asking forgiveness takes ego out of the picture and introduces humility. (We'll get more acquainted with humility in Step 6 of the recipe.)

Once you've broken free of ego's hold, you are boosted into the second level of Love, which is (look at the chart)...Compassion. Compassion sees that the person you've judged is doing the best he or she can at this moment and you can help him or her be lifted up, by sharing your vision, your non-judgment, with them. You don't have to *say* anything, or *do* anything—simply *be* non-judgmental. This not only helps other people be lifted up, but it boosts you into the highest expression of love, which is what? (See chart.) Acceptance. Unconditional acceptance (knowing) is a total letting go, and it brings pure peace.

This Love side of the chart can be used with judgment, anger, resentment, jealousy, guilt, envy…all the children and grandchildren of fear, but fear itself, the granddaddy, is stronger than all the others, and it takes the other side of the heart (Trust) to handle Grandfather Fear. He's a ghost, a *no-thing* and can only be seen through the faithful eye.

The first step up, once you've identified the fear in Observer, is Blind Faith. Blind Faith is barely opening the eye. It's trust with a little "t," and ego grabs you quickly from this level. To deal ego out, you must get understanding.

To deal ego out, you must get understanding.

The wise Chef Solomon said, "In all thy getting, get understanding." Understanding Faith allows you to see the fear as *nothing,* and trust the law, the Lord, to handle it. As you see the law working, over and over, you begin to know that it's infallible, and you become blind to "the cares of the world." You cease being care *full*—full of worry and anxiety and fear—and become care *free*—happy, joyful and loving.

Myrtle Fillmore, co-founder of the Unity movement, who, by the way, did her cooking without a kitchen, had a favorite saying. Whatever was happening, no matter how negative the appearance, she would say, "Count it for joy!" Chef Myrtle was one of the most trusting souls ever to walk the planet, and she did *plan it!* She practiced her trust until it was automatic, and the joy just oozed out through her life!

As you continue to work with this "I Deal" way—the "Heart Chart," it becomes shorter, and easier. Let's wrap up this section by making a practical application. Let's say you're to meet someone for dinner at 7:00 p.m. You're at the restaurant on time, and they're not. What might you be experiencing? "They're always late" would be a judgment, and if there's an emotional charge on it, it could be sifted out.

Go to Observer. "Here's *(your name)* experiencing judgment." Go to Forgiveness…"Forgive me for judging you." Go to Compassion…"They're being exactly the way they need to be." Go to

Acceptance and Unconditional Love. When they do show up, you're at peace, with no judgment—and if they never show up, that's O.K., too!

Let's continue in the practical example. It's now 7:30 and you could be feeling some anger or fear. If it's anger, you go to Observer and deal it out with Love, much as you did with judgment. If it's Fear, you go to Observer, then step up to Blind Faith.

In Blind Faith you know you're supposed to trust God, and you do, for awhile, but you gradually slip back into Fear and begin to panic— call the police or go searching. A more peaceful alternative is to move up to Understanding Faith. In this consciousness, you see them surrounded in light and protected from harm. You're Trusting with a capital "T," understanding that whatever is happening is what needs to happen according to the law (the measure). You may still want to call the police or go searching, but it's not motivated by fear. You have a peaceful desire to help, if needed.

This peaceful understanding boosts you into the highest level of trust—Acceptance—where you know, "without a shadow of a doubt," that everything is perfect! It's all O.K. You know it in your heart and you are at peace and in joy. No more worry, no more anxiety, no more fear. As you practice this process, it gets quicker and quicker until you can begin to use:

"The Quick Draw"
("O" — "O.K.")

The ability to use this short method comes after much practice of the "I Deal" way. In the Quick Draw, you automatically go to Observer whenever any charged input comes to you. When you feel an emotional charge, you go to Observer and automatically "pull the trigger" of acceptance. The verbal expression is, "O" (Observer) — "O.K." (Acceptance).

I believe that God created traffic as a testing ground for emotional control. Even the calmest people seem to "lose it" when someone suddenly pulls out in front of them, and they begin ranting and raving, "wailing and gnashing their teeth!" Of course, one could reestablish peace using the "I Deal" way—the "Heart Chart," going to Observer, saying, "Here's   *(your name)*   being upset" or "feeling anger," then going to Forgiveness (asking forgiveness…"Forgive me for judging you"), to Compassion (seeing that they were doing the best they could in that moment), and finally to Acceptance…pure love (and a smile). That works.

The Quick Draw shortens the process dramatically. Someone suddenly pulls out in front of you, you say "O" (Observer) — "O.K." (Acceptance) and smile! That's how quickly it can be processed. "O" — "O.K." Then bless them on their way, thankful that they missed you. The Quick Draw is the perfect solution to "road rage." Instead of drawing a gun…you draw Love!

Another example might be that you and your spouse (or friend) were planning a trip and they decide, at the last minute, they don't want to go. The *re-action* might be anger; the *response: "O" — "O.K."* Or, let's say you go to work tomorrow and the boss says, "You're fired!" What's your response? "O" — — — "O.K." The dash between "O" and "O.K." would be longer, as many more emotions are involved, but if you've been practicing letting go, you know that the universe will always supply you with what you need, including a better job. "O" — "O.K." will process the input quickly and keep you in joy and at peace, with no emotional upset.

> **"O" — "O.K." will keep you in joy and at peace, with no emotional upset.**

It takes practice, but your reward will be in heaven, here and now! You will be the master chef you're designed to be—"Perfect," Jesus said, "as your Father in heaven is perfect." (Matt 5:48) Perfect peace in every now moment is the goal of the **Peace Soup** recipe. Sifting out the emotions is a vital step in preparing the soup.

"But!"

"But!" ego says, "Won't living without emotion make me 'cold' and 'unfeeling?'" No, ego, it makes you warm and loving! Life won't be the wild, heavy, "up and down roller coaster ride" of the past. It will be the feather-light, magic carpet ride of the present.

"But!" ego says, "This is beyond me. I'm only human!" No, ego, you're not "only human," you are *divine*. You're a child of God, "created in His/Her image and likeness," and you've inherited all of God's attributes. You are Pure Love—so act the part. Your destiny is to be able to say, with all the conviction of Jesus, "I am the son (daughter) of God, and I am therefore perfect as my Father in heaven is perfect. I am created to express love, joy and peace and, by God, I'm going to do it!" He said in John 14:12 (rev. ver.), "If you follow My recipe you'll cook up the same soup I prepare, and yours will be even better (greater) than Mine."

"But!" ego says, "That's blasphemy! You're saying you're God!" That's what *they* (the old conditioned beliefs) told Jesus, and he quoted the scripture, "Do not your scriptures say, 'Ye are gods.'" (John 10:34) Ye gods! He was right! And when they crucified Him for His beliefs, He invoked forgiveness, compassion, acceptance and trust when He said, "Father, forgive them, for they know not what they do." (Luke 23:24)

"Do not your scriptures say, 'Ye are gods?'"

"But!" ego says, "This is a hard teaching. I don't believe I can be like Him!" Repent, ego, change your belief. "My yoke is easy," He said, "my burden is light." You *can* stop the pain and suffering, but only if you're willing to give up your old ways and embrace the new. Are you ready for perfection?

"Not quite," ego says, "it's too big a step."

Another Baby Step
"Preferential Treatment"

If the Quick Draw ("O" — "O.K.") is a big stretch, there's another short method that many have found helpful in taking the charge off and sifting out the emotions. Ken Keyes recommends this method in his HANDBOOK TO HIGHER CONSCIOUSNESS. As you saw in Step 4 of this recipe, Chef Ken defines "addiction" (the cause of all suffering) as "an emotion-backed demand." He says, "Every time you are emotionally uncomfortable in any way, life is warning you to get rid of an addiction." In order to neutralize the emotion, he suggests that we upgrade the demand to a preference.

Upgrade the demand to a preference.

"I *prefer* that you don't do the thing that bugs me so much, but if you keep doing it, it's O.K." Preferences still allow you to have your wants, but if you don't get them, you're O.K. with it. You may have a few little expectations, maybe a judgment or two, but they're only preferences, with no emotional charge, no attachment (addiction), no suffering.

Just remember that preferences are only a step, a baby step, toward unconditional acceptance, knowing, only love. All these methods and processes are helpful in re-conditioning or enlightening ego, and they become even more beneficial when we practice the technique of meditation that completes this step of the **Peace Soup** recipe. This technique is known as:

Mindfulness

Mindfulness means, "Being fully aware of everything that's happening, without being emotionally involved." The mindfulness technique allows you to practice "full awareness without emotion" in the quiet time of meditation, so that you can begin to carry this awareness into every activity of life.

The purpose of mindfulness is to expand your consciousness and bring you to full awareness of the appearance and dis-appearance of thoughts, emotions, sounds, feelings, moods—anything and everything that's going on within and without. It allows your true Self to watch—observe—everything that's going on. As I said earlier, it's like watching a play. The actors on the stage are your thoughts, feelings and emotions, and you're in the audience watching. The actors get involved in the plot, get buried in the plot, but the *true*

Mindfulness allows your true Self to watch—observe—everything that's going on.

you is able to stay un-attached, alive and alert, in joy, at peace, seeing the whole picture, loving and trusting it all!

This tranquil, calm, peaceful state of mind leads to a more "intu-itive" insight into the true nature of life, and away from the turmoil and tribulation of the world. It helps you get in tune, in resonance, in har-mony, with the higher vibrations of peace, joy, love and trust. Without integration through the process of mindfulness meditation, the "Heart Chart" is only an intellectual activity and, as you've discovered, "You can't get to heaven in the intellect!"

In order to practice mindfulness, you must first have developed your powers of concentration and learned to discipline your mind through the earlier techniques in this recipe. As you have seen, the undisciplined mind tends to wander anywhere and everywhere. It can-not be kept under control or directed; it follows any idea, any thought, any distraction. The earlier techniques have developed the discipline, and now mindfulness sets the mind free. True freedom can only come through discipline—self-discipline.

True freedom comes through self-discipline.

Before getting to the actual practice of the technique, I would like to share another story with you. This is the story of another Zen monk who was travelling through the jungle when he became aware of two tigers crashing through the undergrowth, coming his way. He decided to run away but he soon came to a canyon, and discovered it was much too deep to jump down and too wide to jump across, and the tigers were getting close. He found a vine that was hanging over the edge of the cliff and quickly let himself over the side and away from the danger above. The vine went all the way to the bottom of the canyon and he thought he could just climb down and be safe, but when he got about half way down, he heard a growl com-ing from the canyon floor. He looked down and discovered there were two more tigers waiting for him at the bottom!

"I'll just hang here for a while," he thought, "and the tigers, either above or below, will get tired and leave, and I can escape." What he had not counted on was that just below the ridge of the cliff there was a tiny ledge, and perched upon the ledge was a giant rat, and the rat was gnawing on the vine! The monk could feel the vine begin to give way, little by little, and the rat kept gnawing, and the tigers kept growling, and just at that moment, he looked at the canyon wall. Not two feet away from him there was growing the most beautiful wild strawberry he had ever seen. He reached over, picked the strawberry, and enjoyed the most delectable fruit he had ever tasted...

This is the ultimate expression of mindfulness—being in the now moment, experiencing total peace and pure joy, no matter what's going on. This is known in mindfulness as *nirvana*. Literally translated, nirvana means "no-wind, to blow out." This relates to the breath, which, as you discovered in Step 3 of the recipe, holds the key to life, the key to peace. If you hold your breath, grasp it, try to possess it, you die. When you release it and flow with it, you live!

Nirvana means "no-wind, to blow out."

Life is a process of flowing *with* the current, not against it. When you resist the flow, you become fatigued, anxious, fearful. When you go with the flow, you are peaceful, allowing the current to *carry* you, gently down the stream.

In mindfulness meditation, you go with the flow, you do not resist thoughts or emotions or other distractions, nor do you "try" to conquer them. You simply observe them! Mindfulness is being the Observer.

Mindfulness is being the Observer.

By observing the thoughts and emotions in a calm, detached manner, you are able to move beyond them. When there is a thought, there is always something beyond the thought—the thinker, that which perceives the thought. In mindfulness, you separate the thinker from the thought and the thinker begins to *realize* what the *real-I-is*.

Mindfulness allows you to see the thought flow, and distinguish between superficial, emotional, attached thoughts, and the true Self. Increasing your Self-awareness, then, allows you to become Self-realized! Self real-I-zation is the essence of enlightenment.

The Three Aims of Mindfulness

According to tradition, there are three major aims of mindfulness.

1) Expand the consciousness. Actually, consciousness *is* expanding all ways, and that can be a problem. There is no control or balance when ego and intellect run the show, so the kettle gets filled with all sorts of ideas and beliefs that spoil the soup. The mindfulness technique helps you to filter out, sift out, the ego stuff. You learn to let it go and let the *good* stuff, the *God* stuff, expand! The Truth is the yeast that "leavens" the soup. Mindfulness expands awareness of the truth and gives more fullness to life.

2) Develop detachment from emotional thought. Thoughts rise and fall, they appear and disappear, and each thought has an effect on your consciousness. It's good to think—thinking is a valuable tool, but it's not *you!* The true Self does not think, it knows. So in order to access the true Self, you must still the thinking process. You cannot do this by blocking thought out (remember the alligator), you do it by letting thought flow through. You process it and deal it out! You learned how to do this *intellectually* with the "I Deal" way—the "Heart Chart." The mindfulness technique will help you to internalize it and allow your True Self to complete the process and make it truly *auto*-matic.

All great discoveries come from this liberated state of mind.

3) Liberate the mind. The limitations that are placed on you by your b.s. (belief system) are totally removed through the practice of mindfulness, and you are free to think new thoughts, unlimited thoughts! All great discoveries come from this liberated state of mind, beyond rational thought, beyond ego. The intellect only knows what it knows, and its process is to continually rearrange what it knows. The liberated mind is free to search the unknown without fear. The mind soars into realms that are completely beyond anything ever experienced before. It brings you into a new consciousness that is fresh and exciting, and free!

With these three aims in mind, you are now ready to enter into the process that's called:

The Mindfulness Technique

This technique is the easiest of all the techniques you've learned, and it's also the most difficult! It's easiest because it's so simple and there's no particular order to remember. It's difficult because it requires the discipline you've developed using the previous techniques, and without this discipline, mindfulness is not possible. Mindfulness fills up your Flow Bowl, and it's the result of drawing from the other bowls— the Awareness Bowl, the Control Bowl, the Balance Bowl. Mindfulness allows you to be the champion of the Flow Bowl and move on to the Souper Bowl, the Peace Bowl, the Bowl of **Peace Soup**.

As I said, there is no order to mindfulness. It happens spontaneously, as it comes up. If a thought comes to mind during the mindfulness meditation, you simply identify it as "a thought," and let it go. If a sound comes in, identify it, and let it go. If a vision or a feeling or whatever comes to your awareness, you observe unemotionally, you process it, and release it. Here's how you do it:

Begin by sitting in your meditative position, with your head balanced and upright on your shoulders. Be aware of your breathing...deep in the diaphragm...the abdomen rising on inhaling and falling on exhaling. Acknowledge that movement in your mind...be aware of the rising...falling, rising...falling. Don't think the words "rising" or "falling"...just be aware of

---

the movement of the diaphragm (for about 45 seconds).

As you are aware of the rising...falling motion, feel a peaceful warmth emanating from the abdominal region (for another 45 seconds).

Now become aware of the whole body and, as you inhale, think, "Aware of the body in"...as you exhale, think, "Aware of the body out." Continue this body awareness for about 60 seconds, then calm and relax the whole body by thinking on inhaling, "Calming in"...and on exhaling, "Calming out." Calming in...calming out...for another 60 seconds.

Now return your awareness strictly to your breathing— only the rising...falling, rising...falling of the diaphragm. From this point on, for the next 20 minutes, continue with your awareness of the breath only...the rising...falling, rising... falling.

If an intruding thought enters the mind, just be aware of "thoughts, thoughts," or "I am thinking," then return your awareness to the motion of the abdomen...the rising...falling, rising...falling.

If an intruding sound enters your awareness, think "sounds, sounds" or "I am hearing sounds," then return your awareness to the motion of the abdomen...the rising...falling, rising... falling.

If any visions come to your awareness, such as lights, colors, people, places, things, simply be aware of "seeing, seeing," then return your awareness to the motion of the abdomen...the rising...falling, rising...falling.

If during your meditation you are aware of feelings such as peace...or love, think, "peace...peace," or "love...love," then return your awareness to the motion of the abdomen...the rising...falling, rising...falling.

If anything else comes to your awareness, simply move to

Observer, identify it (without emotion), then return to your breathing...the rising...falling motion.

After about 20 minutes, begin to allow your breathing to become longer, and as you inhale, think, "Slowly opening my eyes do I breathe in," and as you exhale, "Slowly opening my eyes do I breathe out." As you think this, gently allow your eyes to drift open and, once they are open, sit very quietly and do not move. "Slowly opening my eyes do I breathe in...slowly opening my eyes do I breathe out."

Now pick a spot on the wall, or on the floor, and look at it very closely. While doing this, think, while inhaling, "Sitting quietly do I breathe in," and while exhaling, "Sitting quietly do I breathe out." Sit very still for about 90 seconds...concentrating on the spot...then you may begin to move and stretch.

That's it! You can see how simple and easy it is, *if* you've developed the mental and physical discipline to be still, using the previous techniques. If you're still having a lot of thoughts, go back and practice the Zen or Yoga discipline exercises you learned in Step 3 of the recipe. If ego still has a hold on you, and your intellect is still in control, practice the koan or zenrin from Step 4.

Mindfulness is the ultimate technique in that it is *no* technique. You're ultimately not *doing* anything, you're just *being*. When you become adept at mindfulness, being fully in control of your mind and body, and having sifted out the emotions, you are ready to add the final and most important ingredient to your soup. It's the essential ingredient in every recipe of all the master chefs. Without it, there is no peace—no soup! When you stir in this ingredient and keep its consistency uniform throughout the kettle, you'll be ready for your "Master's degree," the degree of Master Soup Chef! So let's explore...

Mindfulness is the ultimate technique in that it is no technique.

Step 6

The Final Ingredient
The Cause of Peace

There is one ingredient that all the master chefs have agreed upon as essential to their recipes for peace. Master Chef Jesus stressed the importance of *all* the ingredients in His recipe, but He *command-ed* that we include this ingredient: "One commandment I give unto you," He said, "that you love one another as I have loved you." (John 15:12, rev. ver.)

LOVE is the supreme ingredient of this Peace Soup recipe. We touched on love briefly in Step 5 with the "I Deal" way—the "Heart Chart," but love is such an important ingredient, and so little understood, that it requires a whole step in the preparation of the soup.

Love is the supreme ingredient.

Without love, there is no real peace. Love is the "pearl of a great price," the celestial spice that gives the soup its distinctive flavor, the divine flavor of **Peace Soup**.

As I explained in Step 5, in this recipe we see love as a feeling, not an emotion. It expresses through the feeling nature, but it's actually *beyond* the feelings, beyond everything, even beyond description! In its truest sense, love is God. Love is in-finite, and the finite mind (the in-tellect) of man is incapable of knowing what love is.

When we understand this infinite aspect of love, we can see more clearly why the techniques we've learned that "still the mind" and "stop the chatter" are so vital to our ability to know love and establish peace. Without stillness, one cannot truly be in love and at peace. "Be still and know...that I am...Love...." (Psalm 46:10, rev. ver.)

Love is the final step in preparing the recipe, not only because it is the most difficult thing in life to master, but also because it requires the awareness, control and balance we've established in the earlier steps.

Love is an art...the art of the heart. Love is an art, the art of the heart, and even though the intellect is incapable of knowing true love, the mind of man has created many concepts of what it *thinks* love is, so let's explore some of these concepts to help us see what love *isn't*.

As with all words, when you say "love," the average person's mind will come up with an image, based on their prior conditioning *about* love. "Love," to most people, triggers the image of love between two people, erotic love, or the love of family and friends, or the love of their fellow man. These are all *forms* of love, but they do not always lead to peace, as True Love does. All too often the love of others turns to resentment, to anger, envy and jealousy, to war, family feuds, separation, divorce.

What most people call "love" is really emotional attachment. Most think love needs an object, some-*thing* or some-*one* to love. Everyone's out there looking for that perfect *one,* the *right* person to "fall in love" with. As we've discovered, emotional attachment is the cause of all suffering, and relationship seems to be the area of life where we suffer the most.

It's *so* easy to get at-tached and oh, so painful to get de-tached, because we allow the emotions to rule. In truth we don't want to *fall* in love, we want to be *lifted up* in love! The world has it all backwards. Love is de-tachment, not at-tachment. Love is letting go, not holding on. This is the revelation of revelations:

"LOVE IS LETTING GO!"

It has been said, "If you love something, you let it go. If it's yours, it will return to you. If it doesn't return, it was never yours." Ego wants to hold on to what it loves, and in so doing, smothers it.

There's a story of a little boy who caught a bird. It was a beautiful little bird, the kind of bird all little boys dream of catching. He was so proud of catching that bird and he held it very tightly in his hands so it wouldn't get away, and you can guess what happened—he smothered it, and it died! If he had just opened up and let it go, that beautiful little bird would have flown free for everyone to enjoy.

True love requires freedom. "Letting go" sets everyone free. "You shall know the truth," Jesus said, "and the truth shall set you free." (John 8:32) The truth that you are to know, is that you *are* love! You don't have to *go* anywhere to find it. You don't have to find anyone or anything else to love. All you need to find is your true Self. "Know thyself," the master chefs say, for in knowing your Self, you are knowing God—and God *is* love.

Love is knowing your oneness with God and with everyone and everything in creation. The mystical mind of Charles Fillmore put it this way in his REVEALING WORD: "Love is the pure essence of being that binds together the whole human family. Of all the attributes of God, love **Love is knowing your oneness with God and with everyone and everything.** is undoubtedly the most beautiful. In divine mind, love is the power that joins and binds in divine harmony the universe and everything in it."

We're all part of a hologram, and every part is a full expression of the whole. Love is the *glue* that holds us all together—with each other, with God, with the universe. The goal in this recipe is to let the glue *ooze* out through you, let it ex-press (press out) through every pore of your being! To be loving, you must let go and let God—love—ooze out through you in every activity of life.

A Paradox

The idea that "love is letting go" seems to be a paradox to the rational mind. Lao-Tzu said, "Words that are strictly true seem to be paradoxical." THE TAO says, "Gravity is the root of lightness; stillness is the river of movement." *Love is letting go* is a paradox.

In Taoist and Socratic thinking, the highest step to which *thought* can lead, is to know that we do not know. THE TAO says, "To know and yet think we do not know is the highest attainment; not to know and yet think we do know is a disease!"

The world, and the people who are in it and *of* it, think they know about love, but they don't—they're dis-eased. They think love is an emotion, and the more emotional you get, the more loving you are. But emotions only take one on a roller coaster ride that ends up in a crash! Emotional love says, "I love my wife, but she makes me so mad I could beat her!" And many do, in the name of love.

Spouses lash out at one another in anger and judgment, thinking they can change the other if they just get angry enough, or sad enough, get *emotional* enough. They try to *whip* the other into shape, using emotional love to manipulate. "I know he will change," the

You can never change anyone else.

wife says, "if I just keep working on him!" No he won't. Not as long as *you* keep working on *him*. You can never change anyone else. You can change yourself—that's all! When you change *your* consciousness, the kettle you cook your soup in, the people around you will change, but it's not because you changed *them,* it's because you changed *you!*

Your circum-stances (what "stands around" you) will only change when *you* do. If *you* get worse, *they* get worse. If *you* get better, *they* get better. Improve your love-ability, and those around you become more loving, or leave! You can only have around you that which you are. You only attract to you what your consciousness...your kettle... will hold.

As the great chef "Flip" (Wilson) used to say, "What you see is what you get!" If you see the world through fearful eyes, the world is a fearful place. I know of someone who was afraid of being raped, and she *was* raped—five times! The more locks she put on her doors, the more protection she sought, the more it happened to her. She finally decided to change herself, to wash out her soup kettle, with love. She forgave the rapists (asked forgiveness), established a love consciousness, cooked up a kettle of **Peace Soup** and took the locks off her doors. She was never bothered again.

As I said, we're part of a hologram. The whole universe, the *one* verse, the love song, that keeps playing and swirling around us, contains everything that ever was, or ever will be, and your consciousness determines what you reach in and pluck out. You vibrate at a certain frequency and attract to you what that frequency will allow—frequently! You're similar to a radio receiving station and, if you stay tuned to the same station, the same things keep happening to you, over and over and over. "Why is this happening to me again?" you ask. It's the vibes, man!

You vibrate at a certain frequency and attract to you what that frequency will allow... frequently!

If you want to change stations, you must change your vibration, change your consciousness. That's what the **Peace Soup** recipe is designed to do—not to change you, but to give you the tools you need to change yourself. When you begin to change your thoughts, your words, your actions and your feelings; when you become more loving, more joyful, more trusting, more peaceful, your whole life changes for the better. You begin to vibrate at a different frequency and you attract better circumstances...a more loving environment.

Be aware that when you make these changes, you may move away from some of the people and things you thought you loved. If your consciousness changes and theirs doesn't, you're vibrating at a different frequency and are not compatible any more. It's not that one or the other is better—just different, just tuned to a different station. When you take on a love consciousness, you will interact with more loving people, and the old worldly belief system (b.s.) will be left behind, along with the "old vibes."

Jesus said, "You think I came to bring peace? I came not to bring peace, but a sword, to set man at variance against his father, the daugh-

The Sword of love cuts away the old emotional attachments to the past. ter against her mother, and the daughter-in-law against her mother-in-law." (Matt 10:34) The Sword of Christ is the sword of love, and it cuts away the old emotional attachments to the past. You can never be truly at peace while you're carrying the past with you. Love is letting go of the past, for-*giving, giving* love *for* emotional attachments. "No man, having set his hand to the plow and looking back, is fit for peace," Jesus said. (Luke 9:62, rev. ver.) You can still love the people and the things of the past, but what is love? Letting go! Let go and let God (Love) give you the *present*.

Synchronicity

You're part of the hologram and it's whirling and swirling around you, in and through you, and as you lift yourself up into a more loving consciousness, what begins to happen in your life? You begin to pluck out all kinds of new little good and loving things. All of a sudden, you always seem to be at the right place at the right time (here and now), and exciting co-incidences begin to happen. Your new kettle is beginning to attract little loving happenings that pave the way to an even higher vibration.

Chef Carl (Jung), the Swiss psychologist, was one of the first to explore these co-incidents and he called the phenomenon "synchronicity." He said, "Synchronicity is a causal principle in the universe, a law that operates to move human beings toward greater growth in consciousness."

James Redfield begins his best-selling book, THE CELESTINE PROPHECY, with synchronicity as the *First Insight*. Chef James says this about consciousness growth: "It begins with a heightened perception of the way our lives move forward. We notice these little chance events that occur at just the right moment, and bring forth just the right individuals, to suddenly send our lives in a new and important direction."

Love is the new direction you're heading, and that love will bring you the fulfilling peace and joy you seek. The life of love that this recipe is bringing you will keep lifting you up into higher and higher vibrations, into the heavenly music that you're hearing more and more clearly as you move away from the noise of the world. Love makes a beautiful symphony from every synchronistic event in life.

Love will bring you the fulfilling peace and joy you seek.

East vs. West

Love says that our consciousness is ready to pluck out something new from the hologram, and we're being guided, by love, by God, to move on up—to the *East* side! Love expresses through the feeling nature, which is predominant in Eastern philosophy and emphasized in Christian mysticism. The "paradox" I discussed earlier, that "love is letting go, rather than holding on," comes essentially from Zen and Taoist teachings. Jesus was from the East. Actually, He came from the Middle East and His teachings, while Eastern in tone, are able to blend the East and the West. His soup is a blend, a perfect blend, of the feeling nature and the intellect—with the feeling nature being dominant!

The West is dominated by the intellect, by Aristotelian *thinking*, the East by paradoxical *feeling*. This is expressed in the human body by the left side (controlled by the right brain) representing the feeling nature, the feminine nature, and the right side (controlled by what's *left* of the brain) representing the intellect, the masculine nature.

The West is dominated by the intellect, the East by paradoxical feeling.

The intellect (West-left brain) thinks it can find love in *thought*. What it really finds is *emotion*—emotional reactions, expectations and judgment. As you dis-covered in Step 4 of the recipe, thinking is the "fall"—it's eating of the fruit of the tree of the knowledge of good *and* evil. This *fall* in love is the "original sin, " the belief that you are separate from God—from love. "Nothing is either right or wrong, but thinking makes it so," Shakespeare said. Thinking brings judgment. Judgment and emotion were born with the left brain, in "the fall," and that's when the masculine, judge-mental, intellectual dominance began.

Religion is a conditioned belief system and is dominated by ego.

Left-brained thinking has led to religion. Religion is different from spirituality. Religion is a conditioned belief system and is dominated by ego. This was the consciousness of the religious leaders, the Scribes and Pharisees, that Jesus had so much difficulty with.

"Believe the way we believe, think the way we think, or we'll kill you!" the religionists said to Jesus. "Onward Christian soldiers, marching as to *war!*" the religious hymn says. "Kill the infidels!" the Crusaders declared. "Burn the witches!" the church leaders said in Salem. They're evil! We must fight evil... destroy the enemy!

Is this from Chef Jesus' recipe? Is this what the Christ—Love— teaches? No! It's the anti-thesis—the anti-Christ! We know, in truth, that the anti-Christ is not a person, an *entity,* but anything that is *anti* (against) the teachings of Christ—the teachings of Love. Anyone, any religion (b.s.) that is teaching about "anti-Christ" is teaching fear—nothing! There is nothing to fear in love. "Perfect love casts out all fear," says Chef John. "He that fears is not made perfect in love." (1 John 4:18)

What did Jesus—Love—teach? "Resist *not* evil! Love your enemies! Agree with the adversary. Turn the other cheek. Bless those that curse you!" These teachings are from the Eastern, *paradoxical,* feeling nature, and they sound crazy to left-brain, rational thinking, to the religious ones who are *out there* fighting evil! Spirituality is *in here* loving everyone and everything, and there is no evil, no-thing to resist.

Most wars are *religious* wars. The hot spots of the world are mostly about religious (dogmatic) differences. In some, we even have "Christians" fighting against "Christians!" There are Catholics fighting Pro-test-ants, all pro-testing, all fighting for what they believe (think) is right—in the name of *God.*

Love, true love, knows no fighting, no wars, no protests, no emotion, no resistance—just *peace*. Evil (the nothing) thrives on resistance, as you discovered in Step 4 of the recipe. Resistance keeps the "nothing" alive! Declare war on drugs and what happens to drug use? It skyrockets! Declare *war* on crime and what happens to crime? It increases! Picket abortion clinics and they spring up everywhere! We need to learn to declare *peace,* give the great gift of love, and then watch what happens to drugs, and crime, and abortion, and all the other creations of left brain.

It's interesting that thinking (masculine, left-brain dominance) has also led to what religion has thought of as its antithesis—science. Both religion and science come from the same source, and, with left brain in control, have led the world *head-long* into judgment, fear, prejudice and war. Science created drugs and guns and all the tools of crime and war. But science, when under control of the right brain, feeling nature (love), can bring

Both religion and science come from the same source.

forth all sorts of good and wonderful things. It's not necessary to "beat the weapons into plowshares" when right brain is dominant. They just fade away into no-thing—so, let's stop resisting, stop fighting, let go and love!

Tough Love

"But!" ego says, "If we don't *resist,* if we don't fight, the criminals and war-mongers will walk all over us!" That's right, they might, so the transition from war consciousness to peace consciousness may require a period of *tough love,* but it's still love (power) and not emotion and judgment (force). Tough love is sometimes necessary in the early

Tough love is sometimes necessary in the early stages of True Love.

stages of True Love, and its function is to develop self-control, self-discipline. It may look like force, but the ultimate goal is still letting go—Love.

In his great book, POWER VS. FORCE, Chef David (Hawkins) shows that lower levels of consciousness—the emotional levels (below 200 on his scale)—rely on force, and his research shows that 85% of the population of Planet Earth fall in this lower vibration. The 15% that reside in higher consciousness (above 200) have just recently (in the late 1980s) generated enough power to boost the total consciousness of the population over 200, and *peace* is breaking out! (We'll discuss this more fully in Step 7.)

The prison system of the United States is an example of the use of force in trying to control the *in-mates*. The alternative, tough love, would still require detention, discipline, and control, but with the idea of developing the discipline *within* the *in*-mate—self-discipline...self-control. Left brain, thinking, says, "This is impossible, they're criminals and they'll always be criminals!" Right brain, feeling, says, "They're children of God (Love) and when they're shown love, they'll learn love, and most of them *will* change!"

There was a study done by anthropologists on a society that had no crime. The researchers found that when an individual did something that was disruptive or criminal in nature, the whole village gathered and sat in a circle. Each person, in turn, told the offending person, who was seated in the center, the things they appreciated about him or her. They recounted the good things he or she had done, the good personal qualities. When everyone had finished acknowledging all the things they could think of, they all went back to work. There was no more thought given to the disruptive behavior. The result was a culture without crime.

What would happen if we treated disruptive behavior with love and appreciation?

Does this sound like our penal (penile-masculine—left-brain) system? Does it even sound like how most families or most schools handle disruptive children? What would happen if we treated disruptive behavior this way, with love and appreciation? *Peace* would happen.

Non-Violence

The *non*-violent movements of Mahatma Ghandi and Martin Luther King were a step in the direction of True Love. There was still resistance (albeit non-violent), and these leaders still had to suffer the consequences, but they did it for the same reasons Jesus resisted to get Himself crucified. They had all "been to the mountaintop," and they had no fear. They knew True Love...they knew that life is eternal! They had a dream of *peace,* and they saw that they were an important part of the evolution of love on Earth. Their *apparent* death was necessary in order to help shock the world, lift the world, closer to love.

> **Ghandi and Martin Luther King were an important part of the evolution of love on Earth.**

Love *is* changing the world, and one "spiritual" leader, one Gandhi, one Martin Luther King, one "saint" Teresa, can off-set millions of people who are in the resistant left-brain consciousness of anger, fear, hatred, judgment and prejudice.

Prejudice is an even lower vibration, an even more pri-mate-ive level, than judgment. Prejudice is *pre*-judging. It's judging without any thought, much less any feeling. It comes from an ego, a conditioned belief system, that sees a skin color, a sexual orientation, a religion, a nationality that's *different,* auto-matically judges it as wrong, bad, evil, and wants to condemn it—destroy it—wipe it out! Left-brain, *dog*-matic beliefs engender pre-judice, judgment and emotional re-actions. They also negate True Love.

In the Western religious systems, the *love* of God is essentially the same as the *belief* in God. "Do you believe in God?" the thinkers ask. "Do you believe in God's existence? In God's justice? In God's love?" The love of God is a *thought* experience, a belief.

By contrast, in Eastern philosophy (not Eastern *religion)* and in Christian mysticism, the question is, "Do you *know* God?" To the right brain, the love of God is an intense *feeling* experience, knowing oneness with God and ex-pressing (oozing) this oneness, this love, in

You don't have to be saved. The only separation is in the head...the left brain...the thinker.

every act of living. There is no vicarious atonement (at-one-ment), no church to go through, no priest or pope, or even a Son or Mother of God to go through—just God, just Love, just *you*. You don't have to be *saved*. There is no separation, never has been, never will be! The only separation is in the head, the left brain, the thinker. To the feeling nature, there is only love—only oneness with God.

Chef Carl (Jung) was once interviewed by a panel of religious thinkers, and they asked him, "Do you believe in God?" He paused for a moment and then answered, "No!" "Ahhh," they thought, "we've got him!" But before they could comment, he moved closer to them, looked them straight in the eyes and said, *"I know!"*...and that was all he had to say.

The mystic Meister Eckhart said, "If therefore I am changed into God and he makes me one with Himself, then by the living God, there is no distinction between us....Some people imagine God as if He were standing yonder, and they here, but it is not to be so. God and I, we are one. By knowing God I take Him to myself. By loving God, I penetrate him."

Fun-in-da-mental

Religion is a belief system about God... it is left-brain activity.

The reason I'm bringing up all the beliefs of religion in talking about love is because God is love, and religion is thought, by most people, to be about God, and it *is—about* God! Religion is a belief system *about* God—it is left-brain activity. God, love, spirituality, is right-brain activity. They serve two different purposes. Certainly there's a place for religion in the world. Religion accomplishes many wonderful things and engages in beneficial activity, but religion cannot *know* love, it can only know *about* love.

Religion has a connection with spirituality, just as left brain is connected with right brain, and certainly I'm not saying that religious people are incapable of love. Some of the most loving people I know are religious in much of their life, but their love comes from their heart—their spirituality, their inner knowing—not from their head—their religion, their outer belief system. What I am saying is that left brain—the masculine, thinking nature, intellect—is *incapable* of love. It's not designed for love, it's designed for *thinking*. The problem with religion is that those who embrace it *think* they *know,* and, as the Tao says, "That's a disease!"

> **The left brain is not designed for love, it's designed for thinking.**

Religious people love to argue religion and quote the literal scripture. Intellect loves to argue, debate and play mind games. That's why I call those who follow the strict *letter* of the law...*fun-in-da-mentalists*. They're locked into *their* way being the *only* way. "I'm right and you're wrong!" they say. True Love, non-resistance, says, "I'm *right* and you're *right,* and we're both *wrong!"* As the apostle Paul said, "The *letter* of the law kills....The *spirit* of the law gives life!" (2 Cor 3:6, rev. ver.) When I find someone who wants to debate religion, I don't take *de bait!* I simply bless them and move on to a conversation (meal) with no hook in it!

By now, I hope you realize that what I say about love is all b.s. It's just *my* belief system. It works for me and, as Chef John (Lennon) said in *"Imagine,"* "I'm not the only one." I'm not asking that you embrace my b.s. for yourself. What you believe is between you and God—Love. What I'm pointing out is that left-brain, dogmatic *thinking,* undermines Love, and is even capable of crucifying it! Right brain *feeling* understands that we all see things differently based on our perspective, and it's all right—we can love it all!

The W(hole) Elephant

There's a wonderful little story that illustrates this point. It's a story about seven men who were asked to look through seven different holes in a fence and describe the elephant they saw on the other side of the fence. None of them had ever seen an elephant.

The first man looked through his little hole and saw the tusks. "Well," he said, "an elephant is like two curved spears. That's the way I'd describe it." The second man looked through his hole and saw only the trunk hanging down and swishing around. He said, "An elephant is like a big snake. It looks dangerous!" The third man looked and saw only the eye. "I see the elephant. It's weird!" he said. "It's a black spot in a gray background and it keeps moving. It's eerie!" The fourth man looked through and saw the ear. (It was really ear-ie.) "Oh," he said, "an elephant is like a big plant, waving in the wind." The fifth man saw only a leg and said, "An elephant is like a tree trunk." The sixth man just saw the side of the elephant and said, "It's like a big gray wall with a rough leathery finish. It looks like it might be impossible to climb over." The seventh man saw the tail, and described *his* elephant as being like a rope that's frayed on the end.

"An elephant is like a big plant, waving in the wind."

I'm "frayed" they're *all* wrong, but they all *thought* they were right, and they were, from their point of view. They were all right in describing what they *saw,* but none of them saw the whole elephant—they saw the "hole" elephant. Like all of us, they had "holes in their heads," holes in their belief system. Everyone is always looking through the small lens of his or her own consciousness, and seeing only what *that* lens will allow.

The seven men were basing their belief systems on what they had seen…"with their own two eyes!" If you judge by appearances, what you see with *two eyes*, you're being judge-*mental*. You're seeing two (duality)—right *and* wrong, good *and* bad—and your life is full of darkness. .

"Look with the *single* eye," Jesus said, the eye of oneness, the eye of love, "and your life will be full of light." (Luke 11:34, rev. ver.) You'll see only right, only good. "Judge not by appearances," He said, "but judge righteous (right) judgment." Use the *right* brain, and see that there are many points of view, and they're all wrong (partial), but that's all right! It's all O.K....."O" — "O.K." The right brain won't argue with the other guys who see an elephant as something different. The whole elephant is more than any of us can see through our "holey" fence. Don't be *holey*, be loving...accept everyone and every-thing. Stop "looking through a glass (lens) darkly," as Chef Paul put it, "and come face to face with love...be known as you truly are...as love." (1 Cor 13, rev. ver.)

The whole elephant is more than any of us can see through our "holey" fence.

Is God (Love) Evolving?

The love of God is the ultimate love experience, "the greatest com-mandment"—in truth, the *only* love experience, but even the love of God is an evolving concept. God Himself (Herself, Itself) is evolving!

Early man, pri-mate-ive man, saw God as the Earth or something of nature, the sun, the moon, stars, plants, animals. This was the aware-ness of the oneness with Mother...Mother Nature. Man identified him-self with animals, wore animal masks, worshiped a totem animal or an animal god. This animal god idea evolved into God being more like man, but still animal in nature. The Egyptian gods had the head of a man and the body of an animal or vice versa.

All the ideas *about* God have come from man's longing to stop being separate *from* God, to close the gap created when intellect became active—the Garden of Eden experience in Judeo-Christian tradition.

All the ideas about God have come from man's longing to stop being separate from God.

The god idea evolved further when God (the gods...ye gods!) became super-human. The Greek and Roman gods had super abilities, but they still had human frailties. The Jews and their father, Abraham, spearheaded the next evolutionary step in the concept of God, with the idea of *one* God.

Not just a supreme god, *only one* God, but still a god who was like a man, who created man to be like Him—or vice versa!

The "Old" Testament God of the Jews was a judgmental god, a "wrathful, vengeful, jealous, warring" god, who commanded His people, His *chosen* people (the Jews, of course), to destroy their enemies! The belief became, "Jehovah said, 'Kill the enemy.' So I'd better do it 'Yah Weh' or I'm dead!" This is also the god concept of the Muslim militant fundamentalists who believe their God, Allah, blesses the killing of their enemies.

About 2,000 years ago, a small, mystical sect of Jews came up with a new God concept—the idea that God is like a loving father...still masculine, but a *spirit,* not a man..."like the wind," they said. The intellect still ruled, but it was beginning to be tempered with the introduction of the feminine...*feeling* nature. The masculine God "came down" and impregnated a woman, and their child carried the aspects of both—the masculine *and* the feminine, the intellect *and* the feelings.

That child, the Messiah, Jesus of Nazareth, brought the God concept to a new level, one that we're just now coming

Jesus of Nazareth, brought the God concept to a new level.

to understand. "God is a spirit," He said, "...like the wind." "To know God as I know God, you must love one another as I have loved you. You must know, as I do, that God and I are one, that you and I are one, I in you, you in Him, Him in us...we are all perfected into the one." (John 17:23, rev. ver.)

Jesus said, "If you know God as I do, these things I do, you will do, too, *and even greater things* will you do, for I go to my Father." (John 14:12, rev. ver.) He knew that we would do "greater things" than He, because He knew that the god concept is still growing, still evolving! Our God today is bigger than His god of 2,000 years ago, and who knows what God will be like 2,000 years from now? God only knows!

Loving God is the First Commandment (knowing your oneness with God). "The second," Jesus said, "is like unto it" (the same thing).

"Love your neighbor as you love yourself." (Matt 22:39, rev. ver.) Who is your neighbor? The guy next door? Your family and friends? "No, they're not the ones I'm talking about," He said. "They're easy to love. I'm talking about loving everybody, including your enemies, *especially* your enemies! What reward is there in loving those who love you? Anyone can do that. Love the 'difficult' ones, then you're really loving!" (Matt 5, rev. ver.)

Can you love your enemies, even those who crucify you, as Jesus did? Yes, you can! He gave His life, and His recipe, to show you how to do it. His life and teachings were given to show you how to love. "Judge not," He said. You cannot judge and be in love. "Resist not evil!" You cannot resist anything and be in love. "Agree with the adversary!" You cannot argue or disagree and be in love. Love is letting go.

This *true love* is not easy for the un-*in*-lightened ego to swallow. After all, we've lived in a male-dominated, left-brain, religious society for a long time and the *right hand* is very powerful. Jesus said, "If the right hand (left brain) offends you, cut it off!" He didn't mean to cut it off *literally*. He meant to not give it any *energy*...any *power.*

Stop thinking—that will do it! "Be still and *know.*" His secret was to "not let the right hand know what the left is doing." Shut the right side up, cut it off—and move on up to the East side, the left side, the feeling nature. Mother knows best (father just *thinks* he knows). The male dominance of the world has cooked up a big kettle of Stress Soup, but the feminine is about to pull us out. Mother is the one who really knows how to cook!

The Art of the Heart

As we've said earlier, love is an art and, as in any art, the basics must be learned (understood) and mastered before the artist becomes accomplished. Love is of the heart, the *he*-art, but the *she*-art is equally important. The basics of love require input from both motherly *and* fatherly love.

The basics of love require input from both motherly and fatherly love.

Motherly love is the earliest love a child knows. Mother's love, by its very nature, is unconditional. Mother loves the child, not because it has fulfilled any specific condition or expectation, but simply because it's her child. I'm not saying that all mothers love this way, only that this is motherly love.

Unconditional love is one of the deepest longings of every human being. This is the love we're all searching for, even in adult life. We look for it in our relationships and in our religions, but it can only really come from ourselves. Unconditional love is the love that God gives—the *Mother* aspect of God. If God is seen only as a Father, then this mother aspect is missing and the search continues, usually with erotic and/or neurotic results.

Father is the disciplinarian. Father loves you when you're good and punishes you when you're bad. Father lays down the law, and you're loved according to your merit. Father love then is *conditional* love. Again, I'm not saying that all fathers love this way, but that this is fatherly love.

Most people have been conditioned to see God as "Father" and they live in fear of Father's displeasure. In traditional Christianity, this Father (God) will "fry" His children if they don't obey His rules! I know that I wouldn't condemn *my* children to burn in hell forever for not obeying. Would you? Are we more loving than God? Of course not! Mother-God, motherly love, will always override Father-God before it gets to the point of "eternal condemnation," but the discipline and the laws of the Father *are* important. The rules teach the child how to live effectively. The mature child has a paramount goal, "living according to God's principles." The child thus saves himself when living by the rules, or casts himself into a "hellish" existence if he or she doesn't.

The father's rules teach the child how to live effectively.

Mother-love always forgives the child. Actually, mother-love does not *have* to forgive, because she never sees the child doing anything wrong. Mother's love is unconditional acceptance—all ways. It's that motherly love, in you, that allows you to love yourself, no matter what awful things you've done. It brings the "prodigal son" back to the house—the right-ness, the righteousness, of the Father.

Mother's love is unconditional acceptance... all ways.

It takes both aspects of love, motherly love and fatherly love, to produce a perfectly balanced child of love. If either of these aspects of love is missing or imbalanced in the early life of the child, the child will be imbalanced in adult life. According to psycho-analyst Erich Fromm in his great recipe book, THE ART OF LOVING, "The basic condition of neurotic love lies in the fact that one or both of the 'lovers' have remained attached to the figure of the parent, and transfer the feelings, expectations and fears one once had toward father or mother to the 'loved' person in adult life." "Falling in love," Chef Erich says, "always verges on the abnormal and is always accompanied by blindness to reality, compulsiveness, and is a transference from love objects of childhood."

In many of today's broken homes, there may be only one parent, and the needs of both motherly and fatherly love fall to the single parent. This is not so easy for one person to provide, but it *is* possible, and sometimes even *preferable* to a home with two parents who are always fighting and arguing and abusing one another, and the child(ren), physically, mentally, emotionally or sexually. Perfect parenting, even in the most loving homes, is highly unlikely, so most all of us have work to do in learning love.

Again, I emphasize, "Love is letting go!" It's the children letting go of the parents and what happened in the past, *and* it's the parents letting go of the children! "Your children are not your children," THE PROPHET (Gibran) says. "They are the sons and daughters of life's longing for itself." You don't *own* your children. They're given to you, for a time, to nurture and care for, but as every wise mother bird knows, there comes a time to push them out of the nest, even before it looks like they can fly on their own! You don't do them any favor by continuing to take care of them beyond this very early appointed time.

Being both a child and a parent, I've seen that the child who learns to work his or her way through high school and college is much better able to "work it out" in adult life. Love your children by letting them go early, and letting them go completely—no apron-strings, no emotional attachment, just unconditional love. An "adult-child" is an oxymoron and we don't need to put any more-on our children, oxy or otherwise! Cut 'em loose—with the sword of love!

One on One

All relationships are "workshops on love," or better...*playshops*. Relationships *are* work, but without a conscious lightness, they can get pretty heavy! The one-on-one, "significant other," relationship is the most challenging, and the most rewarding, of all! It's

A married life is like living many lives in one.

not so easy to keep a balanced relationship and keep yourself growing and expanding in consciousness, too. Maybe that's why many of the master chefs lived a single life. A married life is like living many lives in one, and it's a delicate balancing act.

It's that "vibration thing" again. "It takes two to tango." You both have to be on the same wavelength or you can wave good-bye as the relationship falls apart, and the dancers end up in different rooms! How do you do it? How do you stay *together* and stay in love? There are two alternatives. You can either not grow at all (almost impossible in today's fast-moving environment) or you can grow together (also difficult in today's fast-moving environment). The first alternative is unacceptable to one on the path to enlightenment, so let's explore...

Growing Together
(To-get-her!)

This really means growing *in love* together, becoming more and more aware of your oneness with each other, your oneness with God (Love) and your oneness with everyone else. It means becoming ever more *aware,* ever more *in control,* ever more *in balance* in every area of life. It means cooking up a perfect **Peace Soup** together, following the recipe. It works for individuals, it works for couples, it works for groups, it works for everyone. I've always given discounts to couples taking my classes, because I've seen how it's brought so many closer together. They become centered in themselves and centered in the relationship.

True love, in relationship, is possible only if the two communicate with each other from the center of their being. This requires that each one of them experiences *self* from the center of his or her own being. Only in this centered experience is there the aliveness of True Relationship; only here is the basis of True Love.

> **Only in this centered experience is there the basis of True Love.**

Whether there is harmony or conflict, joy or sadness, is secondary to the fundamental fact that two people experience themselves from the essence of their being...that they *feel* their oneness with each other by being at-one with themselves...*in*-dependent rather than outer-dependent.

And keep in mind that all relationships are temporary (temporal) except the relationship with your Self—with God. We come together, in relationship, to learn lessons *with* each other. Some lessons are for the long term...some for a short term. The key is not to force it to be long or short. Keep it here and now, one day at a time. Let it be the loving, learning experience it's designed to be. Each relationship is a lifetime, and each lifetime will end. If the end comes, let it, too, be a lesson in love. How many relationships end in perfect love, without anger, without fear, without guilt, *with* each person supporting the other through the experience? All too few.

If love is letting go, then the experience of separation or divorce must be the most *loving* experience of all. It *can* be, it *will* be, if you follow the recipe. You can continue to enjoy your **Peace Soup** together, even when you part. Isn't that comforting? **Peace Soup** is forever— just like love!

The Blame Game

Blame is something we learned as children, and it's strictly an ego thing, conditioned into our belief system (b.s.). "It's her fault! She made me do it!" "He hit me first, I'm not to blame!" You'll remember the first record of blame in THE BIBLE. Eve said, "The serpent made me eat the fruit!"

Why do we blame others? To keep from being judged, criticized, punished, to escape the wrath of father's anger. Did it work for Eve? No, the Father, the Lord, the Law always compensates our actions, always knows what we do. We can trust that the Law, the measure, will be swift and just, so to blame is futile.

Mother (love) says, "There is no blame. Everyone's doing the best they can do at this moment." There is no *fault* in any of God's children. We're all together (to-get-her) in this adventure called life—there's only *us,* just us, just us for all. I like to say, "It's all *just*...the way it is!"

Through blame, ego separates us... "divides and conquers."

Through blame, ego separates us, "divides and conquers," both the one who blames and the one who is blamed. We don't have to play ego's game, the blame game. We can know, in love, that everybody's right, everybody's perfect, and no-body, no-thing is at fault. Love is God's no-fault insurance!

The New Deal

Love and Trust are the way to Peace and Joy, and the greatest tool I've found for creating and maintaining a healthy relationship is the "I Deal" way—the "Heart Chart" that we learned to use in Step 5 of the recipe. Emotions are the cause of all problems in relationship, and the chart "deals out" the emotions.

Think of any situation that might come up in your relationship that could cause a problem, and you can always deal it out with Love and Trust. When a problem arises, go to Observer, identify the emotion, then move up through the heart. One spouse may think they can't "trust" the other spouse. I say you don't have to trust other people—if you trust

God. You can trust the *order* of whatever is happening. You begin with Blind Faith, but quickly move to Understanding Faith, and then Acceptance, knowing the Truth and being free. Learn to trust God and, in so doing, trust your Self to make the right decisions in a relationship...not emotional decisions, not rational decisions, but *loving* decisions, always letting go.

When a problem arises, go to Observer, identify the emotion, then move up through the heart.

Problems only arise when you're holding on. Let go and the problem *goes*—like magic! In a relationship, if one or the other won't *work,* there is no relationship. A divorce doesn't take place when papers are signed, it takes place when the two stop growing together. If one person won't grow, won't work on him or herself *and* the relationship, it's time for love, time for letting go. Let go and let love build your relationship, or let go and just be alone for awhile and relate with your Self—with God.

Alone = All One

Even in a relationship, one needs to learn to be alone. One of the most important steps in learning concentration and meditation is learning to be alone with oneself, without reading, without watching TV, listening to music, eating or drinking. Being alone is a prerequisite to the ability to love. Being alone is being all one (al-one) with God...love.

The only one you'll always be with is *you.* Have you ever noticed that wherever you go, there you are! When Jesus said, "Love your neighbor as you love yourself," He was indicating that we are always alone, always *all one* with everyone. Loving your neighbor *is* loving yourself! Love is letting go of everyone and everything, including your self, and your self-ish demands.

Thinking one needs someone else to make them whole is one of the great fallacies of the world. So many people are out there trying to find their *other half,* their *soul mate.* The soul doesn't have a mate—it's alone, all one, with every soul. There's only one soul. We're soul mates with

We're soul mates with every-one.

every-*one*. When you feel especially close with another soul, it's because you see yourself in the other. They re-mind you of you, your aloneness, your all-oneness!

If I can't stand to be away from my significant other, then I can't stand alone (all one). I'm attached! The other person might be a "life-saver," and that may be what my life needs to experience, but the relationship is not one of love. In a healthy love relationship, one doesn't *need* the other person and can never be "bored" *with* the other person. The two are *all one* together. Both are fully awake, and being awake is the condition for not being bored, and for not being boring.

Being totally awake and aware of your partner is one of the main conditions for a loving relationship. Listen to them, look them in the eyes, share your thoughts and feelings, touch them lovingly and often. Be alive, alert, awake and enthusiastic about life—that's what we do for love!

Giving Love

There was a popular love song back in the "olden days" that began with these words: "I always give love, and never get love." This is an example of how the world thinks about love. The truth is, you can never *give* love without *getting* love; they're always one and the same activity. The Law of One, of Love, says, "When you give, you receive."

When you give Love, True Love, you get Love, and you cannot get Love without giving.

When you give Love, True Love, you get Love, and you cannot get Love *without* giving, although much of the world is out there *trying*.

They're looking *out there* and hardly ever finding anyone with anything *in here*. Trying to "get" love is a game, a gamble, that never pays off. The sexual imbalance we mentioned in describing the *Balance Bowl* comes from people trying to get without giving. The news is full of reports of elicit affairs, sexual harassment, molestation, incest, rape, sex scandals in business, in religion, in government (politics), in sports…everywhere!

The courts and prisons are filled with people who have "gone off the deep end"—sexually. They're risking life and reputation looking for what? For love, without knowing how to *give* love. They *think* they're looking for excitement, but the true excitement comes not in getting, but in giving love. What's really exciting is that in giving, you get more, too.

The Artist of Love

In love, as in all areas, actions speak louder than words. To give love is to *live love,* not just think about it, or talk about it. Thought, as we've discovered, can only lead to the awareness that thinking cannot give the ultimate answer. One cannot know oneness by thinking about it, only by experiencing it, by living it.

Love is not shown by knowledge or right thought, but by right *action.* The "art of the heart" is learned by practicing right action, but who is to tell you what's right? How do artists develop their talents? They are "in-spired" and they practice! You can be in-spired by becoming still and breathing the truth from within. You are also in-spired by teachings and teachers that come from a high level of consciousness—in this case, a high level of love.

> **Love is not shown by knowledge or right thought, but by right action.**

Chef Emmet (Fox) was coming from a high love consciousness when he wrote his master-piece called POWER THROUGH CONSTRUCTIVE THINKING. On page 275, he shares:

The Golden Gate

Love is by far the most important thing of all. It is the golden gate of paradise. Pray for the understanding of love and meditate upon it daily. It casts out fear. It is the fulfilling of the Law. It covers a multitude of sins. Love is absolutely invincible.

There is no difficulty that enough love will not conquer; no disease that enough love will not heal; no door that enough love will not open; no gulf that enough love will not bridge; no wall that enough love will not throw down; no sin that enough love will not redeem.

It makes no difference how deeply seated may be the trouble, how hopeless the outlook, how muddled the tangle, how great the mistake; a sufficient realization of love will dissolve it all. If only you could love enough, you would be the happiest and most powerful being in the world.

The inspired teachings of the great recipe book (THE BIBLE) contain some high love teachings, especially in the New Testament and particularly in the passage from Chef Paul's First Letter to the Corinthians, a passage so beautiful and so all-encompassing that it has been left pretty much unchanged since it was written.

Whether Paul actually wrote it or not is open to debate (de bait), as essentially the same wording is found in writings that pre-date Paul. No one knows who actually wrote it, and it's not important anyway (except to the left brain). What *is* important is what it says, and the feeling it engenders. I quote the King James English since it is so eloquent:

Though I speak with the tongues of men and of angels, and have not love, I am become as sounding brass, or a tinkling cymbal. And though I have the gift of prophecy, and understand all mysteries, and all knowledge; and though I have all faith, so that I could remove mountains, and have not love, I am nothing. And though I bestow all my goods to feed the poor, and though I give my body to be burned, and have not love, it profiteth me nothing. Love suffereth long, and is kind; love envieth not; love vaunteth not itself, is not puffed up, doth not behave itself unseemly, seeketh not her own, is not easily provoked, thinketh no evil; rejoiceth not in iniquity, but rejoiceth in the truth; beareth all things, believeth all things, hopeth all things, endureth all things.

Love never faileth: but whether there be prophecies,
they shall fail; whether there be tongues, they shall
cease; whether there be knowledge, it shall vanish away.
For we know in part, and we prophesy in part. But when
that which is perfect is come, then that which is in part
shall be done away. When I was a child, I spake as a
child, I understood as a child, I thought as a child; but
when I became a man, I put away childish things. For
now we see through a glass, darkly; but then face to
face: now I know in part; but then shall I know even as
also I am known. And now abideth faith, hope, love,
these three; but the greatest of these is love. (1 Cor 13)

Chef Henry (Drummond) wrote a little book over 100 years ago entitled THE GREATEST THING IN THE WORLD that is based on the above passage on love. As we've seen, love *is* the greatest thing, because God is love! Chef Henry points out that love is the fulfilling of the law. The Jewish law, from Moses, had Ten Commandments, but by the time Jesus was born, left-brain *religion* had increased this to over 800 rules and regulations. Jesus balked at many of the 800 rules and even said, in effect, that the Ten Commandments were outdated. He gave only *one* commandment...Love. Chef Henry writes:

If you love, you will unconsciously fulfill the whole law....Take any of the commandments. "Thou shalt have no other gods before me." If a man love God, you will not require to tell Him that.... "Take not His name in vain." Would he ever dream of taking His name in vain if he loved Him? "Remember the Sabbath day to keep it holy." Would he not be too glad to have one day in seven to dedicate more exclusively to the object of his affection? Love would fulfill all these laws regarding God. And so, if he loved man, you would never think of telling him to honour his father and mother. He could not do anything else. It would be preposterous to tell him not to kill. You could only insult him if you suggested that he should not steal—how could he steal from those he loved? It would be superfluous to beg him not to bear false witness against his neighbor. If he loved him, it would be the last thing he would do. And you would never dream of urging him not to covet what his neighbors had. He would rather they possessed it than himself. In this way, "Love is the fulfilling of the law." It is the rule for fulfilling all rules, the new commandment for keeping all the old commandments, Christ's one secret of the Christian life.

There's a new rule that fulfills all the old rules...Love.

Jesus, in effect, was saying that the "Old" Testament is *old stuff*. There's a new rule that fulfills *all* the old rules—Love. So let the old stuff go, love it, and concentrate all your energy on the new, on love. "That's too easy," Intellect says. "It's got to be more complicated than that!" "Get thee behind me, Intellect...back in the old, dead, past." It is easy. "My yoke is easy," Jesus said...K.I.S.S.!

In the love letter from First Corinthians, Paul lays out the ingredients of love. Henry Drummond calls this the "Spectrum of Love" and says, "Just as you would shine a light through a prism to get a 'rainbow' of colors, so Paul shines love through the prism of his 'illumined intellect' and it comes out on the other side broken up into its elements." The nine ingredients Chef Henry uses in his recipe for love are:

1) **Patience** — "Love suffereth long."
2) **Kindness** — "And is kind."
3) **Generosity** — "Love envieth not."
4) **Humility** — "Love vaunteth not itself, is not puffed up."
5) **Courtesy** — "Doth not behave itself unseemly."

6) **Unselfishness** — "Seeketh not her own."

7) **Good Temper** — "Is not easily provoked."

8) **Guilelessness** — "Thinketh no evil."

9) **Sincerity** — "Rejoiceth not in iniquity, but rejoiceth in the truth."

The **Peace Soup** recipe is a rainbow of love and is designed to bring peace on earth, one loving being at a time. Love is an in-spiration, the breathing of eternal spirit into the temporal world. Each of these nine ingredients in-spires, *breathes in* the loving life, so let's give a quick overview of each:

1. Patience — Chef Henry says patience is "Love passive, love waiting to begin; not in a hurry; calm...for love understands, and therefore waits." Patience is a virtue, a more than ordinary awareness of the presence of God, of Love, in every activity. There is no hurry when God is in charge—just wait, and Love will *move* you when the time is right. Just be patient...

2. Kindness — If patience is "love passive," then kindness is "love active!" Chef Jesus' recipe is filled with acts of kindness, helping people to be more comfortable, healthier and happier. A recent innovation for a more loving world is Random Acts of Kindness Week. What a great idea, but why for just one week? We want to develop a Random Acts of Kindness *Life. Do* things for people—little things that show how loving you are. Every action shows the world *and you* when you are *oozing love*. Again, we echo the words of Dale Carnegie: *"Act* with kindness and you'll *be* kind!"

3. Generosity — This ingredient is "wanting the best for everyone." Henry Drummond says this is "Love in competition with others." Generosity means there is no envy or fear of losing. You give with an open heart—even to the competition...especially to the competition—and there is *no* competition, only co-operation. Everyone is working together for the good of all. How much does the business world need this? How much does *all* the world need it? Generosity happens through you!

4. Humility — "Love is not puffed up" (no pride). "After love has stolen forth into the world and done its beautiful work," Chef Henry says, "it goes back into the shade again and says nothing about it." There is a story about a professor who lived in the cold country of the north. He was very much loved by all the students and faculty, and one year they all got together and purchased a beautiful fur coat for the professor as a symbol of their love. He cherished that coat and wore it every winter day.

One evening, as he was working late, a blizzard was raging outside and he went to the window to look out at the storm. The snow was so heavy that he could barely make out the sidewalk in front of the school, but as he looked more closely, he could just see the figure of a person walking against the wind, and it was obvious that this person was freezing and wore no coat. Without a second thought, the professor ran and got his coat, went out into the storm, wrapped his precious coat around the freezing person and wished him on his way. He never told anyone what happened to his coat, and no one would have ever known, if the janitor hadn't been looking out of another window. That's humility—that's love!

5. Courtesy — "Love doth not behave itself unseemly," Paul said. This is love in society. How much does the world need this now? Discourtesy seems to be the norm. Again, traffic may be the greatest test of love. How do you handle yourself in traffic when someone suddenly drives in front of you, when they are careless or dis-courteous? My friend, Chef Mary (Omwake), has developed a solution to the single finger getting tired and overused in traffic. "Start using two fingers!" she says, "Then see how much more peaceful you and everyone else feels!" Let others go in front of you. "Take the least seat," Jesus said. Love brings peace...all ways.

6. Unselfishness — Chef Henry continues, "Love seeketh not her own. Love does not seek anything. It only gives. 'Seeketh thou great things for thyself?' said the Prophet. Seek them not. Why? Because there is no greatness in things. Things cannot be great. The only greatness is unselfish love." The most obvious lesson (less-on) is that there is no happiness in having or getting anything, but only in giving. "It is more blessed to give than receive," Chef Henry says, "and half the world is on the wrong scent in the pursuit of happiness. They think it consists of having and getting, and in being served by others. It consists in giving and serving others." "He that would be great among you," Jesus said, "let him serve" (Luke 22:26) (Step 7 of the **Peace Soup** recipe).

7. Good Temper — "Love is not easily provoked." We dis-"cussed" anger in Step 5, and it's interesting that it shows up in this discourse on love, but I believe that it goes much deeper than "not easily provoked." This qualification comes from the intellect…left brain. True love cannot be provoked at all, *ever.* Anger is *not* love, even tough love. Anger is *emotion* and it comes from ego, always! Good temper is probably the ingredient of love that needs the most work, so if you feel anger coming on, bring out the "I Deal" way—the "Heart Chart" and process the anger. Practice makes perfect—perfect love.

8. Guilelessness — "Love thinketh no evil." According to Chef Daniel (Webster), "guile" means "slyness and cunning in dealing with others…craftiness…being deceitful and tricky." Guile-*less-ness* is seeing life through "rose-colored glasses." Everything's good…everything's *God!* Love "sees no evil, hears no evil, speaks no evil." The world (ego) might say it makes a *monkey* out of you, but love knows better. As we discovered in Step 4, there is no evil. Guilelessness is knowing the truth and being free.

9. Sincerity — "Love rejoiceth in the truth." Chef Henry says that sincerity allows one to "Rejoice not in what he has been taught to believe; not in this church's doctrine or in that; not in this *ism* or in that *ism;* but *in the Truth*." How do you know what "The Truth" is? No one can tell it to you, you can't read it in any book, including *this book, THE BIG BOOK or THE BIBLE!* Only God—Love can reveal the Truth to you, in your own heart!

Love Is in the Cards

Benjamin Franklin is one of the giants in American history, one of the founding fathers, and a true genius in every sense of the word. "Old

Benjamin Franklin had a recipe for developing genius.

Ben" had a recipe for developing genius. It was his "13–Week System of Learning." When he wanted to learn everything possible about a subject, become an expert in it, he would gather all the information he could find about the subject and then divide it into 13 sections. He would then study a different section each week for 13 weeks. He would saturate his mind with the data from one section all day, every day, for a week.

Then he would forget about it completely and move on to the next section the following week. He forgot about it *consciously,* but the subconscious mind continued to work on it. He would continue this process through the 13 weeks, saturating his mind, then forgetting, until he had completely covered the subject. If he considered himself an expert at that point, he would move on to another subject; if not, he would begin the process all over again with Section One, doing more research on each section.

The secret of this system is in the power of the subconscious mind. Remember in Step 1 of the recipe, when we learned to relax with Autogenic Training? This technique is the most effective method of relaxing I know about, for the same reason Chef Ben's system is so effective. In Autogenic Training, we become totally aware of the part of the body we're working on, tense it, then relax it, then state our affirmation about it. For instance, beginning with the right foot, we affirm, "My foot is relaxed, I am relaxed, I am at peace with my body." Then we forget that foot and move on to the left foot *consciously,* but the subconscious mind keeps on relaxing the right foot.

Developing A Higher L.Q.

Would you like to become a genius in love? By now, you can see the benefit of this, to your Self and to everyone and everything else. I'm going to suggest that you utilize Chef Ben's system to become an expert—in love! Instead of working to increase your I.Q. (intelligence quotient), you're going to increase your L.Q. (love quotient). We have already discussed the first 9 of the 13 sections in the "Spectrum of Love" by Chef Henry (Drummond) outlined above.

Instead of working to increase your I.Q., increase your L.Q. (love quotient).

What would happen to your love-ability if you spent a whole week studying about, and practicing, patience? What if you were to go to the library and read all you could find about patience and then make up *love quotient cards,* with the word "Patience" in big letters? What if you put them everywhere you go during the day—on your alarm clock, on the mirror where you shave or put on your makeup, on the breakfast table, on your refrigerator, on the dashboard of your car, on your desk at the office, in your wallet or purse, on your golf bag or tennis racket…everywhere?

What would happen if you saturated your mind with patience for a week, then forgot about it *consciously,* and let your subconscious mind take over? What would happen if you did the same thing with kindness, generosity, humility, courtesy, unselfishness, good temper, guilelessness, sincerity, each week letting go, *consciously,* and *pumping iron* subconsciously? Your *love quotient* would become awesome. You would develop the highest possible L.Q. and, in the process, alter your life and the world!

I have outlined the first nine sections; you can come up with the other four, or you might want to use the ingredients of Love we work with in the "I Deal" way—the "Heart Chart": Forgiveness (forgive me); Compassion (seeing) and Unconditional Acceptance (knowing). The thirteenth and final week can be a week of *oneness!…*exploring and feeling oneness with God, oneness with people, oneness with nature, oneness with the universe.

If, after 13 weeks, you are totally *in* love, totally perfected, you will ascend. You'll be hanging out on the mountaintop with the mas-

If, after 13 weeks, you are totally in love...totally perfected... you will ascend.

ter chefs Jesus, Buddha, Krishna, Lao-Tzu, Gandhi, Martin Luther King, Mother Teresa. If, however, you don't make it to ascension, start again, another week of Patience, more research, more practice...

With Chef Ben's system for genius, you are saturating your soup with the final and most important ingredient, Divine Love, and your recipe is almost ready. There is just one more thing to do to completely integrate love into every activity of your life, overcome all temptation and put ego behind you—for good.

The Final Technique
"Emotional Replacement"

The final technique in the **Peace Soup** recipe follows closely those we learned and mastered in Step 5, the "I Deal" way—the "Heart Chart" and the Mindfulness Technique. A variation of this final technique, called "micro-mindfulness," has been taught for many years as an adjunct to mindfulness. Micro-mindfulness is simply the ability to call back the serenity you've developed through mindfulness meditation, at any time and under any condition. You can do this by simply centering your awareness in the rising...falling motion of the abdomen and re-membering the peace that mindfulness brings. Micro-mindfulness can be done anywhere, in any position, with eyes open or closed. It's a very valuable and effective tool, indeed.

Chef Emmet (Fox) developed another variation that he called "The Golden Key." It has been a literal life saver to many who are caught up in a problem or a negative situation. "The Golden Key" helps one to switch gears and, instead of thinking about the problem, they think about God. I have been suggesting The Golden Key for many years as a quick alternative to those who have not yet completed the **Peace Soup** recipe. A problem some people have with this alternative is believing in God, or knowing what or who God is.

In the final technique, what I call *Emotional Replacement,* I feel we have an even more effective method. Instead of substituting a *thought* of God for an emotional problem or situation, we replace it with a *feeling*. This is similar to the Stress Replacement we learned in Step 1 of the recipe. In Stress Replacement we used a situation that would normally cause stress, as a trigger to relax.

With Emotional Replacement, when an emotion comes up (fear, or a child or grandchild of fear), we go to Observer, identify the emotion, and immediately replace it with a feeling of love, joy, peace or trust. You find this replacement feeling by remembering a very positive or joyful experience you've had in your life and "calling up," or re-calling the feeling. You then take this feeling into your breathing, being aware only of the rising…falling, rising…falling of the abdomen and breathing the feeling for a few breaths. The transformation from emotion to feeling can come very quickly and, with practice, can become auto-matic. The feeling re-places the emotion.

The transformation from emotion to feeling can come very quickly.

Thanks to Chef Doc (Lew Childre) and my friends at the Institute of HeartMath, I have recently added a subtle pro-gression to Emotional Replacement which I feel gives the soup that final little sprinkle of flavor that rounds off the recipe and makes it appealing to everyone. Here is the final touch of brilliance that I've added to give the soup the taste of perfection.

After a few breaths using Emotional Replacement, concentrating on the rising…falling motion of the abdomen and breathing the feeling of joy and serenity, remembering a joyful, peaceful experience, gently shift the breath to the heart. In effect, you are breathing the "feeling," the joyful, loving experience, *through the heart.*

Gently shift the breath to the heart.

I believe that the heart is not only the receiving station for in-spiration, but it is also the transmitter of love energy. This final technique sets you up perfectly for Step 7 of the recipe. Using the "art of the heart" (love), you have created a masterpiece—your peaceful life. As a master chef, you have established a life of love, joy, trust and enlightenment. Your soup now has all the needed ingredients and it's exuding the sweet aroma and the rich, smooth, flowing texture of *pure peace*. Finally, you're ready for...

Step 7

Serving the Soup

Playing in the Souper Bowl

In reviewing the **Peace Soup** recipe, you can see that you've just completed the longest journey that one can ever undertake—the journey from the head to the heart. In this journey you've seen that the head (intellect), if given full rein, will get you lost, and that the heart is the compass that leads you home. This journey in consciousness began with the *fall from grace*—when we began to think for ourselves.

The heart is the compass that leads you home.

The longest journey has taken you on the adventurous, thrilling, roller-coaster ride through the physical, mental, emotional wilderness, and brought you full circle, back *up* into grace, into the promised land, the land "flowing with milk and honey" (peace and joy). This is the *new Jerusalem* Chef Jesus talked about in the final step of *His* recipe, His *revelation to John.* "Salem" means *peace;* Jeru–salem is the city of peace.

You began your journey to peace and joy with the soup kettle pretty well caked with the residue of old Stress Soup. The first step of the recipe saw you peeling the onion by removing the outer/physical layers of stress using autogenic training, moving gently through the body, one section at a time…tensing…relaxing…affirming peace. In Step 1, you also learned how to use The Ladle correctly in stirring the soup, speaking only positive, healthful, happy words—words that create peace, love, trust, joy.

The process of Step 1 prepared the way for the healthy soup stock that you mixed in through Step 2, where you explored the mind/body connection and how we are programmed for stress by the image makers of the world. In Step 2, you learned the four basic rules of the body and how to follow these rules in creating a robust soup stock. The technique you learned in this step was auto-suggestion...using the Laboratory of the Mind.

Step 2 gave you the base into which you could fold Step 3, the secret ingredient...meditation. You began the journey within, using the discipline exercises from Zen and Yoga—breath-counting and/or the mantra—to gain control over thought. Each step of the recipe has led you gently and effectively away from stress and toward serenity.

Each step of the recipe has led you gently and effectively away from stress and toward serenity.

Step 4 brought you face to face with yourself! You met the enemy, the spoiler, and learned how to put him in his place—behind you! The technique you learned was *non*-sense, and it worked like magic to rein in the tempter, the rational mind. This prepared you for Step 5, the final battle, "Armeggedon"—conquering the emotions. You saw fear for what it is— nothing, a ghost—and you learned to deal it out with the "I-Deal" way—the "Heart Chart." The Mindfulness Technique helped you to train yourself to go to that crucial point—Observer—and make everything "O" — "O.K.!"

At that point, you were ready for the final ingredient that has given the soup its true and distinctive flavor...Pure Love. Step 6 overcame all resistance (666) and brought you to your ultimate goal—perfect peace in all situations—through the use of emotional re-placement, replacing *emotion* with the *feeling* of pure love. Now you're ready for Step 7: Serving the Soup.

Being The Prince/Princess of Peace

Master Chef Jesus is, as you've no doubt gathered, the major contributor to this recipe. He may appear a little different to you from the traditional Jesus, the Jesus of Western *religion,* but to me, He is the *real* Jesus! He *breathes* in me, *in-spires* my life, and is my role model. I'm not saying that you have to see Jesus the way I do, or even that you have to be Christian in order to enjoy **Peace Soup**. It's not a religious thing, it's a *spiritual* thing—it's the *spirit* that gives it life. All the great chefs have *the spirit.*

This final Step 7 is inspired by Jesus' recipe when He said, "He that is greatest among you (the greatest chef) is he that serves (the soup)." (Luke 22:26, rev. ver.) Also, in my favorite chapter of THE BIBLE, the 14th chapter of John, He said, "Peace I leave with you, My peace I give unto you: not as the world gives peace…." The peace He gave was the peace of Christ. Christ in my belief system is *not Jesus,* it's the spirit of God (love) that dwells *within* Jesus, and dwells within *you,* and *me, and every* one of God's children, no matter what their religious beliefs may be. The Christ is the "only begotten" that Jesus talked about in John 3:16.

The second coming of Christ is not, as I see it, *Jesus* coming back, but the Christ nature being expressed (pressed out) through every one of us! So why haven't more of God's children fulfilled their potential as "the Christ?" Again, Chef Jesus gave us the answer in the 17th chapter of Matthew: "Because of your unbelief: for verily I say unto you, if you have faith as a grain of mustard seed, you shall say unto this mountain, remove hence to yon-

> **The second coming is the Christ nature being expressed (pressed out) through every one of us.**

der place; and it shall remove; and nothing shall be impossible to you."

How much faith does a tiny grain of mustard seed have? *100 percent!* It *knows,* without a shadow of a doubt, what it really is, and what it's designed to *be*—"a mighty tree where birds come to nest." (Matt 13:32) To *be* the Christ, to ex-press the Christ, you must know what you are, just as fully and as strongly as a grain of mustard seed knows what it is.

We are all children of love. Each of us is the princess/prince of peace, and we're now ready to give the peace of Christ to the world, just as Jesus gave it to us, and, as we've discussed, Jesus wasn't the only chef who gave peace.

Krishna's Peace

The master soup chef, Lord Krishna, put it this way in His discourse with His disciple, Arjuna:

Better, indeed, is knowledge than mechanical practice, better than knowledge is meditation, but better still is surrender of attachment to results, because there follows immediate peace.

The one I love [is one] who is incapable of ill will, who is friendly and compassionate, living beyond the reach of eye and mind, and of pleasure and pain, patient, contented, self-controlled, firm in faith, with all his heart and all his mind given to me, with such a one, I am in love.

Not agitating the world or by it agitated, he stands above the sway of elation, competition and fear. He is my beloved. He is detached, pure, efficient, impartial, never anxious, self-less in all his undertakings, he is my devotee, very dear to me. He is dear to me who runs not after the pleasant or away from the painful, grieves not, lusts not, but lets things come and go as they happen. That devotee, who looks upon friend and foe with equal regard, who is not buoyed up by praise, or cast down by blame, alike in heat and cold, pleasure and pain, free from selfish attachments, the same in honor and dishonor, quiet, ever full, in harmony, everywhere, firm in faith, such a one is dear to me. (*from THE BHAGAVAD GITA, 12th chapter, "The Way of Love"*)

Lord Krishna had a wonderful recipe. You may choose his, or

another, or others'—Buddha, Lao-Tzu, Confucius, Mohammed…any *in*-lightened one or "ones." You'll know which is right for you, without anyone else telling you!

Peace, true peace, can only come through Love (God), so you can't go wrong when you've cooked up a true **Peace Soup**, no matter whose recipe you've followed. As Chef Jesus said, "It's by your fruits (soup) that you are known.…" (Matt 7:20, rev. ver.) Your soup is ready now, you've completed the recipe, the aroma is heavenly, the taste is sublime, the texture is smooth and flowing, it's ready to be served in…

"The Souper Bowl"

As we've seen, life is designed to be *fun*. It's a game that continues eternally and, when we learn the rules and play by the rules, everybody enjoys it, and everybody wins! There are no losers in the Souper Bowl game. We're all helping one another in the stadium of life, and there's a heavenly host in the stands cheering us on.

In the first six steps of the recipe, we've gone through training camp and learned the rules and techniques for playing the game. We played regular season games by applying what we learned, in our personal lives. Now we're ready for the post season, where we not only incorporate the benefits of peace more fully into *our* lives, but share the good soup with others.

It's time to ask not "what's in it for me," but "what's in it for others." Jesus' golden rule is the measuring chain for this Souper Bowl game. We want to play the game with the fervor of Chef Jane (Bartholow), whose philosophy is to "treat everyone as if it were *their* last day on earth!" As another great chef put it, "Let your bliss be in service to others."

Serving the soup is the most gratifying part of the recipe, and it's also the most *fun*. I've been cooking and serving this soup for over 30 years, and I can attest that it is most gratifying seeing others preparing the recipe and enjoying the results in *their* lives, and then sharing their peace with others. This sharing, one with another, is a never-ending process, and the ways of serving are unlimited. We'll all be coming up with new *plays* continuously. The following are a few pages from the *playbook* for the Souper Bowl game:

Serving Images

In the early steps of the **Peace Soup** recipe, you saw how powerful the imagination is, and you developed the ability to image only good things for yourself and others. You learned to stir the soup gently with *the ladle,* speaking only positive, up-lifting words. You also learned to picture the perfect soup, knowing that the subconscious mind cannot distinguish between what's real and what's imagined.

The server is an example of what he or she is serving.

Now you can use what you've learned for yourself, to help others who have not yet learned the recipe for a peaceful life. You can serve the soup by "spooning" it into their kettles, very gently, subtly. You don't *tell* them what to say or do, or how to be—you *show* them! The server is an example of what he or she is serving.

Images are contagious! When your mind is filled with good, healthy images, when you're thinking loving, peaceful, joyous thoughts, others pick up on the vibration and are affected by it. In the Souper Bowl game, there is no negativity whatsoever. That's why everybody wins. The soup spoons you use in serving **Peace Soup** are the little positive images you place in the bowls of others.

You may offer little "alternatives" to any negativity another may be expressing. When someone says, "This is bad!" you simply reply, "It's not so good." This sounds as if you're agreeing, but you've just effected a subtle shift to: "It's not so good, but it's getting better." You've just made a "first up" (there are no downs) in the Souper Bowl! Using this technique and others you've learned in the recipe, you continue to "lighten up" the game for everyone.

When you're in traffic, you now know to flash *two* fingers as a sign of peace and you can also bless those who curse! If someone utters a "curse" word, say, "Bless you," just as though they had sneezed. If you should step out of bounds and curse (yourself), immediately *bless yourself*. Someone says, "Damn it!" You say, "Bless you!"…another first ~~down~~ up!

Bless those who curse!

After a few good plays, the other person may catch a pass, see what you're doing, and decide to join in the game, that's a touch ~~down~~ up! But they may resist. They may even get *angry*. This is why you must be gentle. If you encounter resistance, the response is "O" — "O.K." (non-resistance). You always "agree with the adversary," as Jesus said, but the seed has been planted and ultimately, when you leave them alone, they *will* come home like Bo Peep said, "wagging their *tales* behind them."

In serving the soup, you do not let yourself get caught up in the worldly images, the worries and fears, "the cares of the world," as Jesus called them. (Mark 4:19) You remain an *uplifting* element. "If I be lifted up, I will draw all men unto myself," He said. (John 12:32) In the Souper Bowl game, you lift the whole world up with you! Each one you help in turn lifts others as the soup is tasted and digested by more and more people. In the Souper Bowl, you become the image maker, and your positive images are felt by everyone—everywhere!

Serving Serenity

The strength of character you set as a goal in Step 1, serenity, is now a reality in your life and you really don't have to *say* or *do* anything— just *be*…serene. You serve others by simply being at peace, in every situation, under all conditions.

Remember the words of James Allen. "Who does not love a tranquil heart, a sweet-tempered, balanced life? It does not matter whether it rains or shines, or what changes come to those possessing these blessings, for they are always sweet, serene and calm." In the Souper Bowl, *you* are the "last lesson of culture…the flowering of life…the fruitage of the soul…" that Chef

You serve others by simply being at peace… in every situation… under all conditions.

James described. There is no more "self," only "Self"—the true nature of your being.

In the Souper Bowl (serving the soup) you are fulfilling your response-ability to act from your highest nature, as "the Christ, the Messiah, the savior of the world." To ego, this sounds like an impossibility, like too great a responsibility, but there is no ego in the Souper Bowl, and to the true Self, this sounds as natural as breathing! In this game, the spiritual nature is the *superstar,* the "M.V.P." You act from perfect awareness, perfect control, perfect balance, perfect flow.

You are finally fulfilling Chef Jesus' instructions in his SERMON ON THE MOUNT: "Be ye therefore perfect, as God within you is perfect." (Matt 5:48, rev. ver.) In this state of perfection, everything's happening *on purpose* and *in order.* Whatever you need is available to you in the moment you need it. You are "in tune" with the rhythm of the universe, and you remain "calm, steadfast, serene...."

In the gospel according to Thomas, which "The Church" decided not to canonize, God is described as "a movement and **God is "a** a rest." Can you feel the rhythm of this phrase? It's the **movement** essence of all music, the essence of life, "a movement **and a** and a rest." This is what the Souper Bowl requires of its **rest."** players, a natural rhythm that is aligned with life itself and allows everything to appear synchronistically, when and where it's needed. Serving serenity is being able to move with the natural flow, from one event to another, without spilling a drop of precious **Peace Soup**.

Serving Love

A COURSE IN MIRACLES says that there are only two activities one can be involved in—"giving" (serving) love or "crying out" for love. Most of the people in our lives are crying out for love, and you, as a **Peace Soup** chef, are always ready to serve love.

As you saw in Step 6, love is the most important ingredient in the recipe, *be-cause* without love, there can be no peace! You practiced this essential element of the game, diligently, in Steps 5 and 6, using the "Heart Chart" and the "13-week system" of Chef Ben. Now you're ready to take love into a higher dimension in the Souper Bowl.

You may be familiar with the little bracelet that's so popular in the "Christian" world—the "W.W.J.D?" bracelet. It's a reminder to always follow the example set out by Jesus by asking "What Would Jesus Do?" when faced with a stressful situation or a temptation to "sin." This is an exciting concept, and I highly endorse it as a *step* in the direction of love; however, a problem arises, I believe, in the interpretation of what Jesus would do in a given situation. Unless you want to get yourself crucified, I don't know that you really *want* to do what He would do. He had his role to fulfill and we each have ours.

His one commandment to us is to love, so I would like to suggest that you follow this commandment in establishing a key play for the Souper Bowl by asking, "What Would Love Do Now?" (W.W.L.D.N?). This play came from the playbook of Chef Mary (Omwake) and I've found it very effective in always being ready to serve love. You may inscribe it on a bracelet, or a plate, or a cup, or a soup bowl, but most importantly, you want to inscribe it in-delibly *in your mind and heart,* so it's the first thing that comes up for you when you're confronted with a challenge…*W.W.L.D.N?*

When the tempter (ego) brings you to the point of re-action—fighting, flighting, arguing—you automatically respond instead by asking W.W.L.D.N? Love would surrender, let go, give *up* (to God)! If someone strikes you on the cheek, what would love do? Turn the other cheek? Yes, and then *love the striker.* He or she's crying out for love! If you're tempted to be afraid or to worry, what would love do? Trust, let go, *know* the truth and be free. *W.W.L.D.N?* allows you to be responsive, quick on your feet, understanding, compassionate, accepting, able to head off any trouble before it starts.

238 / PEACE SOUP

The Love Button

My friend, Chef Wally (Famous Amos), a cookie chef as well as a soup chef, likes to use the example of a button he saw me wearing at one of his workshops. The button simply says, "Love is the answer," and then in smaller letters, "What was the question?" Wally Amos knows the truth about love and he serves it everywhere he goes. Most people think it was his recipe for cookies that made him "famous," but it was really his *love* that did it! (It's also what made the original cookies so good.) Serving love is what we're all designed to do...it's what life's all about—it's all about love!

LOVE is the answer. What was the question?

In my classes and lectures, I always say that if you answer any question with "love," you'll always be right. I'm now suggesting, as a key play in the Souper Bowl, that you wear an imaginary "love button" right over your heart, shining your inner "love light" on everyone you meet. Show the world where your heart really is—"in love" with everyone and everything! *God* is love, and that's what you're ex-pressing—your godliness (ye gods)!

The L.Q. Cards

The Love Quotient cards we developed in Step 6 can be a very helpful tool in serving love. I developed these cards to help each of us become an expert, a genius in love, following the recipe of Chef Ben. In the Souper Bowl, you play with a *full deck*. As you'll remember, there were 13 ingredients of love that you used to complete Chef Ben's recipe. Now, for the full deck, you have four of each card, or a total of 52 cards. (Sound familiar?)

In the Souper Bowl, you play with a full deck.

The first nine cards are the nine ingredients in Henry Drummond's *Spectrum of Love*. The 2 is patience, 3—kindness, 4—generosity, 5—humility, 6—courtesy, 7—unselfishness, 8—good temper, 9—guilelessness, and 10—sincerity. The face cards are Jack—forgiveness,

Queen—compassion, and King—acceptance. The Ace, naturally, is oneness!

The Love Quotient cards can bring a whole new dimension to any game of cards—gin, poker, blackjack, bridge, hearts—as they are a *bridge* to the *heart*. Every time a dealer deals the cards, they're dealing love!

The Love Quotient cards will be an integral part of **Peace Soup— The Game**™, a board game incorporating the steps of the recipe and the tools involved, in an exciting, adventurous and educational way. **Peace Soup—The Game**™ fine tunes our skills, so we can all be more effective in the Souper Bowl.

In **Peace Soup—The Video Game**™, instead of *killing* the enemy, you will "shoot 'em with love!" You will learn to *love* the enemy into sub-mission...then to re-mission...and finally to ad-mission of who they really are—*a souper being*, playing in the game of life. Everyone learns to play by the rules...and life is fun again!

"Shoot 'em with love!"

Serving Health and Healing

In Step 2 of the recipe, you learned how to develop a healthy soup stock by abiding in the rules of the body. In the Souper Bowl you dis-*play* your strength, your health, your good soup stock, by being a living example of health and healing. You eat good, healthy food and say "nay" to the poisons. You get plenty of rest and relaxation, eliminate and de-toxify regularly, and move your body by exercising daily.

Be a living example of health and healing.

Even with a healthy soup stock and abiding by the rules, you still may occasionally allow yourself to become imbalanced and develop a sickness or dis-ease. When this happens, don't see it as something "bad" or "wrong" but as an opportunity to *practice healing*. When Jesus said, "Physician, heal thyself" (Luke 4:23), I believe He was saying that we are to set the example for others by *healing ourselves*. We learn to heal naturally through energy (inner "G") work, instead of using drugs, surgery or radiation—the cures of the world.

I had the opportunity to heal a condition that I had developed in my body from my early years on the S.A.D. (Standard American Diet). Almost everyone living in the technologically advanced cultures has been affected by the artificial substances that have been introduced into the environment. In the autopsy reports of soldiers as young as 20 years of age in the Vietnam War, there were already signs of clogging of the arteries (atheroschlerosis).

Even though I had been eating healthily for the previous few years, the "clogging" caught up with me. I began feeling a shortness of breath and a tightness in my chest, so I went to a cardiologist for a check-up. During the "stress test" I was only able to walk on the treadmill for a few short minutes before he stopped me and ordered more tests, including an angiogram (taking pictures of the blood vessels from inside).

The pictures indicated that I had blockages in three of the arteries around my heart, and the cardiologist immediately called in...*the surgeon.* You can imagine what their recommendation was. "Immediate triple bypass! There is no other solution," they said. "If you don't do it, you might not make it much longer."

Knowing me from the recipe, you can imagine, also, what *my* response was. "Thanks, but no thanks. I believe there *is* another solution, so I'm going to pass—Bye!" I thanked them for the diagnosis, paid them their fee, and walked out of the hospital. I now knew what the problem was, and set about finding what I had to do to overcome the dis-ease and heal my body.

"I'm going to pass...Bye!"

I will admit that the ghosts of fear made an appearance during the o.r.-deal, and I knew I could give in to the ways of the world, or deal out the emotions. I was able to move to Observer and then up into Trust, knowing that I would be "O" — "O.K." no matter what happened. I was able to see this experience as a great test for the recipe, and an opportunity to demonstrate my ability to serve the soup through healing (myself).

I began, of course, with increased prayer and meditation, knowing the truth of perfection and letting the love of God do the perfect healing work through me, without ego's interference. I was guided almost immediately to what I needed. It came "out of nowhere" (now-here) in the form of a book by Chef Carlson (Wade) entitled INNER CLEANSING: HOW TO HEAL YOURSELF FROM JOINT–MUSCLE–ARTERY–CIRCULATION SLUDGE. His recipe includes an increase in eating the *cleansing* foods, such as raw garlic and onions and, as I followed the recipe, my improvement was rapid, even spectacular! My cholesterol and triglycerides went from a "crisis" level of well over 300, to normal (150-175), *in just 17 days.* No drugs, just food. The card-iologist was impressed, but didn't recommend it to his other patients. I wonder why?

Soon after this, I was introduced to *chelation therapy* and spent three hours, twice a week for 20 weeks, sitting patient-ly while the E.D.T.A. (ethylenediaminetetraacetic acid) solution slowly "dripped" through my circulatory system, cleaning out *all* my blood vessels, not just the three around my heart. Each week I could feel myself becoming clearing and clearer, freer and freer. (For more information on chelation and heart health, you may want to read IS HEART SURGERY NECESSARY? by Chef Julian Whitaker, M.D.)

After many months of diligent work, I went again for tests. The results—no blockages whatsoever! My circulatory system was clear, my cholesterol was normal, and I could walk on the treadmill for 20 minutes, uphill, increasing speed every three minutes, hardly breaking a sweat! I feel "souper" and I share this test-I-monial as an illustration of playing in the Souper Bowl. I'm not proud, but I am *pleased,* and forever grateful, for the **Peace Soup** recipe and the love of God in allowing me to set this demon straight! I see it as a *touch up* in the Souper Bowl—how exciting!

I'm not proud, but I am pleased, and forever grateful.

Serving health and healing, of course, isn't always this dramatic. It may come in the form of something as simple as not letting a cold "get you down," or stopping the flu in its tracks using nutrition, or taking *well days* off from work instead of sick days. It may be served by talking about health instead of sickness. Earl Nightingale says in THE STRANGEST SECRET: "Don't tell anyone about a sickness except your doctor, he's the only one who needs to know!" Talking about sickness *perpetuates* sickness, and the whole world talks about it, and perpetuates it. There is no talk of sickness in the Souper Bowl unless it's in showing an example of healing.

Healing (serving) also may not come in the form of getting well. Death, too, can be a healing experience. As we know, the fear of death is no-thing, a ghost, and the death experience is a normal part of eternal life. Serving healing through an easy death can be one of the most beautiful demonstrations. I saw this in the wisdom of my mother, Chef Imogene, when she was diagnosed as having breast cancer. She decided that she had lived a long and happy life and that she wanted a short and easy death experience. She said "no" to surgery, radiation and chemo-therapy, called her family together in a celebration of life, and announced that she had chosen *death* as her healing.

Death, too, can be a healing experience.

Of course, this decision was not an easy pill for most of her family to swallow. Each member had an opinion. We all loved her very much and wanted to keep her with us...but we also respected her, admired her, and ultimately thanked her, for her decision. We grieved, yes, but we were able to grieve *with* her, instead of just *for* her. She passed quickly and easily. We were so blessed. Thank you, Mom, for serving your soup so wonderfully.

The healing power of a loving touch is also important in serving the soup. A hand shake will transfer some healing energy, but a *hug* will accomplish many wonders. Many people are starving for love and affection and there's magic in a hug that comes from the heart. My friend and teacher, Chef Berny (Dohrmann) suggests that we use "the heart hug." When you hug, instead of your right

There's magic in a hug that comes from the heart.

side touching the left (heart) side of the other person, shift to your right so that your heart and theirs are on the same side, heart to heart. Sex and gender play no part in a truly loving embrace—it's divine energy moving from heart to heart.

You may also want to learn some healing techniques such as Therapeutic Touch, Reiki, or massage therapy. Healing is the movement of energy (inner-"G") in a positive way, and any way you can do this will be valuable to everyone involved.

The measure of one's success in the Souper Bowl game is determined by how much their life, and the lives of those around them, improve. Through the activity of serving health and healing, you are changing the whole world, *lifting it up*. You are feeding everyone from your kettle, your consciousness. "Feed my sheep," Jesus instructed. Feed them *peace*...**Peace Soup**.

Serving Trust

One of the most "fun" parts of the Souper Bowl game, the real "add-venture," is stepping out on faith and trusting the innate goodness of life. The way you serve trust is by saying "yes" to life! When you trust, you can always say "yes," know- **Say "yes"** ing that everything shows up in time, on purpose. To **to life!** ego, this may sound too easy, too dangerous, too chaotic! It seems that you would be bounced around like a cork on the ocean. Ego, however, is not involved in the Souper Bowl. Only the true Self can play. True Self sees the natural order of the universe, and is being guided by the events as they unfold. It's actually the intellect (thinking) that gets bounced around like a cork!

We were exposed to this *play* (trusting) in Step 5 of the recipe. It was presented there as the Quick Draw—the short version of the "I Deal" way—the "Heart Chart." Saying "yes" is making everything "O" — "O.K." We're now ready to bring it out in the big game, in the stadium of life, serving trust.

In the Souper Bowl, when a problem or a challenge comes up, you

don't have to *think* about it anymore. You *know*...it's "O" — "O.K."
The signal you can use is the short-hand signal that used to mean
"A...O.K." In the **Peace Soup** recipe, this signal shows that you're in
Observer mode and into the heart, into acceptance, into love!

Keep in mind that saying "yes" to life may not always mean saying, "Yes!" (although it usually does). I said, "No!" to the doctors, to
the world, but I was saying "yes" to life! My mother's *"no"* was also
"yes." "Yes" is being true to your Self, by letting your true Self be the
guide. Remember what Jesus said: "Let your communication be, yea,
yea; nay, nay: for whatsoever is more than these cometh of ego." (Matt
5:37, rev. ver.)

If I had *thought* about the triple bypass, asked my friends, neighbors, family and other doctors what *they* thought, my decision may
have been different, as would my mother's decision. That would have
gotten ego involved, and OPOs (other people's opinions), and we
would have had to *suffer* the consequences. Beyond "yea, yea; nay,
nay" are the *nothings*, the ghosts of fear, and they will bring sure defeat
in the Souper Bowl game.

A common example of *no* being *yes* is when someone comes to
you asking for some money—a loan or a "hand out." The true help they
need may require that you not give them the money. It's usually easier
to be an enabler than to say "No!" Always be sure it's your true Self
that's giving the answer, not ego. How do you know? *You know.* That's
why you're in the Souper Bowl! If you're not sure, just say "yes" and
continue to work on the basics in the first six steps of the recipe.

Trusting is knowing. Trusting *is knowing,* as you learned through use of
the "I Deal" way—the "Heart Chart," but it takes a lot of
practice, a lot of preparation and *perspiration*, to really
let go and trust. We see in Jesus' experience in the
Garden of Gethsemane on the eve of crucifixion, that even He "sweat
blood" before He was able to truly let go through prayer and meditation. He finally came to the real-I-zation that He could trust God's will,
always, and His example, through that experience, shows us how we all
can serve trust, by being trusting.

Serving through Prayer

Prayer, as you discovered in Step 3 of the recipe, is a different activity than meditation. In "effective prayer," you are using the power, the connecting energy (inner "G"), you developed through meditation. Prayer is the channeling of the contact you make with Divine Mind—pure awareness, cosmic consciousness, God—into the manifest world, for the benefit of anyone and/or everyone.

The Souper Bowl game is played in the Souper Dome (Divine Mind) and on the "field of pure potentiality," as Deepak Chopra calls it. The activity of prayer draws the energy onto the playing field and makes "all things possible!" True prayer moves love (God) into the arena of life and every "play-*er*" becomes a "pray-mate!" There is no opposition in the Souper Bowl, no resistance, no competition—just co-operation. You don't pray that *your* team wins, you pray that everybody wins!

True prayer is not beseeching God to give you something, or *do* something for you—it's recognizing that everything is already done, you already have it all! True prayer is *thanksgiving*. God (love) knows what you need before you ask, so you don't need to ask, just give thanks for what you have, knowing that what's needed will

True prayer is thanksgiving.

come in the moment it's needed. You know, as Chef Jesus knew, that God's will is always being done. "Thy will, not mine," recognizes that there is only *one will*. How do you know what God's will is? Just look at what's happening—that's God's will!

Scientific prayer brings a new dimension to the "pray-ers" (those who pray). You don't have to *beg* for God's mercy—you *know* that God *is* mercy, and that mercy is *in* you and *through* you all-ways. Your work is to be a "clear" channel for God's healing love. In serving through prayer, you have reached the level of the master chef and there is no doubt, no fear, no faltering along the way. You *know,* and that knowing moves spirit (energy), and performs miracles.

Prayer works! We've known this for a long time in a limited way, usually in blind faith, but now even world consciousness is moving into understanding faith. In the Souper Bowl, you're "blind again." You

We've been guided to form a prayer grid around our wonderful planet Earth.

know the truth, and *you're* free, and helping others to be free.

We've seen this demonstrated so vividly in the last few years as we've been guided to form a *prayer grid* around our wonderful planet Earth, and *peace* is the result! In the 1980s, I had the honor and privilege of working and praying with John Randolph and Jan Price and "The Planetary Commission" as they organized the New Year's Eve prayer vigils for world peace. Millions of people around the world joined in praying together (to-get-her) at exactly the same time (Noon Greenwich Mean Time) and the results were powerful and dramatic! The Berlin Wall was dismantled, the Iron Curtain fell, the Cold War ended, and Communism lost its grip on millions of people.

This is only the beginning, as we now concentrate our prayer energy on the environment and the saving of the natural resources of our Mother Earth. There is no limit to what we can accomplish in serving through prayer. This is our response-ability as players (pray-ers) in the Souper Bowl.

Serving the soup (Step 7) is about serving the world—*peace*. In the Souper Bowl, you're keeping The High Watch, and you're not alone. Multitudes of "heavenly host" are keeping the watch with you, and the *glow ray* of the spirit of love "shines 'round about you." You are supported from the stands of the Souper Dome by multitudes of angels. They're all ready to help you serve the soup, and prayer calls them into the game!

Serving Light

As we've discovered, most everyone is sleep-walking through life, in the dark, in a hypnotic trance induced by their old conditioned beliefs (ego) and re-in-*forced* by the image makers and the appearances of the world. Most people see life "through a glass, darkly," as Chef Paul observed, and life seems hope-less, futile, a drag! The drag-ons have them in the dungeons, and your light, shining in the darkness, is just what's needed to *save* them, to wake them *up!*

"You are the light of the world," Jesus said in His great coaching session on the Mount. "Let your light shine...to glorify your higher Self... which is God (love) within you." (Matt 5:14-16, rev. ver.) He didn't say you will *become* the light,

> **"Let your light shine...to glorify your higher Self... which is God (love) within you."**

He said you *are* the light. In the Souper Bowl, your light is so bright that it dispels all darkness. There is nothing in the universe more powerful than light in manifesting truth. As God said in the big "inning," "Let there be light!"

The big game requires that you become totally aware of the Christ Light that you are, and shine that light into every situation in your life. Wherever there is a need, there is your light shining! If you drive by an incident (there are no accidents) in the traffic, you don't "rubberneck" to see what's *wrong*. You see it *all right*. You surround the whole situation with white light, knowing that perfect healing is taking place for all concerned.

In the morning, when you first wake up, you surround yourself, your family, your home, your office, your car, your friends, your planet, everything, with light! In the evening, just before falling asleep, you do the same thing. You may want to learn this little prayer from the recipe of Chef James (Dillet Freeman). He calls it "The Prayer for Protection" (you can pray the same prayer using "you" or "us")...

> **The light of God surrounds me.**
> **The love of God enfolds me.**
> **The power of God protects me.**
> **The presence of God watches over me.**
> **Wherever I am, God is.**

Serving light is a full-time activity, but it never drains you. You are a pure channel for light that is unlimited. You also know that "as you serve, so is it served to you." You always get what you *de*-serve.

Whatever you receive is a result of (de)service. I say, "If you don't like the return, change your serve." In the Souper Bowl, you serve an ace (oneness) every time!

Serving Joy

Again, you can only serve that which you *are*. You are perfect joy, and in the Souper Bowl you're always *on*, always positive and up-beat, happy, smiling, de-*light*-full! There are no frowns, no dark moments, no down time. Again, ego will say that this is not possible, and it's *not*—for ego! Ego is vanquished before you reach the Souper Bowl, and all there is, is God (love). "With God, all things are possible," even eternal joy...*especially* eternal joy.

If you are still experiencing lows, it's O.K. It just means you're in a regular season game, still getting ready for the Souper Bowl, still preparing the soup. Keep practicing the plays and you'll make it to pure joy. Keep it light, lace it with humor and sing *joy songs*.

In the Souper Bowl you serve joy much as Tinker Bell serves her pixie dust. I always love the scene in *The Wonderful World of Disney* where "Tink" touches the Magic Kingdom with her wand and everything turns golden. That's what serving joy does for *your* magic kingdom, your life, and the lives of those around you. You have the power to light up the world with your enlightened joy!

You can't be down when the corners of your mouth are up.

Nothing touches the souls of others like a smile. It's been proven that you can't be *down* when the corners of your mouth are *up*. One characteristic that distinguishes a player in the Souper Bowl is that eternal smile. God is always tickling us—let go and laugh!

Serving Grace

The ultimate act of serving is *grace*. The players (pray-ers) in the Souper Bowl are in-finitely *grace-full*. Grace is not *beyond* the law—it's the *full-filling* of the law. "I am the fulfilling of the law," Jesus said.

"I came not to destroy, but to fulfill." (Matt 5:17) That's what we're doing by serving grace. We're full-filling every bowl from grace, the highest level of consciousness we know—the Christ consciousness.

In the final step in the Great Recipe Book, THE REVELATION OF JESUS CHRIST, it's written that "144,000 will be lifted up." This is not a number, it's a symbol! 144,000 represents the consciousness of those who have completed the spiritual work necessary to make it to the highest level of consciousness, to grace. Twelve is the number that represents *spiritual completion.* Twelve times twelve (144) means that one has learned and practiced the less-ons, and has become adept at serving. It's spiritual completion on all levels. One thousand re-presents the

> **144,000 represents the consciousness of those who have completed the spiritual work.**

infinite "one." Twelve times twelve times one thousand (144,000) means that one is infinitely accomplished in expressing Christ consciousness and is ready to serve the grace of Christ.

As the illumined intellect of Paul said, "Christ *in you,* your hope of glory." (Col 1:27) "This is the mystery," he said, "which hath been hid from ages, and from generations, but now is made manifest to His saints." How many saints are there? 144,000! Everyone who does the necessary work is a saint. Serving grace in the Souper Bowl is being a saint, at home, in the Souper Dome!

Tag...You're It!
"The Hope of the New Millennium"

By doing the work in completing the recipe, and cooking up your peaceful life, you are lifting the whole world up with you. The great Master Chef, Jesus, said, "And I, if I be lifted up from the earth, will draw all men unto me." (John 12:32) He came to show you how to do it, then He *tagged you*— instructed you to "take up the cross and follow Him." The cross is not a symbol of suffering and

> **The cross is a plus sign, not a minus sign!**

shame. It's a plus sign, not a minus sign! Crucifixion is driving the cross through the "skull" (Golgotha...intellect). It's crossing out the old ways of ego, and expressing the true self—resurrecting the Christ!

In doing the work of establishing peace in your life, you are remembering the truth about your Self that has been forgotten in the darkness and despair of *Earth* consciousness. Chef Ernest (Holmes) has given this illustration of the journey:

> A parable is told of an angel who came to visit the earth. He found himself in the usual stream of human activities, and he listened to the conversations of people. For the first time, he heard negative comments. Someone who was supposed to be an authority said that there might be a war, and human life would be destroyed. And he read in the newspaper of a great epidemic of illness. And someone who certainly should have known, explained in great detail that financial hardships were certain to limit all of us. He heard that there was not enough food to go around; the world was not going to be able to produce food for everyone, and people were going to starve to death.
>
> He began to wonder if these things might not be true, and even as he entertained the thoughts of negation to which he was listening, the brightness of his angelic presence faded into dark shadows. His form seemed to shrivel, and looking at himself he saw that he was dressed as a human being, walking the earth in fear, doubt and uncertainty.
>
> And so the weary years went by, years of unhappiness and impoverishment and dread, years so filled with anxiety that he wished he were dead, that some oblivion might forever swallow him up. And yet, in the midst of all this, something within him remembered that he was once an angel of God, living in a heaven of beauty

and a place of peace and joy, living in a Garden of Eden which God had provided for him. And remembering, a great determination arose within him to somehow or other find his way back to this lost paradise.

The determination grew into a great hope, and as hope was renewed, a light seemed to shine in the distance, and he seemed to have the courage to travel toward the light! And gradually a miracle took place. As he travelled toward the light, he found that the shadows were being cast behind him, until finally he so completely entered the light that no shadows were cast at all, and he realized he had been asleep, that he had had a bad dream from which he was *awakening!*

As with all parables, the character is *you!* You are the angel who has been asleep and is just now awakening to your true nature. Millions more are awakening at this time, causing a "surge" of energy that is changing our experience of life. We are in a new age of enlightenment on Planet Earth, and the critical mass that is shifting all consciousness into peace has been reached! The 1,000 years of peace, promised in the BOOK OF REVELATION, is upon us *now.* (1,000 is forever.)

The critical mass that is shifting all consciousness into peace has been reached!

Eternal peace and abundance are being made man-I-fest as we wake up, one by one, to "the truth, the way and the life." The Christ spirit that dwells in our hearts is pressing out through us and into the world. Peace is the reflection of God's healing light, and this light is shining in the earth now as never before. Those who are awake can see it, can feel it. Those who are asleep cannot.

Your awake consciousness is the crucial factor in your ability to serve the soup. When your kettle is full, you can serve a never-ending flow of goodness into the world. When you *fall* asleep, block the flow with negativity, the soup sours and is not fit for consumption. We've come to the point, in this final step of the recipe, where there is no more sleep, just rest—eternal rest.

On the Sabbath day, the seventh step, we rest. This doesn't mean that we're not active. The Earth doesn't stop spinning on the Sabbath.

It's play-day... pray day... pay day!

God doesn't stop moving, stop loving. It's the *work* that stops—it's done. It's time to play, to pray. The Sabbath is *Holy*...you are *whole*. It's play-day... pray day...pay day!

The Revelation

The recipe is complete, you've created the peaceful life for yourself and are now serving it to others. You know your true Self and are ready for the new Jeru–salem, the new city of peace. In this new consciousness of peace there is only *one* tree, as contrasted with the *two*

There is no duality... no more separation... only oneness... only love.

trees in Eden. There is no duality, no more separation—only oneness, only love. You have now "overcome the world" as Jesus did, and there is no more tribulation.

With the **Peace Soup** recipe, you have eliminated the "tree of the knowledge of good *and* evil," the tree of judgment. All that remains is the Tree of Life, the Christ life. The fruit of this tree

is *grace*. It comes through the heart and expresses (presses out) into the lives of the saints, the enlightened ones—*you!*

THE BOOK OF REVELATION is a cryptic book, and is in no way intended to be taken literally. It is a book about consciousness (as is the whole BIBLE) and it is being played out in the lives of all of us. It's the final book, and it's about the *end of time*. As we've seen, there is no time in the enlightened consciousness. There is no clock in the Souper Bowl game, there is no end, and everything is happening in *no time,* in the "twinkling of an eye," the all-knowing single eye of Christ. The whole-"o"-gram is seen in its completeness, its fullness.

You have a key role to play in the "giant leap for mankind" that began when man broke free from the earth and set foot on the moon. The world is not the same for you as it was for your fore-fathers, and you are not the same, either! You are the *new man (woman)*, the divine expression of God, and you know it, just as the *pattern* for the new man, Jesus, knew it, and all the great masters know it. You may be persecuted for your knowing by the old world, but you are *blessed* in the new world!

"Blessed are they which are persecuted for righteousness sake: for theirs is the kingdom of heaven," Jesus said in His *Attitudes of Being.* Heaven is yours, right here and now. Heaven is the peaceful life that you've developed with this recipe and are now serving in the Souper Bowl. You are a peace-maker!

You are a peace-maker!

"Blessed are the peace-makers; for they shall be called the children of God." (Matt 5:9) You are a perfect child of God and are *in*-volved in the mystical rhythm of life...the melody of life. To keep the melody and the rhythm going, you stay in tune by continuing to practice the techniques of peace, and by keeping your energy balanced. Keep your mixing bowls full and draw from them often, as you cook up and serve new batches of **Peace Soup**. It's a never-ending process, and it keeps cycling you higher and higher.

Continually taste test the soup before serving it to others. Remember what our premise was at the beginning of the recipe— "Peace on Earth begins with the peace *you* establish." You are the standard bearer, and the new *standard* is perfection. "Be ye therefore perfect, as your Father within you is perfect." (Matt 5:48, rev. ver.)

"To be or not to be," is not a question anymore. You *are* peace! You *are* the recipe and you *are* the soup. It's all totally digested and flowing through your mind, your body, your life! You are a *souper being*, in tune with the universe, the *one* verse, and everything in it. You are omniscient, omnipotent, omni-*present*. You are the greatest gift the world can ever receive. You *are*, as God *is*, indescribably delicious!

You have emerged from the cocoon of Earth consciousness as the

beautiful, multi-colored butterfly, as you flutter-by everyone, expressing the full spectrum of God's pure love-light! You are revealed to the
world in all your glory, the glow-ray of God! You *are* "in that chosen
number, as the saints go marching in!" So be it! So *be* you!

Peace...
Chef Jerry 💗

Afterword

So now you have it! The full recipe for peace. It is complete and capable of handling any situation that may come up for you in your eternal growth process. In my experience (my life), I have not come upon any problem, any challenge, that I could not handle with the **Peace Soup** recipe. However, as I've said all along, it takes *practice!* The techniques work, when you work them.

As we enter the new millennium, and the new Jeru-salem, not everyone is ready to come along peacefully. Some are hanging back in the shadow(s) with the old conditioned belief system (ego) and will have to be *dragged* (from the drag-ons), kicking and screaming. There will be much "wailing and gnashing of teeth!"

If you find yourself "entering into temptation," you may find it helpful to have a master chef to bounce your situation off of, so we've established the Peace Soup Inner-net Cooking School™, a school for aspiring soup chefs. The faculty of the school consists of master chefs, those who have become adept in the techniques, and are living the peaceful life.

If you feel you have mastered the techniques and are playing a good game in the Souper Bowl, you may want to serve further by helping your fellow chefs who may still be working their way up through the regular season games. You can qualify as a *master chef* by requesting and completing a one-page "pro"-file from the **Peace Soup** web site…**www.peacesoup.com.**

If you are just beginning to cook your soup and you feel you need some help in your learning pro-cess in the "regular" season or, if you're a *master chef* needing a special play for the Souper Bowl, you will be assigned a helper, again *by request,* on the "inner-net." Remember, we're all in the soup together, ready and willing to help…all ways.

Bibliography

A Course in Miracles. Glen Allen, CA: Foundation for Inner Peace, 1975.

Allen James. *As a Man Thinketh.* New York: Grosset & Dunlap.

Baroody, Theodore A. *Alkalize or Die: Superior Health through Proper Alkaline-Acid Balance.* Waynesville, NC: Eclectic, 1991.

Becker, Robert O. *The Body Electric: Electromagnetism and the Foundation of Life.* New York: Morrow, 1985.

Bryant, M. Darrol, ed. *Huston Smith: Essays on World Religion. "Essay on Buddhism."* New York: Paragon House, 1992.

Carter, Al. *Rebound to Better Health.*

Cheraskin, E. and W. M. Ringsdorf, Jr. *Psychodietetics: Food As the Key to Emotional Health.* New York: Stein & Day, 1974.

Chopra, Deepak. *The Seven Spiritual Laws of Success: A Practical Guide to the Fulfillment of Your Dreams.* San Rafael, CA: New World Library, 1994.

Clason, George. *The Richest Man in Babylon.* New York: Hawthorn, 1955.

Cole-Whitaker, Terry. *What You Think of Me Is None of My Business.* New York. Jove Publishing, 1991.

Diamond, John. *Behavioral Kinesiology: How to Activate Your Thymus and Increase Your Life Energy.* New York: Harper & Row, 1979.

Your Body Doesn't Lie: How to Increase Your Life Energy Through Behavioral Kinesiology. New York: Warner Books, 1979.

Drummond, Henry. *The Greatest Thing In the World.* New York: Grosset & Dunlap, 1981.

Dyer, Wayne. *Four Pathways to Success* [sound recording]. Carlsbad, CA: Hay House Audio, 1997.

Fillmore, Charles. *Revealing Word: A Dictionary of Metaphysical Terms.* 2nd ed. Unity Village, MO: Unity Books, 1994.

Fox, Emmet. *Power Through Constructive Thinking.* 11th ed. New York: Harper & Brother, 1940, 1932.

Fromm, Erich. *The Art of Loving.* New York: Harper, 1956.

Gibran, Kahlil. *The Prophet.* New York: Knopf, 1923.

Hawkins, David. *Power vs. Force*. Veritas Publishing, 1987.

Hay, Louise. *You Can Heal Your Life*. Santa Monica, CA: Hay House, 1987.

Hill, Napoleon. *Think and Grow Rich*. No. Hollywood, CA: Melvin Powers, Wilshire Book Co., 1996.

Hudson, Robert. *The Center of the Wheel*. Birmingham, AL: Enlightened Quest Publishing, 1998.

Jafolla, Richard and Mary-Alice. *The Quest: A Journey of Spiritual Rediscovery*. Unity Village, MO: Unity Books, 1993.

James, William. *The Varieties of Religious Experience: A Study in Human Nature*. New York: Modern Library, 1994.

Jampolsky, Gerald. *Goodbye to Guilt*. New York: Bantam Books, 1985.

Keyes, Ken, Jr. *The Handbook to Higher Consciousness*. 5th ed. Berkeley, CA: Living Love Center, 1975.

Kipling, Rudyard. "If." In *The Best Loved Poems of the American People*, pp. 65–66. New York: Doubleday and Company, 1936.

Kübler-Ross, M.D., Elisabeth. *Death: The Final Stages of Growth*. New York: Simon & Schuster, 1986, 1975.

On Death and Dying. New York: Touchstone Publishing, 1997.

Lucas, George (Writer and Executive). (1970). *The Empire Strikes Back* [film]. Los Angeles: Lucasfilm Ltd Production—A Twentieth Century Fox Release.

Maltz, Maxwell. *Psychocybernetics: A New Way to Get More Living Out Of Life*. Englewood Cliffs, NJ: Prentice Hall, 1960.

Moody, Raymond A., M.D. *Life After Life: The Investigation of a Phenomenon—Survival of Bodily Death*. New York: Bantam Books, 1988.

Nightingale, Earl. *The Strangest Secret* [sound recording]. Chicago: Nightingale Conant Corp, 1988.

Ponder, Catherine. *The Prosperity Secrets of the Ages*. Marina del Rey, CA: DeVorss, 1986.

Price, John Randolph. *The Planetary Commission*. Boerne, TX: Quartus Books, 1991.

Superbeings. 2nd. ed. Boerne, TX: Quartus Books, 1991.

Rayne, Janeson. *Don't Have a Cow: How to Thrive In a Post-Cow World*. General Store Publishing House, 1997.

Redfield, James. *The Celestine Prophecy*. New York: Warner Books, 1994.

The Tenth Insight. New York: Warner Books, 1995.

The Celestine Vision: Living the New Spiritual Awareness. New York: Warner Books, 1997.

The Secret of Shambhala: In Search of the Eleventh Insight. New York: Warner Books, 1999.

Sears, Barry. *The Zone*. New York: Regan Books, 1995.

The Bhagavad Gita: A New Translation by P. Lal. Calcutta: P. Lal, 1971.

The Tao Te Ching of Lao-Tzu. New York: St. Martin's Press, 1995.

Toffler, Alvin. *Future Shock*. New York: Random House, 1970.

Wade, Carlson. *Inner Cleansing: How to Free Yourself From Joint–Muscle–Artery–Circulation Sludge*. Englewood Cliffs, NJ: Prentice Hall, 1992.

Watts, Alan. *Psychotherapy, East and West*. New York: Random House, 1975.

Weil, Andrew. *Eight Weeks to Optimum Health: A Proven Program for Taking Full Advantage of Your Body's Natural Healing Power*. New York: Alfred A. Knopf, 1997.

Natural Health, Natural Medicine: A Comprehensive Manual for Wellness and Self-Care. Boston: Houghton Mifflin Co., 1990.

Whitaker, Julian M. *Is Heart Surgery Necessary?: What Your Doctor Won't Tell You*. Washington, D.C.: Regnery Publishing, 1995.

Young, Robert O. *One Sickness, One Disease, One Treatment*. Alpine, UT.

INDEX